# Second Language Acquisition/Foreign Language Learning

# MULTILINGUAL MATTERS

Age in Second Language Acquisition
  BIRGIT HARLEY
Bicultural and Trilingual Education
  MICHAEL BYRAM and JOHAN LEMAN (eds)
Bilingual Children: From Birth to Teens
  GEORGE SAUNDERS
Bilingualism and the Individual
  A. HOLMEN, E. HANSEN, J. GIMBEL and J. JØRGENSEN (eds)
Bilingualism in Society and School
  J. JØRGENSEN, E. HANSEN, A. HOLMEN and J. GIMBEL (eds)
Bilingualism and Special Education
  JIM CUMMINS
Communicative Competence Approaches to Language Proficiency Assessment
  CHARLENE RIVERA (ed.)
Cultural Studies in Foreign Language Education
  MICHAEL BYRAM
Current Trends in European Second Language Acquisition Research
  HANS W. DECHERT (ed.)
Dialect and Education: Some European Perspectives
  J. CHESHIRE, V. EDWARDS, H. MUNSTERMANN, B. WELTENS (eds)
An Ethnographic/Sociolinguistic Approach to Language Proficiency Assessment
  CHARLENE RIVERA (ed.)
Introspection in Second Language Research
  C. FAERCH and G. KASPER (eds)
Key Issues in Bilingualism and Bilingual Education
  COLIN BAKER
Language Acquisition: The Age Factor
  D. M. SINGLETON
Language Acquisition of a Bilingual Child
  ALVINO FANTINI
Language Distribution Issues in Bilingual Schooling
  R. JACOBSON and C. FALTIS (eds)
Language Planning and Education in Australasia and the South Pacific
  R. B. BALDAUF and A. LUKE (eds)
Language Proficiency and Academic Achievement
  CHARLENE RIVERA (ed.)
Learner Language and Language Learning
  C. FAERCH, K. HAASTRUP and R. PHILLIPSON
Methods in Dialectology
  ALAN R. THOMAS (ed.)
Modelling and Assessing Second Language Acquisition
  K. HYLTENSTAM and M. PIENEMANN (eds)
Placement Procedures in Bilingual Education
  CHARLENE RIVERA (ed.)
Raising Children Bilingually: The Pre-School Years
  LENORE ARNBERG
The Role of the First Language in Second Language Learning
  HÅKAN RINGBOM
Schooling in a Plural Canada
  JOHN R. MALLEA
Variation in Second Language Acquisition: Discourse and Pragmatics (Vol. I) and
Psycholinguistic Issues (Vol. II)
  S. GASS, C. MADDEN, D. PRESTON and L. SELINKER (eds)

**Please contact us for the latest book information:**
**Multilingual Matters,**
**Bank House, 8a Hill Rd,**
**Clevedon, Avon BS21 7HH, England**

**MULTILINGUAL MATTERS 58**
Series Editor: Derrick Sharp

# Second Language Acquisition/Foreign Language Learning

Edited by

# Bill VanPatten and James F. Lee

**MULTILINGUAL MATTERS LTD**
Clevedon · Philadelphia

**Library of Congress Cataloging-in-Publication Data**
Second language acquisition : foreign language learning /
edited by Bill VanPatten and James F. Lee.
　　p. cm. (Multilingual matters ; 58)
　　Bibliography: p.
　　Includes index.
　　1. Second language acquisition. 2. Language and languages
—Study and teaching. I. VanPatten, Bill. II. Lee, James F.
III. Series: Multilingual matters (Series) ; 58.
P118.2.S43 1989
418′.007—dc19　89-3170


**British Library Cataloguing in Publication Data**
Second language acquisition – foreign language learning
(Multilingual matters; 58)
　　1. Foreign language skills. Acquisition
　　I. VanPatten, Bill II. Lee, James F.　　401′.9
　　ISBN 1-85359-054-1
　　ISBN 1-85359-053-3 Pbk


**Multilingual Matters Ltd**
Bank House, 8a Hill Road　&　1900 Frost Road, Suite 101
Clevedon, Avon BS21 7HH　　　Bristol, PA 19007
England　　　　　　　　　　　USA

Index compiled by Meg Davies (Society of Indexers)
Typeset by Photo·graphics, Honiton, Devon
Printed and bound in Great Britain by WBC Print, Bristol

# Contents

Preface ................................................................ ix

Introduction ......................................................... 1

1   'Second' and 'Foreign' in Second Language Acquisition/
    Foreign Language Learning: A Sociolinguistic Perspective
    *Margie Berns* ................................................... 3

PART I: SOME PERSPECTIVES ON SECOND LANGUAGE
ACQUISITION/FOREIGN LANGUAGE LEARNING ............ 13

A:  VIEWS FROM FL

2   Theory and Research in Second Language Acquisition and
    Foreign Language Learning: On Producers and Consumers
    *Bill VanPatten* ................................................ 17

3   What is Foreign Language Learning Research?
    *Claire J. Kramsch* ........................................... 27

B:  VIEWS FROM L2

4   Second and Foreign Language Learning: Same, Different or
    None of the Above?
    *Susan M. Gass* ............................................... 34

5   Models, Processes, Principles and Strategies: Second
    Language Acquisition Inside and Outside the Classroom
    *Roger W. Andersen* .......................................... 45

PART II: FRAMEWORKS AND APPROACHES TO
RESEARCH ISSUES ............................................................. 69

A.  USING L2 AND FL DATA IN INTERLANGUAGE RESEARCH

6   Linguistic Theory and the Acquisition of German Negation
    *Lynn Eubank* ................................................................. 73

7   Word-Order Transfer, Metalinguistic Awareness and
    Constraints on Foreign Language Learning
    *Terence Odlin* ................................................................. 95

8   The Acquisition of Clitic Pronouns in Spanish: Two Case Studies
    *Bill VanPatten* ................................................................. 118

B.  LANGUAGE USE INSIDE AND OUTSIDE THE CLASSROOM

9   Coexisting Discourse Worlds: The Development of Pragmatic
    Competence Inside and Outside the Classroom
    *Mary E. Wildner-Bassett* ................................................ 140

10  Foreign Language Learning: A Social Interaction Perspective
    *Frank B. Brooks* ............................................................. 153

11  On Topic Choice in Oral Proficiency Assessment
    *Susan Cameron Bacon* ..................................................... 170

PART III: FROM RESEARCH AND THEORY TO
PRACTICE .......................................................................... 181

12  In Second Language Acquisition/Foreign Language Learning,
    Nothing is More Practical than a Good Theory
    *Sandra J. Savignon* ........................................................ 185

13  Prefabricated Speech for Language Learning
    *James R. Nattinger* ........................................................ 198

14  A Role for Communicative Competence and the
    Acquisition–Learning Distinction in Translator Training
    *Don Kiraly* .................................................................... 207

15  Can Foreign Language Learning Be Like Second Language
    Acquisition? The Curious Case of Immersion
    *Linda Schinke-Llano* ...................................................... 216

16  Conservation of Language Resources
    *Russell N. Campbell and Kathryn J. Lindholm* .................... 226

CONCLUSION .................................................................... 240

17  Contexts, Processes, and Products in Second Language
    Acquisition and Foreign Language Learning
    *Bill VanPatten and James F. Lee* .................................... 240

References ................................................................ 246

Index ...................................................................... 269

# Preface

Second language acquisition (SLA) and foreign language learning (FLL) have been and continue to be viewed by many as largely unrelated fields of research or at best being only weakly connected disciplines. Over ten years ago, Frechette (1976: 377) noted that, 'By and large, observation of classroom practices and talks with classroom teachers have revealed that many feel a large portion of [SLA research] efforts are of little relevance to them'.

While it is undeniable that early psycholinguistic research in SLA, which concentrated on morpheme studies and error analysis of the speech of learners of English, was limited in scope, is it true some 12 years later that SLA research offers little to those in FLL? Recently, Higgs (1985: 202) voiced a concern similar to Frechette's observation:

> the majority of the research literature cited in support of the claims for the Input Hypothesis [e.g. Krashen 1982] assumes a second language or an immersion environment, not a foreign language situation . . . Offering this same literature in support of a foreign language pedagogy extrapolates what is arguably true for one kind of environment into a very different environment, with few experimental data.

This perception implies that the psycholinguistic development found in SLA is somehow different than that found in FLL and that a different theory of psycholinguistics (and probably any other field of language study) is somehow necessary to account for FLL. Yet, there are three aspects of Higgs's comment that deserve attention. The first is that much of current reaction among foreign language (FL) professionals to SLA research and theory-building is a reaction to Krashen's Monitor Theory (in particular his Input Hypothesis). It is not a reaction to SLA research in general and most FL professionals have had little to say about other models proposed to account for SLA, e.g. Schumann's Acculturation Hypothesis, Andersen's Nativization Model.

The second important feature to note in Higgs's statement is that few empirical data have been collected on the psycholinguistic development of foreign language learners. If this is true, then the question is raised as to just what SLA researchers and FL researchers have been investigating and, if they have been pursuing different issues, why this is so.

The final aspect of Higgs's comments that we will mention is that FL professionals are largely concerned with teaching. That is, all SLA research and theorizing tends to be filtered through the lens of pedagogy. Seemingly, research on non-native language learning is only of importance to the FL profession if it has some direct consequence for the classroom. Within this context, research on FLL has been directed almost exclusively at the investigation of methodology. As VanPatten *et al.* (1987: 1) point out:

> Underlying this emphasis on methodology has been the basic assumption that classroom language learning, like a clear plastic bag, reveals the nature of the instruction that is poured into it but without shape or color of its own. What students learn and how well they learn was assumed to be primarily a result of how they were taught.

We should point out here that, beyond the confines of the United States, concerns about the relationship between SLA research and theory and other fields of language study have been raised as well. Sridhar & Sridhar (1986), for example, have observed that SLA research/theory and research on indigenized varieties of English (IVEs) have tended to ignore each other, resulting in an 'absence of dialogue'. These authors note that SLA cannot be all-encompassing if it ignores IVEs and that researchers in IVEs do not contribute empirically or theoretically to language acquisition studies. Kachru (1986: 35) has also remarked on the limits of SLA research and theorizing. Using a non-Western perspective, she notes the absence of a non-Western context in building toward a theory: 'Unless the data base of research in these areas is expanded, the claims to universality of research findings in second language acquisition will remain suspect for most of the non-Western world'.

While acknowledging the world context of foreign language learning, we believe that the time is ripe for second and foreign language specialists in the United States to begin critically examining the relationship between SLA and FLL. On 3–4 April 1987, a conference was held at the University of Illinois at Urbana-Champaign which was dedicated to exploring this relationship and to bringing SLA and FLL researchers together. Three general questions were posed to reflect the themes of the conference. Do classroom language learners, without access to a second language speech community, necessarily follow different paths in the acquisition of linguistic structure compared to those who acquire a second language either naturalistically or in a natural environment where instruction is also used? Are SLA and FLL fundamentally different in terms of the processes used to internalize language? What is the relationship between SLA and FLL at the level of theory?

A total of 39 papers were presented from researchers in the United States, Europe, Japan and Australia. Included in that number were prominent research voices, selected to ensure that both SLA and FLL perspectives would be present to address major issues: the two keynote addresses (Andersen and Savignon) and a special panel of four speakers (Gass, Kramsch, Valdman and VanPatten). While we tried to provide as much thematic unity as possible to the organization of the conference, we soon saw that many scholars and researchers had their own related questions concerning the relationship between SLA and FLL. With the presenters bringing not just psycholinguistic but also sociolinguistic, ethnographic, psychometric and other perspectives to the theme of the conference, the three unifying themes blossomed to include other issues, such as:

(1) How can the relationship between SLA and FLL be conceptualized? Indeed, how are the disciplines of SLA and FLL themselves conceptualized?

(2) Where does SLA overlap with FLL? Where do they differ? What are the common concerns? What are the divergent concerns?

(3) What research needs to be undertaken to explore further the relationship between the two?

(4) What problems are there in applying SLA (or FLL for that matter) to foreign language education?

(5) Is classroom language learning the province of educational theory? Is there a theory of classroom language learning that is different from a general theory of classroom education?

(6) What are the parameters and limitations of classroom language learning? What can or does instruction impact on?

(7) Is FLL an independent field of research? Should we be working toward a separate theory of FLL? Is the classroom setting so unique that SLA research can not be applied to it?

With these additional questions, the papers treated a variety of topics including interlanguage theory and description, fossilization and accuracy, the social context of language learning, strategies, reading in a non-native language, application and evaluation.

Because of all the various subthemes, not all of the papers presented at the SLA/FLL conference could be included in this collection, but we are pleased to note that some are appearing elsewhere in both FLL- and SLA-orientated journals. The 17 papers that we have gathered here were all presented at the conference, with the exception of VanPatten's 'The Acquisition of Clitic Pronouns in Spanish: Two Case Studies'. We are grateful to the University Press of America for allowing us to reprint that particular article here. We also thank the editors of *Issues and Developments in English and Applied Linguistics* at the University of Illinois for allowing us to publish a special short collection of four papers in the Spring 1988 issue of their journal. We would also like to thank William Prokasy (former Dean of the College of Arts and Sciences), the Miller Endowment Committee, and Ivan Schulman of The Department of Spanish, Italian and Portuguese, all of the University of Illinois, for major sources of funding for the conference. In addition, the following also provided monetary support and we recognize their contributions here: the School of Humanities, the College of Education, the Department of Educational Psychology, the Department of French, the Department of Linguistics, and the Division of English as an International Language. Special thanks also go to Jane Berne, one of our graduate students in Applied Linguistics in Spanish, who not only helped to make the conference a success, but also helped with the manuscript for this collection at various points in its development. And finally, thanks to Marita Romine, the Administrative Assistant in our department who, if she doesn't have the answer to a question, will find it out for you.

Bill VanPatten and James F. Lee
*Champaign, Illinois, USA*
*July 1988*

# Introduction

We begin this collection of papers with a discussion of what the terms 'foreign' and 'second' language mean. Citing Stern's (1983) distinction of the two terms, Berns explores in Chapter 1 whether or not the terms are adequately descriptive of what really happens among learners of another language. By examining the learning and use of English in three different settings, Berns concludes that a dichotomy of contexts is insufficient to explore the complexities of language settings and offers instead the notion of a cline or continuum of settings. What is clear from her discussion is that the terms 'foreign' and 'second' are meaningful and useful only to researchers and other 'outside' observers. But when one assumes the learner's point of view, neat research distinctions of black and white fade into shaded areas of varying degrees of greyness.

As we ponder Berns's remarks, we are immediately drawn to a description of Spanish in the United States, generally described as a 'foreign' language. Our question is: 'Foreign to whom?' Within the borders of the United States, Spanish displays each and every one of the characteristics of use outlined by Berns for English in Japan, West Germany and India. We might consider, for example, that Spanish in Alaska is much like English in Japan. Spanish in Los Angeles and Dade County, Florida, on the other hand, is much like English in India. And finally, Spanish in places such as Chicago, New York and Dallas is akin to English in West Germany. Yet, like the English that Berns discusses, it could very well be that some learners in both Alaska and Dade County share similar profiles in terms of purpose and real opportunities for use outside the classroom. That Spanish exists in a community outside the classroom does not mean that non-classroom input and interaction are sought by the learner; and that Spanish does not 'exist' outside the classroom does not perforce keep a learner from seeking outside input and interaction. Within the same community, then, individual as well as group profiles regarding purpose and language use can emerge.

It is important to point out that Berns is mostly concerned with language use, i.e. the communicative and interactive nature of learner behaviour. Couched in a sociolinguistic framework, Berns's contribution is unique in this volume and therefore stands alone. What remains to be seen (and, indeed, this is touched upon by several of the papers in this

1

collection as well as being addressed in our concluding remarks) is just how important a clarification of the terms is for research and theory in SLA or how important it is for curriculum development. The reader is encouraged to keep Berns's discussion in consideration as each contribution is read, delaying any assessment of distinctions and contributions until the end.

# 1 'Second' and 'foreign' in second language acquisition/ foreign language learning: a sociolinguistic perspective

MARGIE BERNS

*Purdue University, West Lafayette, Indiana, USA*

Second language acquisition/foreign language learning can be explored from a variety of perspectives. The psycholinguist, for example, seeks to discover cognitive characteristics of the learning/acquisition of some feature of language; the psychometrician searches for a way to measure validly and reliably a learner's progress toward competence in a language; methodologists and applied linguists exploit available knowledge about language learning/acquisition and devise plans and techniques based upon this knowledge for the classroom.

Sociolinguists, too, find second language acquisition and foreign language learning a productive area for research. Their interests relate to the social and cultural factors that influence, for example, the choice of languages to be learned, the particular models of those languages that classroom learners are to approximate, and the differences in degree of language proficiency learners achieve.

One sub-area of sociolinguistics that has been especially rich in providing insights into the social dimension of second and foreign language development is the study of non-native varieties of English. Recent studies of English in Africa (e.g. Magura, 1984) or Asia (e.g. Lowenberg, 1984) identify a variety of sociocultural factors that contribute to the learning of English in countries in these regions. They also suggest a reconsideration of the familiar 'foreign–second' dichotomy used to characterize language learning contexts. Such a reconsideration is the focus of this paper. Following Stern (1983), the distinction will be made between languages learned with reference to a speech community outside (foreign) or inside (second) the national or territorial boundaries in which the learning takes place. Descriptions of English language learning and use will be presented as a basis for examining the adequacy of the dichotomy as a means of describing language learning contexts.

The three descriptions of English in non-native contexts will be in the form of 'sociolinguistic profiles'. This method for description was first suggested by Ferguson (1966) as a means of systematically representing the complex nature of language use in a speech community. Sociolinguists (e.g. Kachru, 1983) have productively applied the method to identify salient functional characteristics of non-native English contexts that distinguish non-native varieties from one another as well as from native varieties, e.g. British or American English.

The three profiles referred to will include features typical of most sociolinguistic profiles: the users of the language; the uses they make of it, i.e. the function the language performs; their motivations for learning the language; and their attitude toward it. (More detailed and extensive accounts than those offered in this discussion are available in Stanlaw, 1982, and Morrow, 1987, for Japan; in Berns, 1988, for West Germany; and in Kachru, 1983, for India.)

## English in Japan: On Uplifting Pastimes and Language as Communication

A useful starting point for a sociolinguistic profile of English in Japan is the overview provided in Helgesen (1987). While English language instruction beginning in junior high school is universal in Japan, he explains, the degree of competence learners develop is relatively restricted. This is due, in part, to the role of English in the school curriculum. English is a subject tested in the college entrance exams, which are highly competitive. These exams rarely contain a listening or speaking component and focus instead on the knowledge of grammar and translation skills. As a result, language instruction is geared towards preparation for the exams and not towards the development of communicative ability. Once students who do choose to continue English study enrol in English courses at the university, they find that oral communication is given perfunctory attention. Two additional educational factors affecting the development of communicative ability are large class size and the tradition of rote-learning, which contribute to a neglect of interaction through English between teacher and learner or learner and learner in the classroom.

In addition to being a subject at school and at the university, English classes are a popular free-time activity. Due to the high social value placed on education in general in Japan, English study, along with flower arranging and calligraphy, is considered to be an 'uplifting' pastime and is therefore a popular hobby (Helgesen, 1987:208). Helgesen stresses that the emphasis is on *study* rather than *use* when describing English as a free-time activity. This attitude also prevails among viewers of Tokyo television station's English broadcasts, which are not seen as an opportunity to use English to get information or for entertainment. Rather, viewers consider these broadcasts primarily as an opportunity to improve their knowledge of English (Ohtani, 1978). Thus, English is learned for the cultivated status it bestows upon an individual, not for its usefulness as a tool for communication.

A different view of the ability to use English is that prevailing in the domains of business and commerce, where English is recognized as essential to Japan's emergence as a world economic power. English is considered necessary for the *kokusaijin*, or 'international people', who are believed to be in a better position to understand the world and to share knowledge of Japan. As a consequence, English is frequently required in the workplace. Many companies and language schools offer classes for employees in a wide range of businesses and enterprises. Kobe Steel, for example, has its own English language course, established in response to a study which indicated that almost all Kobe Steel employees use English at some point in their career (Baird & Heyneman, 1982). Those who are sent overseas need English for face-to-face communication, e.g. in business meetings and on social functions. Those who stay in Japan use English as they sell and service products, make the documents used in engineering, and correspond in English with their overseas customers. Company-based language instruction is tailored to these needs.

English instruction is available to a variety of Japanese in private language schools. Learners at these schools may include oil company technicians who want to learn English in order to instruct Burmese and Saudi engineers in petroleum processing; hotel staff interested in better serving guests attending international conferences; cable manufacturers in need of English to explain optic cable capabilities to potential clients; research hospital doctors interested in attending and participating in medical conferences conducted in English; and employees of local tourist attractions who learn English in order to make tourists' visits more informative and enjoyable.

## English in West Germany: Across Domains and Social Groups

English plays a significant role as a language of wider communication in the everyday lives of Europeans. Its use is not as restricted to a particular domain (commerce) or group (employees in international companies), as in Japan. Rather, as Edelhoff (1981) has emphasized, in Europe English is a means of communication for all types and classes of people across national frontiers.

West Germany offers an excellent example of the use of English in Europe. English is part of all school curricula; is used to some extent in all media; is the source of extensive word borrowings; is available through contact with native and non-native users within West Germany in a variety of domains and for a range of purposes; and is learned to varying degrees of competence by West Germans of all social, economic and educational levels.

English is taught in the state schools beginning generally at grade five. It is the first foreign language in most German states, except those bordering on France. In contrast with Japan, emphasis in language classes in West Germany is on the development of written and oral communication skills as well as on the interpretation of texts. While not widespread, there is some recognition of the potential use of English within the West German context in the materials and texts available to learners. These materials may include the lyrics of popular songs, comic books, or letters exchanged with penpals. Although English is not the medium of instruction in most West German schools, a considerable and increasing amount of informal activity that could be termed instructional or educational is conducted through trade and professional journals that carry a steadily increasing number of articles in English.

English also functions for West Germans as a 'link language' with speakers of other languages and dialects within the pluralistic context of Europe. Families and individuals of all levels of education who have contact with other Europeans through vacations or social contacts often find English the *lingua franca* for personal interaction. Children frequently have penpals in other European countries and carry out their correspondence in English.

Other opportunities for using English outside the classroom available to West German learners of English include: contact with English through the media, e.g. television, radio, and films; the presence of American and British military personnel stationed at bases throughout central, and southern and northern Germany; and frequent contact with British speakers as a result of the proximity of Great Britain. West German teachers of English often take advantage of this proximity for frequent trips to Britain on their own or with school groups or for organizing visits from British schoolchildren.

West Germany's dependence on trade relations with others to keep its economy alive is a key motivation for learning English within the business community. As Smith (1987) reports, English is the most important language for international communication. It is often the language of routine phone calls, letters, telexes and conversations in firms doing business outside West Germany. Job opportunities may depend on knowledge of English, whether it be in a pharmaceuticals firm or a restaurant serving the 9 million or more tourists visiting West Germany annually.

In response to the need for English language skills related to jobs, some West German companies, like their Japanese counterparts, have established in-house language courses which focus not only on knowledge of business English vocabulary, routines and correspondence matters, but include training in communicating through English. A training course, for example, may cover such interactions as negotiations and presentations, and such behaviours as turn-taking, making a point, interrupting, or summarizing that are required in international meetings where English is the *lingua franca*.

## English in India: National and International Language

In large part due to its colonization by the British, the role of English in India is quite different from its role in Japan or West Germany. In the educational system, English is taught at every stage of education in all states of India. In 23 of India's states and union territories, English is the medium of instruction in the schools. It is also the medium of instruction in most institutions of higher learning. Textbooks in English are standard at the tertiary level of education.

While English is used for international communication, the numbers of those using it for this purpose is a small part (an estimated 3%) of the 18 million Indians who are English-using bilinguals. The majority of English speakers use it in primarily Indian contexts with Indian participants for typically Indian situations. That is, English is used for national purposes. It is a primary unifying force, a link language, in a country which has more than 1600 dialects and 15 languages recognized as major by the Constitution.

National uses of English are realized officially in the legal system and administrative network of India. Attempts have been made to introduce regional languages in high courts and lower courts, but the Indian Bar Council has opposed such a move, claiming that it is vital to the existence of the All-India Bar that one language (currently English) be used. The Council claims that English ensures 'national integration' and 'all-India standards' within the legal system.

In administration, English and Hindi are the two languages used for interaction all over India. In broadcasting, these are the only two languages used by All-India Radio. Of the 15 major languages used (English included), book production from 1974 to 1979 was greatest in English and is increasing annually. During 1978, 152 of 196 scientific journals (78%) and 239 of 275 engineering and technology journals (87%) were published in English. Of seven daily newspapers, four are printed in English, with English language newspapers of some type published in 23 states and union territories.

A significant area in which use of English has expanded is in literature. Over the past 40 or 50 years, literature in English written by Indians has come to be regarded as national literature. The novels of Mulk Raj Anand, Raja Rao, and R.K. Narayan exemplify achievements in the literary domain. Development in this area is due in part to the increase in bilingualism in English which has expanded the size of the potential audience for this literature.

## Reconsideration of the Dichotomy

Given these profiles of use and users of English in three diverse sociocultural contexts, which term, 'foreign' or 'second', would more accurately describe how English is learned? Is it learned and used with reference to a speech community inside or outside the country?

If a foreign language is learned with reference to a speech community outside the country in which the learning is taking place, then Japan appears to qualify as a foreign language learning context for English. There are few opportunities for use of English in Japan to encourage the development of a non-native English-speaking speech community which would serve as a reference group.

If a second language is one learned with reference to a speech community in the country in which the learning is taking place, India is clearly a second language learning context for English. Ample opportunities for use of English are available and a non-native English speaking speech community consisting of educated Indians serves as a reference group.

What of English in West Germany? As in Japan, English is generally considered a foreign language. Yet, West Germans, unlike Japanese, have opportunities to use English and have more contact with English, and the use of English serves interpersonal as well as professional purposes for them; learners do not have to wait to go abroad or become employed in international firms to use English. Given this distinction between West Germany and Japan, is it perhaps more accurate to describe English in this context as a second language?

It is difficult to compare West Germany to India within the notion of English as a second language. English is not the medium of secondary or tertiary education, is not the language of law and administration, nor has it become a literary language. At the same time, the context of West Germany is not strictly analogous to that of Japan because of the contact West Germans of a range of social groups have with English within the borders of their country.

How best to describe this complex situation? One approach to describing the status of English in West Germany is to use the notion of a *cline*, or continuum. With a cline the problems of the 'either/or' approach can be avoided and a productive means of characterizing the status of English in various contexts is made available. On this 'cline of language status' one pole could be designated 'foreign' and the other 'second'. Japan could be placed on the cline near the foreign language end, India near the second language end. West Germany could be placed near the midpoint, indicating that English has neither a strictly foreign nor a strictly second language status.

While the notion of a cline offers a means of describing English in a context such as West Germany, it does not characterize the one use of English common to the three profiles. As the reference to Saudi and Burmese engineers and international conferences illustrates, use of English, even among Japanese, may include speaking English with other non-native speakers. In fact, as Helgesen (1987: 209) points out, when opportunities to use English do present themselves in Asia, the speech partners are more likely to be two non-native speakers using English as their only common language. For these speakers, English is a means of international communication. It is neither strictly a foreign nor strictly a second language in the domain of business, trade and commerce since the speech community in which English is used consists of Japanese and non-Japanese, Germans and non-Germans, Indians and non-Indians i.e. the international English-using speech community. The use of English for communication across national boundaries for business and commercial purposes requires the introduction of an additional term to supplement the terms 'foreign' and 'second'. 'International' has been suggested and is frequently used to characterize this role of English.

## A Perspective Within a Perspective

The sociolinguistic perspective of this paper has served as an overall approach to the question of what the terms 'foreign' and 'second' mean for English in non-native contexts. The potential pedagogical significance of the sociolinguistic profiles and the reconsideration of the foreign–second dichotomy come from another perspective, that of the learner, which is embedded within this broader perspective. It is the perspective of the learner that can provide useful insights and suggest implications for language teaching practice since, as shown by the profiles, it is the learner, as a group or as an individual, who determines the purposes a language may serve.

These insights and implications relate to language teaching in a number of ways. As the three profiles above suggest, a speech community does not necessarily consist of native speakers; assumptions cannot be made that a learner will want to identify or use a language with a native-speaking speech community. For example, a learner may have the goal of using French with African speakers of French. If this is the case, it may be more important for a learner to become more competent in interactions with non-native speakers, which would have consequences for teaching. It may prompt reconsideration of standards for pronunciation, for example, since a non-native speech community is likely to have its own norms. Or it may at least require that learners be exposed to the varieties of a language and the diversity of its speech community.

The profiles also show that speakers may assume one of a range of roles in using a language, e.g. business partner, engineering instructor, administrative clerk, or penpal. Not every learner will want or need the range of skills or level of proficiency to fulfil all roles. The competence required for work as a tour guide differs from that of a manager in an international steel company.

The implications of role diversity for a variety of teaching contexts can be related to the range of purposes a learner in a foreign language context may bring to the classroom. Motivations for learning may be as various as wanting enough language to satisfy basic needs for travelling abroad, acquiring just enough of a native-like accent to perform an operatic role convincingly or getting the vocabulary necessary to communicate with a grandparent who is not bilingual in the learner's language. That is, a learner may want to assume the role of a tourist, opera singer, or interested grandchild. Perhaps success in fulfilling these roles should suggest the standards for determining a learner's success.

A sociolinguistic perspective can offer insights into the nature of language learning within a culture or society. It can provide a description of purposes for learning that challenges familiar views of why languages are learned and used and who learns and uses them. The sociolinguistic perspective taken for this discussion is actually the perspective of the learner. In the profiles, taking the learner's perspective for learning English in a non-native context illustrates that purposes for learning are not homogeneous across contexts and that purposes within a context may vary from one individual to another. The awareness of variation that such a perspective provides into English learning contexts and the recognition that the perspective of the learner is productive for understanding the nature of learning in these contexts need not be restricted to the learning of English. It seems that the perspective of the learner, which identifies purposes for learning, is viable and valuable for the learning contexts of all languages, whether they are considered international, foreign, second or something in between.

# Part I:
# Some Perspectives on Second Language Acquisition/Foreign Language Learning

Putting order into inquiry is not an easy task. And when an attempt is made to relate diverging disciplines, one is confronted with a task akin to putting *mega*-order into *mega*-inquiry. Addressing the question, 'What is the relationship between second language acquisition (SLA) and foreign language learning (FLL)?' encompasses more than just intellectual issues. In fact, behind the question lurks a sociology of each discipline, a sociology that helps in part to define the very nature of each discipline's inquiry.

To understand the relationship between SLA and FLL one must consider the professional and intellectual goals of the various disciplines represented. Why disciplines differ (or why they overlap) is generally dependent on what the intended goals are for the research. This is most clearly evident in the major division of the present collection: research and theory on the one hand, and curriculum and application on the other. In the first division, the goal (indeed the goal of almost any discipline's programme of research and theory) is to describe and explain adequately the phenomena under scrutiny with the intended result being an increased knowledge about the phenomena. In the other, the prospective goal is to influence teacher behaviour, to impact on the classroom environment. Whether these two goals are mutually exclusive, somewhat related, intricately entwined, or bear some other relationship is a motivating force in this book, as it was in the conference on which the book is based.

The first areas to be explored in this book concern research and the role of research in SLA and FLL and how these disciplines are conceptualized. What exactly are the domains of SLA and FLL research? How might they be characterized? What are the objects of study and how are they related? Are SLA and FLL two different fields?

It will become immediately evident to the reader that how these (and other) questions are addressed is dependent upon the point of departure for each researcher. While VanPatten touches on this in

Chapter 2, a brief observation is important here: the perspectives taken by individual authors are coloured by whether they come from second language research (e.g. non-classroom language acquisition, childhood bilingualism, English as a Second Language (ESL)) or from foreign language research (e.g. classroom ethnography, research on methodology). Each discipline has a tradition of inquiry and scholarship founded upon 'parent' disciplines (e.g. linguistics, psychology, education).

Even within each of these two major disciplines, researchers' perspectives are coloured by particular language backgrounds. The point can be made with the example of two researchers participating in a conference on learner language (interlanguage) development, each from a different language background: ESL and Spanish as a second language (SSL). During the course of the conference, the ESL researcher is advocating a research paradigm based on current linguistic theory; in particular she is arguing for a strong role for what has come to be called 'parameter setting'. On the other hand, the SSL researcher presents a model based on human information processing to describe and explain what he sees in second language acquisition. Both researchers argue with and challenge each other as to the explanatory adequacy of the differing perspectives, and an outsider would rightly ask: 'Is it possible to have such vastly different and competitive perspectives on the same thing?' But closer examination reveals that these researchers are influenced by the characteristics of their distinct language backgrounds such that in reality they may not be exploring 'the same thing'. English, for example, is a language 'heavy' with syntax and many of the syntactic properties of English have received detailed investigation from theoretical linguists. In contrast, Spanish, while containing interesting syntactic properties as well, is a language 'heavy' with morphology, in particular verbal morphology. For decades Spanish linguists have explored the rich functional and formal aspects of this morphology. These researchers' approaches to explaining interlanguage development have been influenced by what they view as basic features of the language. In a sense, one might say that neither researcher is completely wrong in attempting to describe and explain language acquisition, but at the same time neither is entirely correct.

In this volume, these and other orientations are sometimes made explicit by the individual researchers, but others remain subtle and implicit. No reader of research can blindly argue for or against a particular perspective without first examining what can be considered the sociological background of each perspective. Thus, the reader is urged to go beyond the issues and questions addressed by each author in this section to examine just what the points of departure are for each and what the stated or implied goals of the inquiry are. In this way the reader can better assess the conclusions about the relationship between SLA and FLL.

With this in mind, we have purposefully placed the papers in this first section in two subsections. The first is titled 'Views from FL' and, as will become apparent, an unstated subtitle is 'A Place for FLL Research'. Tackling the issue of 'mega-order' as opposed to specific issues, these papers contain two different approaches to looking at SLA and FLL from a foreign language (FL) perspective. VanPatten argues that SLA has tended to be biased in its object of study, having focused too much on English. He suggests that only research on the processes and products of different languages in different contexts can yield an adequate theory of SLA, and he suggests an important role for FL learner data in testing hypotheses and claims. Thus, for him, the relationship of SLA and FLL is one of increased research partnership with an explicit goal of working towards a theory of language acquisition. Kramsch, on the other hand, addresses the kind of research needed in order to understand better the specifics of classroom language acquisition. She claims that FLL must have an agenda for research differing from that of 'current SLA' so that teachers of languages are better equipped for understanding classroom learning. She does not, however, argue for a divorced relationship between SLA and FLL, but instead calls upon SLA to include a broader research agenda to round out teachers' education. It is here that an observation on FL tradition is in order. The classroom context of FL research has always pulled FL professionals towards inquiries that benefit the teacher. VanPatten and Kramsch both wish to see SLA and FLL researchers working together, but from different directions. VanPatten wants FLL research to be more concerned with theory, while Kramsch wants SLA to be more concerned with classroom teaching.

The second subsection is titled 'Views from L2'. Immediately we see the influence of an established second language (L2) research agenda on the two perspectives offered here. Gass outlines two general sets of variables in language acquisition and examines how each might be the same or different depending upon the context (environment) of the language acquisition situation. She argues against any simplistic 'same' or 'different' approach to relating SLA and FLL and asks that researchers investigate the extent of similarities and differences. In a similar vein, Andersen rejects a simplistic 'same' or 'different' approach and offers one model by which researchers might begin to explore language acquisition in different contexts. Through this model, it may be possible to explore the similarities and differences mentioned by Gass. Like VanPatten, Gass and Andersen's contributions are motivated by research and theory and, like Kramsch, their view of the relationship between SLA and FLL is one of a mutually beneficial research agenda. In short, VanPatten and Kramsch offer us the justification and place for FLL research, while Gass and Andersen offer frameworks that incorporate FL data.

# 2 Theory and research in second language acquisition and foreign language learning: on producers and consumers

*University of Illinois at Urbana-Champaign, USA*

## Introduction

According to Ellis (1985:5), '*Second* language acquisition is not meant to contrast with *foreign* language acquisition. SLA is used as a general term'. He then proceeds to inform us: 'It is, however, an open question whether the way in which acquisition proceeds in these different situations is the same or different'. I find this citation somewhat ambivalent and believe it reflects a schizophrenic nature which is not particular to Ellis but to many second language (L2) professionals. On the one hand, we would like to use one term to cover all language acquisition situations. Yet, at the same time, we feel the need cautiously to qualify our term because we have not provided adequate evidence that one term can really be used for all acquisitional environments. What, then, is the relationship between second language acquisition (SLA) and foreign language learning (FLL)?

The relationship between SLA and FLL that I would like to explore is one involving theory-building, that is, a theory about the processes underlying acquisition which in turn relies on empirical research for support. (For present purposes, I will follow the convention of using SLA to refer to language acquisition in a native-speaking environment

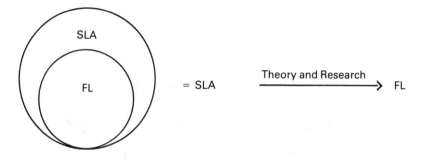

FIGURE 2.1 *The producer–consumer relationship*

and FLL in a non-native classroom environment. In addition, where necessary, FLL will be contrasted to foreign language (FL) teaching, the former referring to what the learner does with language, the latter being what the teacher does in the classroom.) In the theoretical domain we encounter concepts such as input, interaction, the role of universal grammar and so-called 'parameter setting', language transfer (identification and causes of), fossilization, socio-affective background, and others. The central questions which underlie theory construction in all language acquisition situations are: how and why people acquire languages; which conditions are *necessary* to language acquisition and which, in contrast, are *beneficial*; how we can account for different outcomes; and what the constraints on language acquisition are at different stages of development and where these constraints come from (for a discussion of theory-building as a process, the reader is referred to McLaughlin, 1987, Chapter 1).

Currently, the relationship between SLA and FLL is a unidirectional one in which theory and hypotheses flow from SLA to FL *teaching*. This can be schematized as in Figure 2.1. In this relationship, FLL is subsumed under SLA and is thought to be some special type of language acquisition context. (Quite unclear in this scheme of things is the relationship between FL, English as a foreign language (EFL), English as a second language (ESL), untutored SLA, and the formation of pidgins.) Thus, since FLL is a 'subset' of SLA, then whatever is true for FLL must also be true for SLA, but not vice versa. This suggests, then, that *all* the products and processes involved in FLL must be accounted for and explainable by SLA research and theory.

This schematic representation is reminiscent of earlier accounts of the relationship between linguistics and applied linguistics where those in applied linguistics were considered to be *consumers* of theory and research and were concerned only with *practical* applications (see, for example, Corder, 1973, and Wardhaugh & Brown, 1976). Thus, those in FL teaching seek out knowledge from SLA research and theory and then seek ways in which to manipulate the classroom environment to 'improve' instruction.

There are at least three assumptions underlying this relationship that deserve discussion: firstly, that SLA has answers to questions about language acquisition; secondly, that SLA has a truly cross-linguistic perspective; and thirdly, that acquisition is not a research domain of the FL profession. What I will argue here is that the relationship between SLA and FLL that has dominated the field is an artefactual one which rests upon debatable (if not incorrect) assumptions. I will then outline what I perceive should be the relationship between SLA and FLL and then suggest that only in the FL context can SLA theory find the answers to some rather important questions in theory.

## Second Language Acquisition: Questions and Answers

To begin, it is unquestionable that SLA does not have answers to the fundamental questions of non-primary language acquisition. How and why people acquire languages is a question which is still unanswered and will probably go unanswered for some time. Even in the field of child first language acquisition different theories and approaches to the issues of acquisition remain in competition. As is typical of any young field of research, SLA has rightfully spent some 18 years generating question after question, posing more than it has been answering, and thus setting up a research agenda. If we pick up any empirically based research paper, if it is written true to style, it ends with a conclusion or summary section in which the limitations of the research as well as areas in need of future investigation are outlined. What SLA *has* accomplished in the last decade and a half is to turn attention away from simplistic accounts of habit formation and primary language (L1) interference and to isolate some of the factors which apparently influence non-primary language acquisition, thus leading us to ask better questions than could have been asked in previous years.

In order to demonstrate how questions in this field have multiplied over the last decade and a half, let us take one factor thought to be essential to language acquisition: communicatively centred input. Since our attention was first focused on input in the mid- to late 1970s the following questions (not presented in any particular order) have been asked:

(1) Is meaningful input necessary? if so,
(2) does it have to be simplified?
(3) does input have to be comprehensible?
(4) does it have to contain $i + 1$?
(5) is there a silent period?
(6) what out of input becomes intake?
(7) does input have to be negotiated?
(8) does input differ among age groups?
(9) does input differ among cultures?
(10) is meaningful input enough?
(11) and generally, what are the limits of input as a factor in SLA?

While we could list more questions, I will conclude with a citation. In 1985, Susan Gass & Carolyn Madden published a volume titled *Input in Second Language Acquisition*. In that volume are 25 papers that treat input from either an empirical or a theoretical perspective. The volume concludes with a summary by Larsen-Freeman in which, on the last page, she lists ten areas (at least) in need of further research. Clearly, we do not have the answers to our questions about communicatively centred input except to say that it is an essential ingredient for language acquisition.

Now, what happens when this particular aspect of SLA is 'applied' to the FL context? The result is a flurry of claims about what should happen in the classroom, e.g. we get 'input methods'. This is not to say that the particular claim that meaningful input should be provided in the classroom is unwarranted. I merely wish to point out that any claim beyond that is quite probably premature. We have yet to really understand how interaction with input results in a language system. That is, we still have not sufficiently filled the gaps in our information about the following chain of events and relationships:

$$input \rightarrow intake \rightarrow acquisition \rightarrow language\ use[1]$$

What I find worthy of concern from this example is that the FL community does not respond with a research agenda about input in the classroom, but responds instead with a consumer's eye focused upon instruction. I do not mean to underestimate or denigrate the 'applicational' aspect of SLA research and theory. Indeed, as I have argued elsewhere (VanPatten, 1986a; 1986b; 1987a; 1987b), there are implications for classroom practice derived from SLA research and theory. But these implications are principles that are broad in scope, setting constraints on teaching and curricula rather than dictating what to do on a day-to-day basis. To continue in the vein of input-related issues, an example of one such principle is as follows. For successful language acquisition, learners need access to input that is communicatively and/or meaningful orientated and comprehensible in nature. (This particular principle is followed by three corollaries with research citations that expand upon the principle.) What I suggest this principle means is *not* that an input approach is best, only that there must be meaningful input present in the environment. In fact, the corollaries that follow the principle help to point out the weaknesses of specific methodologies such as Total Physical Response and other comprehension-based methods in their extreme form.

## On the Cross-Linguistic Nature of Second Language Acquisition Research

The second assumption underlying SLA theory and research is that it is truly cross-linguistic. This, like the first assumption, is demonstrably false. If one examines the publications of American journals that treat non-primary language acquisition, one is struck by the overwhelming preponderance of papers that use learners of English for their data base. If the papers are theoretical rather than research-orientated, they use the English language as their source of linguistic data. In Gass & Madden (1985), out of the 25 papers included, only three involve looking at learners of languages other than English. With the exception of the cross-linguistic series published by Newbury House and some occasional papers in *Studies in Second Language Acquisition*, SLA in the United States is a theory and research agenda of *the acquisition of English*. (Such, however, is not the case in Europe and Australia.)

This observation begs the question whether there is any problem with this. I believe that there is, from both a theoretical and a practical perspective. As an example, let us take the claim made in the 1970s that the acquisition of morphemic structure was determined by frequency of occurrence in input (Larsen-Freeman, 1976). This looks to be the case in a language like English, which has five verb inflections and one noun inflection. But what if the data base comes from a typologically different language such as Spanish, where morphology plays an important role in marking semantic features of language which in English are marked lexically or by word order? Spanish has some 46 verb inflections, five noun inflections, four forms for the definite article, two copulas, and between two and five forms of a pronoun for a given person number (dependent on case and/or syntactic function). In my research on the acquisition of *ser* and *estar* (VanPatten, 1985a; 1987b), for example, I have argued that Larsen-Freeman's position on frequency is incorrect with reference to the acquisition of Spanish and that, while certainly important, frequency of occurrence is not the primary factor in morpheme acquisition but instead exists in a *hierarchical relationship* to other factors. What I have argued is that frequency is only a factor once the relative communicative value of a form is assessed by the learner's language processor. In the case of *ser* and *estar*, for example, *ser* (the more frequent copula) does show up in the output of learners and is 'acquired' before *estar*; however, this only happens because *ser* and *estar* are of equivalent communicative value to the learner. But when two forms are of contrasting communicative value (i.e. one form *means* something in a sentence and the other does not) then the form with greater value tends to be acquired first regardless of frequency. (This is the only way to explain, for example, the acquisition of certain verb morphemes as opposed to adjective–noun concordance, the latter being more frequent than some verb morphemes which are nevertheless less or equally frequent compared with agreement markers on adjectives. It also explains the early absence in the output of a language learner of those forms that have exact or parallel L1–L2 usage but are meaningless, e.g. the earliest stage of sentence formation where copulas are absent in learner language even though the learner's L1 possesses an obligatory copula.) When this perspective is then applied to English morpheme development, we find an alternative explanation which accounts for the same data (see VanPatten, 1984). Clearly, research on morpheme acquisition is one area that could benefit from a cross-linguistic foreign language perspective.[2]

The FL community, then, assuming that SLA is either cross-linguistic or has justifiable cross-linguistic projections, may accept conclusions based on the data from ESL learners that are not readily applicable to FL teaching or are not adequately explanatory for FLL.

## Acquisition Research in Foreign Language Learning

The third assumption, that acquisition is not a research domain of the FL profession, derives, I believe, from the history of the two disciplines. SLA is firmly established in two disciplines of inquiry: linguistics and psycholinguistics. It has also been linked historically to two related research domains: child language acquisition, and pidgins and creoles.

The FL community also has linguistics as the backbone of modern language teaching, contrastive analysis (e.g. the backgrounds of Robert Lado, Robert Stockwell, Donald Bowen, Robert Politzer and William Bull). However, these roots were abandoned and replaced with something else: educational research. Sometime in the 1960s, schools of education blossomed and soon thereafter special degree courses in foreign language education were born. What then happened is that FL professionals turned their attention away from both what language is and how languages are learned, and focused their attention instead on the manipulation of instructional variables and methodology.

I would hasten to add here that I am not suggesting that educational issues are unworthy of attention or that the manipulation of instructional variables is unimportant. Nor do I wish to suggest that the work of those who have graduated from schools of education or who are conducting research in educational issues does not merit attention. Indeed there are some very important aspects of teacher behaviour and curriculum design that have been challenged by research and have profoundly influenced the language teaching profession, e.g. Savignon's classic study on communicative competence. I merely wish to point out that, for the most part, the FL profession has not been investigating the range of questions about language and language acquisition that have been asked in SLA.[3] While SLA has persevered in a quest for the 'how' and the 'what' of language acquisition, most professionals in FL have either assumed what these were or ignored them. Thus, the processes underlying acquisition itself have never really become a focus of inquiry in the FL profession. The result is a schism between two fields resulting in a biased approach to looking at language learning, that is, the over-emphasis on English in the case of SLA, and, in the case of the FL profession, an over-emphasis on methodology.

## Towards a New Relationship

As can be expected from this discussion, what I would like to suggest here is that the FL profession needs to cease being only a consumer of SLA research and theory and start becoming an active contributor, making FL learning just as important as FL teaching. Indeed, it can be argued that there are some questions asked in SLA that are best answered or even only answerable by researching *foreign* language learners and not *second* language learners.

For instance, let us take an empirically testable question such as the following: Is meaningful input itself sufficient to make alterations in a learner's linguistic system over time? If we attempted to investigate this with a rigorous longitudinal study in an L2 context, we would immediately be struck by the confounding variables outside the classroom. What about input sources outside the classroom? How could we control for interaction outside the classroom? How could we control with *whom* a learner interacts? What about literacy? What about different L1 backgrounds? The list of questions could go on. But, in a foreign language context, these extremely crucial variables are already controlled for us. We could, for example, set up a long-term (e.g. two- to three-year) study where learners are tracked across several different kinds of curriculum, one in which meaningful input is the be all and end all of the classroom, another in which input is mixed with explicit instruction, and another where meaningful input is virtually absent and focus is on production from the earliest stages. In all three contexts, homework and outside exposure are matched to classroom environment. Since we are controlling here for what happens outside the formal context, we are providing a much more exacting research design than could ever be achieved in an L2 context. It is important to note, however, that we are not testing methodology here, nor teaching variables, but those factors which SLA has already suggested are important in the construction of any theory of non-primary language acquisition. In addition, by using the FL context we may more easily get at the problems posed by language typologies. I could envision the research just outlined involving English as an FL, Spanish as an FL, German as an FL, and Japanese as an FL. In this way we see typological differences such as whether the language is underlyingly subject-initial or verb-initial, whether the language is morphologically rich or poor, whether the language is right- or left-branching, and whether the language has flexible or rigid word order. In addition, we would be including typological differences that go beyond the sentence level, i.e. discourse differences and communication differences based on the interface between culture and language.

While research of the kind just outlined may be hampered by practical concerns (e.g. funding), the point is that it is the FL context that can eventually serve as the testing ground for some of the hypotheses in SLA. And if these hypotheses are unsupported, then research in FLL may offer up new ones. What is clearly needed, then, is for the theorist–consumer relationship between SLA and the FL profession to be abandoned and for, firstly, the FL profession to promote language acquisition research with research paradigms in developmental psycholinguistics, sociolinguistics, discourse interaction and general communication;

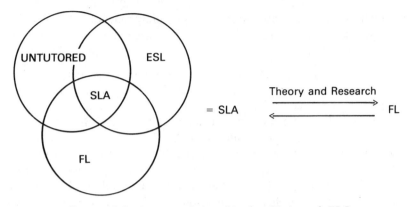

FIGURE 2.2 *A new relationship for SLA and FLL*

and secondly, SLA researchers to seek out FL professionals as partners in both research and theory construction. My schematic representation, then, for this relationship would look something like that in Figure 2.2.

From this scheme, it should be evident that FLL has aspects which are contextually different from other non-primary acquisition types, e.g. the constraints imposed on discourse by the setting. At the same time, FLL overlaps with untutored language acquisition in that there are persons who learn what are typically FLs in this country in an untutored setting somewhere else, e.g. German as an L2 in Germany, French as an L2 in France. In other areas, FLL overlaps with ESL in the context of English as an FL in such countries as Japan and Colombia. ESL and untutored language acquisition overlap in areas which are not pertinent to FL, e.g. the acquisition of English in the United States without the aid of formal instruction. But central to this entire scheme is that there is a learner who is capable of participating in any of the three contexts. It is what that learner *does* that is *common* to all contexts which forms the *core* of SLA theory and thus, in Figure 2.2, SLA is placed in the small area where all three contexts overlap. In a certain sense, we could even suggest that a theory of SLA must be a product of research in different contexts of non-primary language acquisition rather than a precursor.

What can we do to help build bridges? While this chapter is concerned with FL contributions to SLA theory, let us first mention the practical side. ESL and FL teachers need ways in which to interact such that common aspects of non-primary language teaching can be delineated, e.g. instead of meeting independently, there might be joint meetings of various regional and national FL organizations and ESL organizations.

We might encourage those currently pursuing teaching degrees in a language also to pursue a minor in the other discipline, e.g. FL teaching majors with ESL minors.

On the empirical side, researchers need to cross fields and test hypotheses in other contexts, e.g. we could set up special panels and colloquia at the Second Language Research Forum and at the annual international Teaching of English to Speakers of Other Languages (TESOL) meeting. In such contexts, both L2 and FL researchers could provide their perspectives and/or empirical research on various issues of SLA. And most importantly from my perspective as a professional in FL, the FL community needs to offer theory-testing research to SLA. Perhaps research interest sections, modelled on the TESOL interest sessions, could become integral parts of the annual meetings of various FL organizations such as the American Council on the Teaching of Foreign Languages. Hopefully, if such joint ventures are pursued, Ellis's need for caution in terminology will be obviated and one day we might even arrive at a comprehensive theory of non-primary language acquisition.

## Notes to Chapter 2

1. See, for example, the discussion in Chaudron (1985), Sharwood Smith (1986) and VanPatten (1989).
2. I do not mean to suggest that my account of morpheme acquisition is the only possible alternative to Larsen-Freeman's. Instead, I am simply demonstrating how a cross-linguistic FL research agenda can offer insights in SLA. In this volume, see Andersen (Chapter 5) for different comments on morpheme acquisition.
3. Interestingly, one often hears FL professionals lamenting that researchers in SLA ignore educational concerns or, as is generally said, researchers ignore those 'in the trenches'.

# 3 What is foreign language learning research?

CLAIRE J. KRAMSCH

*Massachusetts Institute of Technology, Cambridge, Massachusetts, USA*

As foreign language (FL) teachers turn to applied linguistics to understand the way people learn foreign languages in instructional settings, they encounter two relevant research strands, second language acquisition (SLA) and foreign language learning (FLL) research, that have emerged in recent years. The question, 'What is the relationship between SLA and FLL and what can each contribute to teaching foreign languages in classrooms?' is an important one. Yet, as linguists are busy discussing theoretical issues, language teachers have to help solve urgent matters of foreign language policy with or without the help of SLA or FLL research. For example, in West Germany, a theoretically orientated SLA (Wode, 1985; Felix & Hahn, 1985) vies with an empirical FLL research (e.g. Koordinierungsgremium, 1983; Bausch & Königs, 1983; 1985; Bausch, 1986) for the favours of foreign language teachers and learners while 4.5 million foreigners need to be integrated linguistically and socially into the West German society and economy. In the United States, the two strands of SLA, the universal-grammar-orientated (e.g. Flynn, 1987; Eubank, this volume) and the broader psycholinguistics strand (e.g. Seliger & Long, 1983; Gass & Madden, 1985) seem to have been short-circuited to a certain extent by an FL pedagogy that is responding to urgent national priorities under the pragmatic principle of 'proficiency' (e.g. Higgs, 1984). Here, as in West Germany, the lack of sufficient information on the complex factors involved in FLL has left classroom teachers to their own devices. Turning to FL education, they take some ideas from first or second language acquisition research to the extent that they fit into their procedural agenda, and for the rest they follow general educational methods that work.

## Foreign Language Learning Versus Second Language Acquisition and Foreign Language Education

FLL in educational settings—and I will concentrate on educational settings rather than general instructional settings—is currently the immediate concern of neither SLA research nor FL education research. SLA research, within a theoretical linguistics framework, is concerned mostly with the biological and psychological processes of learners in and out of classrooms. It asks such questions as: How do learners acquire L2 structures irrespective of such external factors as setting, instruction, etc.? What are the universal sequences of acquisition impervious to manipulation because they are biologically founded? Psycholinguistic SLA asks in addition: How is language learning linked to motivation, cognitive development, and the degree of socialization of the learners? In both cases, SLA research is centred on the learner as an independent biological and psychological entity and uses mostly quantitative methods of investigation. Until recently, SLA classroom research has used mostly interactional analysis or analysis of the surface features of discourse. But for a few exceptions, it has not attempted to interpret the phenomena observed in the light of their social context. Classroom studies have been mostly of the 'input–output' variety, correlating, for example, certain learner characteristics or strategies with second language achievement. Furthermore, up to now, most classroom-orientated SLA research has been conducted in English as a second language classrooms, in which the teacher is a native speaker, not in FL classes, for example in American secondary schools.

The other branch of research, FL education, is mainly concerned with the procedural aspects of the transmission of knowledge, be it a foreign language or any other sort of knowledge. The questions it asks are more of the type: How can we better help learners become proficient in a foreign language? (See, for example, Omaggio, 1986.) It is centred on the teachers, not on the learners, and on teachers' needs to conduct foreign language lessons. Neither psycholinguistic SLA or FL education research addresses the essential aspect of FLL, namely the socially and instructionally mediated acquisition of a foreign language in a classroom setting.

## Foreign Language Learning as an Area of Inquiry

As an area of inquiry, the field of FLL is characterized by very specific features regarding its setting, its object of research, its method of investigation, its concept of language and of language learning.

### Setting

In addition to the biological and psychological foundations of SLA, FLL in classrooms is affected by a multiplicity of variables that affect the propensity of learners to acquire a foreign language and the rate of this acquisition. Language is 'internalized' (Snow, 1987) on a grid of interpersonal transactions that are different from the social transactions in which a first language is acquired and in which foreign languages are acquired in natural settings. In a school setting, FLL is seriously affected by such factors as error correction, teaching methods, favoured versus disfavoured communication patterns between teacher and students and between students, turn-allocation across genders, statuses, roles, encouraged versus discouraged kinds of voice, allowed versus disallowed types of creativity and originality (are we encouraging true creativity or mere syntactic productivity?), previous FLL experience of learners (are we dealing with L2 or L3 learners, or with interactional patterns established by previous teachers?); it is also affected by the social background of learners and their degree of literacy and schooling.

### Object of research

The question posed by FLL is not, as in FL education, 'How can we better help learners learn?' but 'How can we better understand the conditions of FL learning and teaching in classrooms so we can change and improve these conditions?' Thus, FLL is orientated towards the learner, but the whole learner, in his or her biological, neurological, psychological, social, affective and personal make-up. FLL takes an integrative view of the learner drawing on a variety of related fields: psycho- and sociolinguistics, semantics, pragmatics, information-processing theory, cultural anthropology and ethnography, literacy studies and the teaching of English as a second language, and even foreign language policy. Its goal is not to control or predict the acquisition of the forms of the language, but to shed light on those classroom conditions that might further or hinder the learners' appropriation of a foreign language.

### Methods of investigation

FLL cannot be content to describe the phenomena observed and submit them to quantitative analysis, as has been done in most current SLA. As Michael Long (1980b) pointed out, SLA has to interpret the empirical data collected in the light of existing or emerging theories about human behaviour, learning, and language learning, using also methods taken from the social sciences: interviews, questionnaires, introspective accounts, diaries, think-aloud protocols. It has to understand both the behaviour of classroom learners and what informs that behaviour. Descriptive anthropological studies, such as interactional analysis, can inform experimental work. Long (1980b: 32) notes, that 'knowledge derived from [interactional analysis] would show not simply *what* the organization of interaction in a classroom is, but *how* it is achieved'. The fact that, as with ethnographic research, the method can create the phenomena it purports to discover, does not, in my view, speak against using such an approach if it does not replace, but supplements, more quantitative SLA methods of research that allow for greater generalization. FLL itself could profit from adopting an action-orientated approach, which searches for a convergence between researcher's and participant's perspectives, thus making the participants—the teacher and the learners— the very agents of the social change needed to effect language learning in the classroom.

### Concept of language

Unlike FL education that is anxious to divide language into a series of separate skills, FLL research must consider language in its total expressive and communicative thrust and deal with the global exploration of the development of communicative competence through the various modalities of speech. It must view the categorization into separate skills as detracting from the global concern with communication, as if we were using blinders instead of telescopes to understand the complex phenomena involved. In addition, FLL must consider language to be quintessentially indeterminate and culturally relative and thus view communication, especially communication between interlocutors of two different cultures, as the negotiation of meanings intended and interpreted within an interactional context. To quote Martin Buber: 'Meaning is not in us and in things, but between us and things, it can happen' (cited in Cook, 1985: 7).

### Concept of learning

Learning, for FLL, is not only a mental process, as it is for SLA, it is a social construct constrained by the conventions of schooling. In classrooms, language learning is a socially mediated process that originates and is ultimately fulfilled, not in the learner's Language Acquisition Device (Chomsky, 1965), but via the support system of the learning environment or Language Acquisition Support System (Bruner, 1985). According to Bruner (1985: 32) 'There is no way in which a human being could possibly master another world without the aid of others, for, in fact, that world *is* others'. If learning another language is mediated by the social environment of the classroom and if, in addition, this social environment is supposed to lead to the reorganization of sociocultural consciousness through the acquisition of foreign cultural meanings (Vygotsky, 1962; Frawley & Lantolf, 1985), then we need much more research into the social context of classroom FLL. Furthermore, classroom learning is, as we know, constrained by institutional parameters. It is related to the ability of the learners to display items of academically defined, and thus socially acceptable, knowledge, to match this knowledge with pre-established norms, to equate it with numbers of chapters in a textbook or items on a syllabus. In the classroom, difficulties in language acquisition are not due to linguistic complexity alone, but to a host of external factors such as lack of experiential background, lapses in memory, high affective defences, and procedural deficits, i.e. the inability to navigate around the established norms of classroom discourse (Allwright, 1980). 'The competence that is sufficient to produce sentences likely to be understood may be totally insufficient to produce sentences likely to be listened to . . . Social acceptability cannot be reduced to grammaticality alone' (Bourdieu, 1982: 42).

Some ten years ago Tarone *et al.* (1976) listed seven limitations to the classroom applications of SLA research. Among them were: lack of data on cognitive processes and learning strategies; limited information about the role of social and environmental variables; and underdeveloped methodology for data collection. Today, I feel, with Lightbown (1985b), that FLL has a specific classroom agenda that is not attended to by current SLA. Lightbown remarked that SLA in its current state can contribute immensely to teacher education, but not to teacher training. I would like to suggest that we would need less teacher training if we had a more interdisciplinary, comprehensive teacher education. Our capacity for teaching teachers how to teach is and will remain as limited as our abilities to teach learners how to learn. What we can do, however, is make them understand why they do what they do and the consequences of what they do. For that, FLL research still needs to continue exploring such questions as:

(1) How do learners acquire lexical meanings, develop concepts

from the foreign lexical and grammatical structures they learn, and pass from one-to-one equivalence to multifunctionality within the L2 system of semantic relations?

(2) What is the relationship between literacy skills, especially decontextualization skills, and the ability to manipulate symbols in a variety of cultural and social contexts?

(3) What is the impact of classroom discourse (teacher–students, students–students interaction) on the acquisition of L2 discourse patterns and on the setting of different sociolinguistic parameters of language in use? Might the meaning of language learning in the classroom reside in the institutional ritual itself (Bourdieu, 1982)?

(4) What is the impact of the acquisition of other modalities, such as writing and reading, on the acquisition of oral communicative competence? In particular, what impact does the literate environment of the classroom have on the acquisition of oral speech forms?

(5) What are the differences in learning strategies at different levels of proficiency?

(6) What is the impact of culturally determined learning styles on the acquisition of foreign cultural forms of discourse? In particular, what is the nature of textbook-mediated language acquisition? For example, how do textbooks help students make links between different aspects of knowledge, pass from one cultural framework to another, construct meanings, etc.?

(7) Language teachers need to know what the difference is between teaching/learning a language and teaching/learning any other subject in school—from maths to driver's education.

(8) Finally, what are the political, economic, ideological and societal forces that compel teachers to teach the way they do *irrespective* of insights gained through SLA/FLL research?

Such a research agenda is hardly touched upon by current research in SLA and has been neglected by FL education. This in part explains why FL teachers feel disenfranchized by current language learning research. I would like to advocate broadening the agenda of SLA to include more systematically the social and societal dimensions of language learning in classrooms. We do not need yet another discipline which teachers would look up to for definitive answers; what we do need is the participation of teachers, learners and researchers in the joint attempt to formulate the questions that are critical to FLL in classrooms.

These questions should be conceptualized at the necessary level of abstraction, so that rather than promoting piecemeal methods that work we can start searching for answers in an integrated manner. For example, the questions should not be: 'How should I teach dialogues?' but rather 'What do I want my students to know, how will I know that they know it, and what conditions can I help create in the classroom that will facilitate both the acquisition and the display of that knowledge? And, if the educational setting does not allow me to create those conditions, how can I change the educational setting?'

# 4 Second and foreign language learning: same, different or none of the above?

SUSAN M. GASS

*Michigan State University, East Lansing, USA*

The question of differential effects of the learning environment on learning outcomes and on acquisition processes has not seriously been addressed in second language acquisition (SLA) research. While it is the case that there has been a significant body of research focusing on classroom language learning (see, for example, Chaudron, 1988, and the sources cited therein), there is little emphasis on separating out the two contexts in which learning takes place (see VanPatten *et al.*, 1987, for a notable exception). In fact, Chaudron (1988) states that besides the obvious differences (i.e. availability of input and interactional opportunities), there is little in the way of actual classroom processes which are dependent on the contexts in which the language is being learned. What differences there may be between second language and foreign language instruction may be programmatically based or an effect of teacher training.

If we consider the issue from the perspective of learning, there are a number of ways in which we can conceive of the relationship between second language and foreign language learning. In this paper I will consider two such perspectives: variables internal to the learner; and variables external to the learner.

## Variables Internal to the Learner

There are two issues which I will address in this section: the task that a learner is faced with; and completeness.

## Learning tasks

It is difficult to imagine a situation in which the fundamental *processes* involved in learning a non-primary language would depend on the context in which the language is learned. In particular, the psycholinguistic tasks learners are faced with, the abilities that learners come to the learning situation with, the potential motivation they bring to the learning task[1] do not depend on the learning situation, whether it be a foreign language classroom, a classroom in a second language environment, or so-called naturalistic 'street' learning in a second language situation. All learners have the capability of taking information from the input and organizing it within the framework of their current linguistic system and modifying and restructuring that system (McLaughlin, 1988). A frequently made distinction in the second language literature is that between learning and acquisition (e.g. Krashen, 1981). 'Learning' in Krashen's sense refers to the conscious learning of explicit rules, as is typically seen within the context of a language classroom, whereas 'acquisition' refers to the internalization of language rules and information. While it may be the case that there are differences between these two ways of using second language information, both occur in as well as out of the classroom and both are essential in the development of a second language (see Gass, in press).

The task facing a second language learner is to come up with a grammar of a second language (grammatical competence)[2] and to develop the ability to put that knowledge to use. In the first case the learner has to determine the abstract structures of a language on the basis of limited exposure to surface structures only. Learners have to know the rules underlying the syntactic, semantic and phonological patterns of the language. In the second, the learner has to develop the skills necessary to translate that knowledge into output (fluency). What does differentiate the two language learning situations is the relative emphasis imposed by the context of learning on the development of knowledge versus the development of skill.

Kasper (1982) and Stenson (1975) have argued that there are qualitative differences between the two learning situations. They note that learners within a classroom context can be led to interlanguage-specific rules, that is, rules which are teacher (or material) induced. Stenson (1975: 54), in fact, argues that teaching procedures trigger processes which result in rules which are *only* evidenced in the speech of classroom learners.

> Students are easily led into making errors in the course of classroom participation by the structure of the situation: there are errors which it is doubtful they would produce in spontaneous speech.

An example which Stenson (1975: 57) cites is as follows:

> Students in one advanced class were asked if they knew the meaning of *any*, and, when all said yes, to give some examples, with the following result: 'In this class there are any students who speak German (= not any, no students)', 'In a private garden anyone can enter (= no one)' and 'Anybody has to work.' Apparently these students were once told something to the effect that *any* is used in negatives, or has negative connotations, and they interpreted that to mean that it was itself a negative word like *never* or *nothing*.

Stenson claims that this error is not found in the spontaneous speech of second language (L2) learners.

Unlike Stenson and Kasper, I would not consider this a result of a different learning procedure since *all* learners generalize from one instance to another; *all* learners misinterpret information. What does differ is the particular instantiation of the process, not the process itself.

### Completeness

The second issue I will address is that of completeness, since on the surface it appears to differentiate second and foreign language learning. A typical view of language learning maintains that one cannot *really* learn another language unless one lives in the country where that language is spoken. Implicit in such a view is that the classroom does not provide a sufficient basis (whether due to the quality or the quantity of the input is not clear) for successful language development to take place, where successful language development is assumed to mean something like 'native-like' competence. The question is whether successful language development ever takes place, given the above definition. I would like to challenge the implicit assumption that 'mastery' of a second language is possible.

The question of completeness, or non-fossilization, has been discussed recently by Schachter (1988). As she points out, it is rare that any second language speaker reaches a state of 'completeness'.[3] She further claims that, while it may be the case that there are learners who appear to be native-like in a second language, if one were to probe their intuitions sufficiently, one would find differences between their linguistic knowledge and that of a 'typical' native speaker.

It is well known that most learners, be it classroom or non-classroom learners, do not attain complete mastery of an L2. Most non-native speakers never reach a point of being indistinguishable from native speakers of a particular linguistic community. What is perhaps the most interesting question is whether native language proficiency by second language learners is *ever* possible. Is it ever possible to have the grammatical knowledge of a native speaker? Leaving aside the vexed question of pronunciation (see Neufeld, 1980), the issue of completeness is one which seems at first glance to be one which may to some degree be determined by classroom versus non-classroom exposure.

However, a closer look reveals that the difference may only be a quantitative one. Even in those cases where a non-native speaker *appears* indistinguishable from a native speaker, subtle differences are present in the form of the linguistic knowledge learners have about the L2. In a recent study, Coppieters (1987) investigated the grammatical intuitions of fluent non-native speakers of French. These were speakers of a variety of native languages. Importantly, they are speakers who had been identified by native speakers of French as fluent French speakers. Yet, when their intuitions about a set of French sentences were probed, these departed from the intuitions native speakers of French have about the same utterances. Similarly, Mack (1986) finds that the semantic and syntactic processing of bilinguals differs from that of monolinguals. While this is not her interpretation, it may be possible to extend the claim about completeness made within the context of second language learning to include bilingual contexts as well—native-like competence is only possible in one language.

Revealing research relating to completeness comes from work by Swain (1985), who looked at the language development of sixth-grade immersion children in Canada. These are children who had been in a French language context for the seven years of their education. Swain assessed their language abilities in a variety of areas, finding that these children performed in a like manner to native speakers in some areas, but not in others. What Swain claims to be the differentiating factor between the non-natives and the native speakers is what she calls comprehensible output. Comprehensible output, or language production, provides 'the opportunity for meaningful use of one's linguistic resources' (Swain, 1985: 248). Thus, the learner, through output, is able to test hypotheses, try various phrases, words, syntactic structures and see if they work. Another function of output is to move development along from a semantic to a syntactic focus. Language production 'may be the trigger that forces the learner to pay attention to the means of expression needed in order to successfully convey his or her own intended meaning' (Swain, 1985: 249).

The reason why immersion children do not show productive competence in the L2 is that they have had little opportunity to *use* the language productively in the classroom. The difficulty in interpreting these results in the context of classroom versus non-classroom learning is that, while it is true that learning in an immersion context takes place within a classroom environment, there is peer interaction outside the classroom as well. None the less, Swain's claim is that the opportunities for language production are limited because the bulk of learning takes place within a classroom environment.

Swain's claims regarding comprehensible output as well as other work on the role of negotiation and interactional learning (Pica, 1987; Varonis & Gass, 1985; Long, 1980a; Gass & Varonis, 1986) point to the fact that second language productive knowledge may be attainable only through interactional exposure to the language. On the other hand, Coppieters (1987) points to the fact that native-like intuitional knowledge or complete native-like language abilities may never be attainable by most learners or even by *any* second language learner. Whether these differences are quantitative or qualitative remains to be seen.

Thus, what on the surface appears to differentiate the two learning situations may in fact only be a difference of degree rather than an absolute difference in which productive competence is possible in one situation, but not in another.

## Variables External to the Learner

In this section I will focus on two areas of research which influence language learning: negative evidence; and input.

### Negative evidence

The major concern in second language research is to seek to understand how learners arrive at a 'grammar' of a second language with only limited information about that language. It is well established that as learners produce utterances in a second language, many 'errors' are made. What is of interest is how learners recognize that an error is in fact an error, a necessary prerequisite for the eventual emergence of correct forms (see Gass, 1988a; Schmidt, 1988).

Theoretically, there are two kinds of evidence available to learners as they make hypotheses about correct and incorrect language forms: *positive* and *negative* evidence (Bowerman, 1987). Positive evidence comes from the speech they hear or read and is thus comprised of a limited set of well-formed utterances. Of the infinite number of possible sentences in a language, a learner hears only a subset. Chomsky (1981a) and others (e.g. Berwick, 1985; Pinker, 1984; 1987) have claimed that there is no way for a learner to determine whether a given sentence is not heard because it is not a possible sentence in that language or it is coincidentally not heard. It is in this sense that the sentences of a language which a learner hears (either a child first language learner or a second language learner) are referred to as the 'positive' evidence on the basis of which hypotheses are formed. On the other hand, *negative* evidence is comprised of information to a learner that his or her utterance is deviant *vis-à-vis* the norms of the language being learned. This can be in the form of an overt correction or an indirect indication of the deviance of an utterance.

It has been argued that for child language acquisition negative evidence is not frequent and is not a necessary condition for acquisition (cf. Pinker, 1987; see Bohannon & Stanowicz, in press, for evidence against this claim). Rather, innate properties which impose limitations on possible grammars have been posited. From a theoretical perspective this is necessary since in the absence of negative evidence it would be an impossible task for a child to arrive at a well-formed adult grammar. In other words, because there is no way through positive evidence alone to limit the range of possible grammatical sentences and since negative evidence is not frequently forthcoming, there must be innate principles which constrain a priori the possibilities of grammar formation.

Birdsong (1987), Bley-Vroman (1989; in press), Gregg (1989), White (1987) and Gass (1988b) have made refinements to and arguments for the role for negative evidence in second language learning (although see Schwartz, 1986 for arguments against the role of negative evidence in adult second language learning; and Gregg, 1988, for arguments against Schwartz). If there were a lack of negative evidence in adult second language learning, one would need to assume that adults have access to the same innate universal constraints or properties as children. However, there is a crucial difference: it is not clear that the assumption of lack of negative evidence in second language acquisition is warranted

(Birdsong, 1987; 1988; Bley-Vroman, 1989; in press; Schachter, 1988). If we consider that negative evidence is present primarily in conversational interactions, then it becomes necessary to investigate the nature and structure of conversations to understand the potential role of negative evidence in the acquisition of a second language. Examples of negative evidence (in this case from a native speaker (NS) to a non-native speaker (NNS)), and both taken from Day *et al.*, 1984 are given in (1) and (2):

(1)

| NNS: | He will be, you know, he will be dirty this March 8. |
| NS: | He will be what? |
| NNS: | Thirty years old. |

(2)

| NNS: | Like the like the the the chop the chop |
| NS: | Chopsticks. |
| NNS: | Yeah, chopsticks. |

Exchanges of the type in (1) (in which, because of the oddity of the phrase, the native speaker indicates to the non-native that the message has not been understood) and (2) (in which the native speaker helps the non-native with an apparently unsuccessful word search) are frequent in conversations with second language learners (see Scarcella and Higa, 1981; Varonis and Gass, 1985; Gass and Varonis, 1986; 1988; Pica, 1987; Long, 1980a). However, to argue that negative evidence is a necessary condition (or even an important aspect of second language learning), it is not sufficient to show that instances of negative feedback to second language learners are frequent. Rather, we must minimally argue that learners, as a consequence of the negative evidence they receive, alter hypotheses about the language (Gass & Varonis, 1988; 1989).

Negative evidence in the second language literature has been conceptualized narrowly, generally referring only to verbal indications to a learner that her or his utterance is malformed, as in (1) and (2) above. If, on the other hand, negative evidence involves subtle non-verbal information as well (a generally unexplored area of second language research), then it may be that the way learners are provided with negative evidence (and hence what learners perceive as negative evidence) differs cross-culturally. Erickson and Shultz (1982), while not dealing with non-native speakers, allude to this when they note that speakers from different ethnic backgrounds attend to different listening and speaking behaviours.

If it can be shown that negative evidence is a necessary condition for successful second language acquisition, then this difference may provide a basis for differentiating second and foreign language learning. Learners in these contexts may have different opportunities for obtaining this relevant linguistic information.

Let us assume, then, that negative evidence is essential to second language acquisition and that it is an important area of difference between first and second language acquisition. What, then, might the difference be between purely classroom learning and learning in a second language environment (with or without classroom instruction)?

Within a foreign language classroom, the negative evidence provided by a native speaker may be at times indirect (as in (3) below) but may also be direct (as in instances of direct correction, e.g. 'That's not right, you should say it like this . . .'), whereas the major type of negative evidence in a second language environment is indirect.

(3)

| | |
|---|---|
| **NNS**: | It is necessary to 'pirsuad' students. |
| **Teacher**: | It is necessary to 'what'? |
| **NNS**: | to 'pirsuad' |
| **Teacher**: | I'm sorry I don't understand the word. |
| **NNS**: | to 'pirsuad', you know, 'convince' |
| **Teacher**: | Oh, persuade, you've done a lot of reading, that's how it's spelled. |

Outside of the classroom one is unlikely to get explicit correction of an utterance (Chun *et al.*, 1982). Let us also assume, following Erickson and Shultz, that different cultures respond differently to listening and speaking cues. It follows that the subtle indirect cues may not be as beneficial to some learners as are more direct indications (e.g. by a teacher) of the deviance of an utterance. Thus, while the amount of information a learner receives outside the classroom may in fact be greater than what a learner receives in a classroom, it may also be the case that that information may be unusable for language development.

## Input

It is in the category of input that major differences exist between second and foreign language learning. In fact, one might be tempted to argue that the major difference between at least classroom and non-classroom learning are the limits of the input. While I would agree with this to a certain extent, there are certainly some fundamental similarities to the structure of the input which cannot be overlooked. In both situations the input is, in some sense, controlled for the learner. In an untutored environment, direct talk to a learner is controlled through modifications of the input (that is, slower rate, limited vocabulary, limited range of syntactic structures etc.; cf. Hatch, 1983a, for an extensive list of features of input modification in foreigner talk); and the interactional structure of talk (that is, clarification requests, comprehension checks, negotiations of meaning etc.; cf. Long, 1980a; Varonis and Gass, 1985). In a tutored environment, the linguistic input is controlled and structured by the teacher (see Gaies, 1977) and by the materials used. Because of these modifications in talk directed to learners, in neither situation are learners confronted with the full range of grammatical structures nor lexical richness of the target language.

However, it must be noted that there may be areas of language which are not amenable to textbook or teacher explanation and which are therefore only attainable from the external environment. For example, Gass (1987) investigated sentence interpretation strategies by speakers of English learning Italian and speakers of Italian learning English. Both learning groups were further subdivided according to learning environment (second versus foreign language). There are important differences between these two languages in the information each uses to establish the grammatical relations among elements in a sentence, and hence, in the way that sentence interpretation takes place. English is a language which uses word order as a major criterion for interpretation, so that a sentence such as 'The picture kisses the girl' can only be interpreted as the picture doing the kissing; Italian, on the other hand, uses agreement as well as semantic and pragmatic factors to sort out constituent relationships. In the data from Italian learners learning English there was no difference in interpretation between the EFL and the ESL groups, whereas in the group of English speakers learning Italian there were significant differences between the IFL and ISL environments on nearly every variable tested. Thus, for the native speaker of English, the variables considered were highly dependent on the environment. Italian speakers had the task of moving from a highly flexible system for interpretation to a more restricted system. The lack of flexibility in English word order becomes immediately obvious to a learner. On the other hand, English speakers learning Italian have to learn not only to extend the range of possibilities of interpretation, but also to determine which of the cues dominates and under which condition.

The data presented in that study suggest that sensitivity to strategies of interpretation is an aspect of learning which is not available through minimal exposure, as one often gets in a classroom or from textbooks. For native speakers of Italian learning English, the sensitivity was rather straightforward in that word order dominates and only one word order is possible in most situations. For learners of Italian the situation is much more complex with more interacting factors to reckon with. This information is unavailable from most textbooks. Rather, it is only discernible from the ambient speech of the L2 community. Blum-Kulka and Olshtain (1986) and Edmondson *et al.* (1984) have similarly argued that certain language information is in need of 'higher levels of contextual explicitness' for acquisition to take place.

This view of the significance of environment differs from typical treatments in which that significance is debated. The effect of the environment is dependent on a number of factors, among which is the language learned, how concrete the information is, and how accessible the information is to the learner. A question of both theoretical and practical import arises: Is the type of interpretation strategy apparent from this study and other similar studies (e.g. papers in *Applied Psycholinguistics*, 8,4) available or perhaps more importantly 'learnable' through explicit instruction? In other words, even if we were able to make some of these factors precise, are they available in other than natural settings? Is there language information which is available only implicitly? If so, in those cases, explicit descriptions would serve little purpose in integration of L2 information.

## Conclusion

As I have, I hope, made clear in the body of this paper, there are both quantitative and qualitative differences in the two language learning situations. Moreover, there are numerous similarities. While foreign language (classroom) learning generally involves a greater focus on form, non-classroom learning involves a greater focus on interactive skill-building. Hence, the former tends to emphasize knowledge over skill, whereas the latter emphasizes skill over knowledge. Clearly, this is a gross over-simplification, but it may be a distinction which in the future will help us to understand the similarities and differences between second and foreign language learning. Our research agenda, then, should not be whether they are the same or different, for the answer is 'yes'. Our major interest should be in the discovery of the extent and nature of the similarities and differences.

## Notes to Chapter 4

1. Clearly, in a situation of second language learning there may be additional learner interest as a result of living in a second language culture; however, the motivation is not necessarily dependent on the situation.
2. This, of course, is an oversimplified view of what has to be learned for it overlooks pragmatic knowledge, sociolinguistic knowledge, etc. However, for the purposes of this paper I will focus on grammatical knowledge in the more traditional view, not from any belief that the others are irrelevant. To the contrary, I would maintain that the claims that I will make concerning the acquisition of grammatical knowledge may be just as applicable to other kinds of language-related information. What differs in the two language learning situations under consideration in this paper is not the mechanisms available for learning, but the availability to the learner of relevant information.
3. The question of completeness raises a number of interesting questions. Most notably, what knowledge does a native speaker of a language have? If native speakers differ in terms of what they 'know' of their native language, then how can we determine non-native completeness?

# 5 Models, processes, principles and strategies: second language acquisition inside and outside the classroom

ROGER W. ANDERSEN

*University of California, Los Angeles, USA*

## Putting Order in Our Inquiry

This paper relates empirical research on primarily natural untutored second language acquisition to the foreign language classroom environment. The goal is to provide a new perspective on how foreign languages can be acquired from natural language input within the limited confines of a foreign language classroom. The model of second and foreign language acquisition presented here is intended to be especially relevant to the Authentic Language Plus Model, being developed by the author, but it is phrased in more general terms that do not require adherence to any specific authentic language model. It does require, however, a model of instruction that allows students to come into contact with authentic language as a major part of their language instruction.

To relate the two types of language acquisition, naturalistic second and tutored foreign language acquisition, requires, I believe, close attention to at least four basic distinctions concerning the models of how a second language is 'acquired' and used; the explicit characterization of the psycholinguistic processes involved in the acquisition and use of a language; the empirical verification of psycholinguistic principles that govern development of the language being learned; and the empirical verification of the strategies learners use to communicate with their non-proficient linguistic competence.

I am assuming that the same processes, principles, and strategies will be shared to a great extent across different settings, different types and ages of learners, and different circumstances for learning and using the second or foreign language. By working with a particular model and the processes, principles and strategies that fit within that model, it should be easier to recognize the effect of setting-, learner-, and language-specific variables on the language acquisition process and the final outcome. I further believe that only by working within such a common framework can we carry out the type of new innovative research that will eventually allow us to intervene more successfully in the acquisition process to bring about faster, more efficient, and more successful learning of a foreign language as the result of such research.

Most of this paper will be devoted to outlining a particular model of second or foreign language acquisition and the processes, principles and strategies that fit within that model. Since these terms could mean different things to different people, let me define as clearly as possible what I mean by each:

1.  *Model*: 'A tentative ideational structure used as a testing device . . .' (*American Heritage Dictionary*, 843).
2.  *Process*: '1. A system of operations in the production of something. 2. A series of actions, changes, or functions that bring about an end or result' (*AHD*, 1043).
3.  *Principle*: '4. A basic, or essential, quality or element determining intrinsic nature or characteristic behavior . . . 5. A rule or law concerning the functioning of natural phenomena or mechanical processes . . .' (*AHD*, 1041).
4.  *Strategy*: 'A method by which people go about solving problems' (Clark & Clark, 1977: 567).

The model I will follow is basically a psycholinguistic model with a socio-interactive component. In taking this approach, I am agreeing with Clark & Clark (1977: vii) that 'one of the principles that gives the field [of psycholinguistics] coherence is that psycholinguistics is fundamentally the study of three mental processes—the study of listening, speaking, and the acquisition of these skills . . .' and that 'another principle that gives the field coherence is that the primary use of language is for communication'. Although processes, principles and strategies eventually must all be elaborated and supported empirically to an equal degree, in this discussion I will focus most heavily on the cognitive operating principles that seem to govern interlanguage construction.

## A Cognitive-Interactionist Model of Second Language Acquisition

Any psycholinguistic model[1] of naturalistic (i.e. non-instructed) second language acquisition has somehow to capture at least the following. First, that learners do attempt to communicate (and often succeed) with a very minimal competence in the second language. Second, that through such attempts to communicate the learner comes to perceive linguistic devices used by native speakers (or more proficient non-native speakers) that previously he had not perceived. Third, that the learner somehow incorporates these new perceptions into his interlanguage system, i.e. his developing internal representation of the language he is learning. Fourth, that this internal representation is initially and even for a long time very different from what it must be for a near-native or native speaker. Fifth, that when he incorporates a new linguistic device (a phonological contrast, a lexical class distinction, an inflection, an auxiliary or subject-verb inversion) into his interlanguage, it fits into the learner's evolving interlanguage system and does not bring with it the full meaning, function and distribution it had in the native speaker's linguistic system. Finally, that over time, the learner gradually restructures his second language linguistic system in terms of increasingly finer congruence with the native target system, provided the conditions are right for restructuring over time.

In earlier work (Andersen, 1979b; 1980; 1983a; 1984a) I tried to capture this view of the creation of an internally consistent interlanguage system through verbal interaction with more proficient speakers of the second language in what I called the Nativization[2] Model. In this model 'nativization' refers to the composite of presumably universal processes and principles which guide an individual language learner in the creation of an internal representation of the language he is acquiring and subsequent assimilation of new input to that gradually evolving internal representation. In the original phrasing of the model (Andersen, 1979b:109) I included reference to an opposing 'force', denativization, which was characterized as 'the gradual restructuring of the learner's somewhat unique and idiosyncratic internal representation of the language he is acquiring in terms of the input he processes during language acquisition'. Nativization constituted development independent of the nature of the target language system and denativization as development towards that target system. Subsequent research has made it clear that nativization and denativization are not two separate processes or 'forces', but simply represent different extremes in the result of the overall process of second language acquisition, which could be plotted along a continuum ranging from furthest from the target language system (the nativized end) to closest to the target language system (the denativized end).

This paper is an attempt to specify more fully the psycholinguistic processes, cognitive operating principles, and communicative strategies that fit within this overall conceptualization of the Nativization Model. I assume that the Nativization Model, being a psycholinguistic model of individual second language acquisition under a variety of different circumstances, applies equally well to a classroom environment. The classroom environment, however, must be one in which the learner has some reasonable access to and control over the input from which he is to acquire the second or foreign language as well as some means of carrying on meaningful communicative interaction at a level suitable for his linguistic competence at any one point in time, so that he can utilize these processes, principles, and strategies effectively to gain access to specific target-language linguistic devices and gradually incorporate these devices into his interlanguage system.

## Psycholinguistic Processes

The basic task in language learning is to get the language that is outside the learner's head into his head. In formal classroom learning, it is assumed that clear, orderly, explicit presentation of bits and pieces of the language in some logical sequence will accomplish this task. In naturalistic non-instructed second language acquisition (SLA), it is assumed that the learner must somehow impose order on the language he is exposed to and make sense out of it, in order to 'get it into his head'. In both settings the psycholinguistic processes involved are usually assumed and seldom made explicit. If we are to relate SLA research to the foreign language setting, these processes need to be made more explicit.

It is clear from such studies as Brown (1973) and Peters (1977; 1983; 1985) on first language acquisition, and Hakuta (1974; 1976), Huang & Hatch (1978), and Wong-Fillmore (1976; 1979) on second language acquisition, that both first and second language learners are fully capable of perceiving and extracting meaningful segments of language from the input directed to them. Such a capacity for perceiving, analysing, storing and somehow organizing in memory meaningful bits and pieces of language without any formal instruction must be an important prerequisite for any language learning. Slobin (1985b) incorporates Peters's (1985) principles for perceiving, storing and tagging such segments of speech into his revised group of 40 operating principles for first language acquisition. These initial basic principles are the first eight operating principles of his group of principles. They are the first group because they are prerequisite to all the others. Four examples of these initial operating principles are (Slobin, 1985b: 1251–52):

*Attention Principles*:
*Sounds*: Store any perceptually salient stretches of speech.
*Stress*: Pay attention to stressed syllables in extracted speech units. Store such syllables separately and also in relation to the units with which they occur.

*Storage Principles*:
*Frequency*: Keep track of the frequency of occurrence of every unit and pattern that you store.
*Units*: Determine whether a newly extracted stretch of speech seems to be the same as or different from anything you have already stored. If it is different, store it separately; if it is the same, take note of this sameness by increasing its frequency count by one.

In addition to perceiving and storing such segments, the learner must impose some organization on them within his memory, so they can be retrieved rapidly and accurately and integrated into the stream of speech during production (as well as utilized during comprehension). Lenneberg (1967: 89–120) has shown how the brain is capable of incredible co-ordination and planning of speech on all linguistic levels in order to access the information stored in memory and integrate it rapidly in linear order in speech production. Somehow when the learner perceives, tags, and stores segments of speech during natural interaction with the providers of input, these segments are stored in such a way that they can be accessed rapidly and thus readily available for integration into spontaneous speech production.

The psycholinguistic constraints on speech perception and production are well known (cf., for example, Clark & Clark, 1977). Within a psycholinguistic framework, Clahsen (1984a) has drawn on three language processing strategies to explain the order of acquisition of a number of word order and negative placement rules in German by non-instructed immigrant workers in West Germany. He concludes that the first interlanguage structures to emerge are those which conform to these strategies. The next structures to emerge in a subsequent stage violate one but conform to the other two strategies, followed by structures which violate two and finally all three strategies. He thus argues that delay in acquisition of certain word order permutations is a consequence of these processing constraints: it takes time for the learner to override these constraints and acquire the mechanism for doing so.

What then does this mean for the foreign language classroom setting? Pienemann (1985; 1987) has carried out studies in a classroom setting to test the hypothesis that instruction will have an effect on acquisition only if the learner has reached the stage where he is 'ready' to incorporate the new rule or structure into his linguistic system. This study, which supports the hypothesis, is based on Clahsen's formulation of the three processing strategies and the German SLA project conducted by Clahsen, Meisel and Pienemann (see, for example, Clahsen *et al.*, 1983b; Clahsen, 1984a; 1987; see also Jordens, 1987, and Taylor, 1987, for possible counter-evidence and alternative interpretations).

A related question is whether the input that is provided for learners in a classroom can be carefully controlled in order to conform to this series of constraints. By this I mean meaningful input supplied for communication, not the usual rules, examples, and paradigms for memorization and practice.[3] A worthwhile hypothesis to test is whether constructions that do not violate these processing strategies are easier to comprehend, imitate, and also produce spontaneously within a classroom context than similar constructions which differ only in terms of the number of strategies they violate. This is, of course, a proposal for research, not a prescription for teaching methodology.

Another more difficult hypothesis to test would be that the bits and pieces of input that are perceived, tagged and stored in memory must be accessed in the input through meaningful communicative interaction for the brain to be able to store these segments in such a way that they can later be accessed rapidly and integrated into a novel utterance at a different point in time. That is, the familiar lists, paradigms and rules of foreign language classrooms are not readily accessible for this purpose precisely because they are not the result of such communicative interaction. Such a hypothesis seems to underlie the emphasis on communicative language teaching during the past decade as well as any teaching approach that attempts to provide an acquisition-rich environment within the classroom (e.g. Krashen & Terrell, 1983).

## Cognitive Operating Principles

I will now turn to the major area of this paper: the cognitive operating principles that govern the path the learner takes in developing an increasingly more native-like and more efficient and successful linguistic competence in a second language. During the past several years I have been influenced considerably by the first-language acquisition work of Dan Slobin in this area (Slobin, 1973; 1977; 1982; 1985b). I will proceed to discuss seven potential operating principles for SLA which I believe are consistent with the psycholinguistic processing framework I have just touched on. Most of them can be related directly or indirectly to one or more of Slobin's operating principles. They are not, however, simply a translation of Slobin's principles into the domain of SLA. In fact, they are more macro-principles in that each one would correspond to a group of more succinct operating principles within Slobin's framework. In addition, two of these principles are mainly relevant to SLA.

Just how many such principles are needed to begin to account for empirical evidence within the field of second language acquisition is a difficult question to answer. For native language acquisition, Slobin has increased his initial seven operating principles (Slobin, 1973) to 40 (Slobin, 1985b). The principles that I discuss here have evolved primarily out of my own research on the acquisition of Spanish and English as second languages, as well as my understanding of related research on other languages. I find they are a major improvement over the two principles I began with several years ago (the One-to-One Principle and the Transfer to Somewhere Principle) and contribute to a further elaboration of the Nativization Model.[4]

### The One-to-One Principle

This principle states that 'an interlanguage system should be constructed in such a way that an intended underlying meaning is expressed with one clear invariant surface form (or construction)' (Andersen 1984a:79). The motivation for such a principle is probably the processing constraints discussed earlier. In fact, the earliest constructions to emerge in German, following Clahsen's (1984a) three processing strategies, conform to the One-to-One Principle. His subjects initially maintained a subject-verb-object word order, even though native German requires verb-subject order in certain contexts, clause-final placement of non-finite verb forms, after any object or adverbial, and final placement of finite verb forms in subordinate clauses.

Native French and Spanish require clitic objects to be placed pre-verbally, but in early stages of SLA of these languages learners maintain the canonical post-verbal position, which conforms to the One-to-One Principle, since full NPs and pronouns alike are placed in the same post-verbal position (see Zobl, 1980b; Andersen, 1983b). In placement of a negator, native English, French, German and Swedish each have language-specific rules which are hard to acquire. For each of these languages learners initially choose the simplest solution, which conforms to the One-to-One Principle: place the negator directly before[5] the entity to be negated (the verb or predicate, for propositional negation) (see Andersen, 1984a:81–82 for further details).

Articles in German and Spanish (and many other languages) encode, in addition to specificity of the referent, gender, number, and, for German, case. Learners, however, initially disregard all but specificity as the relevant meaning to encode (Andersen, 1984b; Gilbert, 1983; Pfaff, 1985; see also Huebner, 1983; 1985). Personal pronouns similarly encode a number of features in native languages like English, German and Spanish. In second-language Spanish, there is a strong tendency to disregard case marking and use the same form (usually a stressed form) for subject, direct and indirect object, and possessives (Andersen, 1983b).

Finally, a number of first and second language acquisition studies (summarized in Andersen, 1986a; 1986b) suggest that learners first use past-reference verbal morphology according to whether the event is punctual (i.e. one simple completed act of limited duration). In first and second language acquisition of English, past morphology (especially strong past) is first attached to punctual verbs (Antinucci & Miller, 1976; Bloom et al., 1980; see Andersen, 1986a; 1986b, for discussion of SLA). In Spanish, there àre two past forms: preterite and imperfect. The preterite is the first form to be used (Jacobsen, 1986; Simões & Stoel-Gammon, 1979; Andersen, 1986a; 1986b). The preterite form is initially restricted to punctual events and, when the imperfect form begins to emerge, it is restricted to states. Both of these cases conform to the One-to-One Principle.

What does a One-to-One Principle mean for the foreign language classroom context of SLA? Perhaps a one-form–one-meaning relation is inevitable as a first entry into a language. If so, a major goal of foreign language research should be to discover what form–meaning relations learners initially perceive and incorporate into their interlanguage. The assumption is that an acquisition-directed language pedagogy should work within such natural tendencies. After discussion of the next principle, I will discuss further what type of research might be productive in this area.

## The multifunctionality principle

The Multifunctionality Principle can be stated as follows:

(a) Where there is clear evidence in the input that more than one form marks the meaning conveyed by only one form in the interlanguage, try to discover the distribution and additional meaning (if any) of the new form. (b) Where there is evidence in the input that an interlanguage form conveys only one of the meanings that the same form has in the input, try to discover the additional meanings of the form in the input.

It might seem strange, after discussing a One-to-One Principle, to suggest that there is pressure for a learner to move towards an interlanguage system where a given form is multifunctional. But such a principle seems inevitable. This is evident from at least two perspectives. First, all native languages appear to incorporate a considerable amount of multifunctionality into their linguistic systems. Second, when a learner moves away from a one-to-one representation of form to meaning it is usually in the direction of multifunctionality in existing forms (along with addition of new forms).

Why should a learner feel compelled to abandon an initial One-to-One Principle? Slobin (1977) has discussed four metaphorical charges to language that any natural language must obey: it must be clear; humanly processible in ongoing time; quick and easy; and expressive. The One-to-One Principle conforms to the first two charges. The multifunctionality principle addresses the second two. The communicative and phatic functions of language require the user to be able to express a wide range of meanings, intentions, and perspectives ('be expressive') and to do so as quickly as possible and in such a way that it is easy for the listener to interpret his or her intentions ('be quick and easy'). These two charges require considerable multifunctionality of forms and constructions. Another way to put it is that by using fewer forms and constructions and letting each one perform a number of different functions, the speaker can get across a richer, more complex message and do it easier and faster.

How, then, does the learner move from a One-to-One Principle towards multifunctionality? One way seems to be that once the learner has incorporated one form into his repertoire (for example, *no* for all uses of negation: *no* the dog, he *no* go), he can perceive alternate forms (e.g. *not*, *don't*) and differentiate the environment in which they occur (e.g. *no* for anaphoric negation, *don't* for preverbal negation and *not* for everything else). That is, having one of the forms in his interlanguage allows him to perceive the multiple forms for that one meaning. In cases where there is one form with multiple meanings, it seems that, in some cases at least, the learner is able to extend the initially limited scope of a form to a wider range of lexical items to which it can be attached by analogy. For example, in natural non-tutored SLA of Spanish, learners begin to use the past preterite verb form for purely punctual, non-durative events and the present form or, somewhat later, the imperfect form, for all other verbs. But once the learner has begun to use the past preterite verb form (e.g. *cayó* 'fell') for strictly punctual and non-durative events he can extend the form to a wider range of verbs that are both punctual and durative (*corrió una milla* 'he ran a mile'), and from there to completely non-punctual but durative events like *jugó* 'he played', using the preterite form now to impose a punctual-type interpretation on the event (contrasting with a durative interpretation: *jugaba* 'he played/he would play/he was playing'; see Andersen, 1986b for more details).

I believe, however, that the ways in which a one-to-one relationship expands into a multifunctional one vary from case to case depending on certain aspects of the native language of the learner and the language being learned, as well as additional principles which I will be discussing shortly. That is, various of these operating principles interact with each other.

The One-to-One Principle, together with the Multifunctionality Principle, should have important implications for innovative new research within a foreign language classroom. If there is a 'preferred' path of development from an interlanguage form or construction that conforms to the One-to-One Principle through various interim structures up to the full native multiform and multifunction system, then a logical hypothesis to test in research is that learners will acquire easier and faster input that is controlled systematically to match this preferred path (i.e. with the input changing as the learners move up to a level where they can efficiently process the more complex input).[6]

I should provide equal time for a counter-proposal and a clarification of what I am proposing. First of all, a counter-hypothesis would state that controlling input (and thus depriving the learner of examples of something he will acquire much later after many such examples) will actually retard development and promote an early fossilized interlanguage, quite the opposite of what one might hope for. This is a logical counter-hypothesis and one that should be pursued in such research. I need also to clarify that I am not proposing that such modification of input is a simple task that any teacher can or should do. This is a proposal for research, not a prescription for pedagogical intervention. Moreover, such a research proposal does not address the possible need for control over the ways the learner should interact with the suppliers of the input and with fellow students to facilitate internalization of the form–meaning relations in the input (on this matter, see Long, 1981; Hatch *et al.*, 1986; and Sato, 1986).

## Formal Determinism

One of the principles which guides the learner from a unifunctional to a multifunctional linguistic system is the Principle of Formal Determinism. Basically this states that when the form–meaning relationship is clearly and uniformly encoded in the input, the learner will discover it earlier than other form–meaning relationships and will incorporate it more consistently within his interlanguage system. In short, the clear, transparent encoding of the linguistic feature in the input forces the learner to discover it.

The example of English negation mentioned earlier seems to be partly the result of formal determinism. Many learners initially place *no* before any constituent to be negated: *no* here; they *no* work; my brother *no* in school, following the One-to-One Principle. When they discover other forms it is because the other forms, *not* and *don't*, are modelled clearly in the input in such a way that they differ from each other and from *no* in their distribution. Evidence for this is that learners generally restrict *don't* to pre-verbal environments (which do not include the copula), *no* to anaphoric use, and *not* to negated constituents such as equative predicates, noun phrases (NPs), adverbs, and the like. Even with such complexities in the input as the imperceptibility of certain contractions, such as 'is*n't*' versus 'is *not*', English seems to offer a clear enough model for which form belongs with which context to allow the learner to abandon his earlier one-to-one system of negation.

In the cases of German and French negation, the clear post-verbal position of the negator (*nicht* in German, *pas* in French) is strong enough to pull the learner away from his earlier pre-verbal position (or, perhaps in many cases, to cause the learner to opt for a post-verbal position from the start).

In second language acquisition of Spanish, I already mentioned the early preference for post-verbal placement of objects even though native Spanish requires pre-verbal clitics. Thus learners will say:

|                   | the police |    | want   | him |
|-------------------|------------|----|--------|-----|
| learners:         | *la policía* |    | *quiere* | *él* |
| native Spanish:   | *la policía* | *lo* | *quiere* |     |

using the same form *él* for subject and object. When learners first begin to perceive the pre-verbal position of clitics (Table 5.1) it is with those clitics that are distinctly and invariantly marked: the first person singular *me* and plural *nos*. These are the same forms for direct object, indirect object, and reflexive. Third person clitics, however, have different forms for each of these functions and also differ according to gender. This complexity delays their acquisition in comparison with the first person clitics.

TABLE 5.1 *Clitics*

|             | *Direct object* | *Indirect object* | *Reflexive* |
|-------------|-----------------|-------------------|-------------|
| 1sg.        | **me**          | **me**            | **me**      |
| 1pl.        | **nos**         | **nos**           | **nos**     |
| 3sg. masc.  | lo              | le                | se          |
| 3sg. fem.   | la              | le                | se          |
| 3pl. masc.  | los             | les               | se          |
| 3pl. fem.   | las             | les               | se          |

In a similar fashion (see Table 5.2) the plural subject-verb agreement markers, *-mos* for first person and *-n* for third, are acquired before first person singular *-o*. The plural agreement markers are consistently and invariantly used across the entire verb inflection paradigm, whereas the first singular inflection *-o* is restricted to present indicative. Thus the formal consistency and clarity of certain forms in the input promote early discovery of them and the meanings they encode. It should be apparent at this point how the principle of formal determinism contributes to the effect of the Multifunctionality Principle.

At the end of the previous section, I suggested that new research be done to test the hypothesis that controlling the input in the foreign language classroom in a manner consistent with the Multifunctionality Principle would promote faster and more accurate acquisition of the constructions so controlled. In effect this would mean altering the natural formal determinism or lack thereof in the unmodified input. Thus a

TABLE 5.2 *Agreement markers on verb*

| | Present | | Imperfect | | Preterite | | Future | Conditional | Auxiliaries | |
| | Indicative | Subjunctive | Indicative | Subjunctive | (1) | (2&3) | | | Perfective | Progressive |
|---|---|---|---|---|---|---|---|---|---|---|
| 1sg. | -o | - | - | - | -é | -í | -(r)é | -(ría)- | he | estoy |
| 3sg. | - | - | - | - | -ó | -ió | -(r)á | -(ría)- | ha | está |
| **1pl.** | **-mos** | **-mos** | **-mos** | **-mos** | **-mos** | **-mos** | **-(re)mos** | **-(ría)mos** | **hemos** | **estamos** |
| **3pl.** | **-n** | **-n** | **-n** | **-n** | **-ron** | **-ron** | **-(rá)n** | **-(ría)n** | **han** | **están** |

related hypothesis that could be tested in a foreign language classroom setting would be that when a given form–meaning relation is infrequently encoded in the input and/or encoded in complex and opaque ways, acquisition of this form–meaning relation can be facilitated by artificially increasing the frequency of the form in the input as well as making the form–meaning relation more transparent (by temporarily excluding from the input the more opaque forms). This is what most good teachers and textbooks attempt to do anyway. The basic difference here is that such a study would attempt to verify empirically whether such control over the input has the positive effect that we commonly assume it to have.

### Distributional Bias

As stated, the Principle of Formal Determinism promotes discovery of the correct form–meaning relationship (from a target language perspective). But there are also properties of the input that promote the incorporation of an inappropriate form–meaning relationship into the interlanguage. That is, the learner misperceives the meaning and distribution of a particular form that he discovers in the input, following the Principle of Distributional Bias:

> If both X and Y can occur in the same environments A and B, but a bias in the distribution of X and Y makes it appear that X only occurs in environment A and Y only occurs in environment B, when you acquire X and Y, restrict X to environment A and Y to environment B.

The case I will discuss has already been mentioned in connection with the One-to-One Principle: the early preference for using past verbal inflections on punctual verbs much more than other verbs. The particular case comes from SLA of Spanish, where more specifically the preterite verb form appears earlier than the imperfect form. This is also true for first language acquisition of Spanish and Portuguese (Jacobsen, 1986; Simões & Stoel-Gammon, 1979). The primary argument advanced to explain this is that unitary punctual events are especially salient and there is a need to distinguish such events formally from other less salient events, through, in this case, verbal inflection. But there exists the possibility that preterite forms are more abundant in the input than imperfect forms. From a study I did of one sample of native Spanish, this indeed seems to be the case: by both a type and a token count, preterite forms clearly outnumbered imperfect forms. Moreover, it also appears that certain of the more frequent verbs occur mainly in one of the two possible past forms, which introduces another bias into the input. For example, punctual verbs like 'break' occur mainly in preterite form, and states like 'know' in imperfect form. It is thus quite possible that an accidental distributional bias within the target language causes the learner to err in the direction of that bias. It is also clear, however, that certain potential distributional biases do not actually lead the learner in the direction of this bias (see Andersen, 1986c for further details).

A design for testing this principle in a foreign language classroom is quite straightforward. Two groups of learners, none of whom have had any exposure to past verb forms in Spanish, could be given identical input except for past verb forms. Group 1 would receive input in which punctual verbs were only encoded in preterite form and non-punctual verbs (states and activities) were only encoded in imperfect form. Group 2 would receive the same input except that each verb would appear equally often in preterite form and imperfect form (e.g. *caer* 'fall' and *ser* 'be' would appear as *cayó*, *caía* and *era*, *fue*). Designing the input so that it is as natural and as communicative as possible is, however, not so straightforward and would require careful piloting. If the Distributional Bias Principle is valid, the learners in Group 1 should acquire the preterite and imperfect forms to the same degree, but restrict each verb to only one of the two forms, whereas Group 2 should acquire some instances of both forms for the same verb: preterite and imperfect forms. This design can be extended also to reflect greater frequency of preterite forms over imperfect forms (as in the native input I sampled) for one group and the reverse (greater frequency of imperfect forms over preterite forms) in the other. A counter-prediction to such studies would be that the inherent semantics of the individual verb strongly controls the tense-aspect inflection that will initially be attached to it.[7]

**Relevance**

The Relevance Principle comes from Bybee (1985). For ease of presentation I will use Slobin's (1985a:1255) Operating Principle version of it:

> *OP (POSITION): RELEVANCE.* If two or more functors apply to a content word, try to place them so that the more relevant the meaning of a functor is to the meaning of the content word, the closer it is placed to the content word. If you find that a Notion is

marked in several places, at first mark it only in the position closest to the relevant content word.

We can explore this principle using the examples of Spanish verb morphology discussed earlier. What predictions could we make with regard to acquisition of verbal inflections for aspect, tense, and subject-verb agreement? Following Bybee (1985:196ff), we expect that aspect would be perceived and internalized earliest, since it is most relevant to the lexical item to which it attached, the verb. Tense would be next, since tense has wider scope than aspect, but is more relevant to the verb than subject-verb agreement, which would be last.

The research I am doing on SLA of Spanish (Andersen, 1986a; 1986b) as well as related studies in first language acquisition (Jacobsen, 1986; Simões & Stoel-Gammon, 1979) supports the prediction that aspect is encoded before tense and that subject-verb agreement does not appear until at least aspect is taken care of and probably tense also. (The status of tense as separate from aspect is problematic, since the inflections in question encode both tense and aspect.) Related work on SLA of English clearly supports the prediction that tense-aspect inflections will generally appear before subject-verb agreement inflections (third person singular -s). However, as discussed earlier, none of these categories (aspect, tense, agreement) is acquired as a whole in one abrupt and dramatic step. And, since some but not all verbal inflections are multifunctional in that they encode not only aspect but also tense and subject-verb agreement, the relative attention paid to any one of these categories by the learner changes over time as the learner acquires greater sophistication in the language.

There is also a logical implication in the Relevance Principle for classroom-based foreign language acquisition. Inflections that are most closely relevant to the content word to which they are attached should be acquired earliest. For example, gender marking should appear earlier for natural gender than for simply grammatical gender and gender marking should appear earlier on the noun (which has the gender) than on any determiners or adjectives associated with the noun (see Andersen, 1984b). For English, the -s on nouns that mark number should be acquired before the -s that marks possession and both these should be acquired before the -s that marks third person singular. This is supported by SLA research (see summary in Andersen, 1978), but the prediction is complicated by the fact that frequency in native English would make the same prediction (Larsen-Freeman, 1976).

**Transfer to Somewhere**

The Transfer to Somewhere Principle states that:

A grammatical form or structure will occur consistently and to a significant extent in the interlanguage as a result of transfer *if and only if* (1) natural acquisitional principles are consistent with the L1 structure or (2) there already exists within the L2 input the potential for (mis-)generalization from the input to produce the same form or structure. Furthermore, in such transfer preference is given in the resulting interlanguage to *free, invariant*, functionally *simple* morphemes which are congruent with the L1 and L2 (or there is congruence between the L1 and natural acquisitional processes) and [to] morphemes [which] occur frequently in the L1 and/or the L2 (Andersen, 1983b:182).

I will provide only one example here, since I have discussed this principle in detail elsewhere (Andersen, 1983b; see also Andersen, 1979a; 1980; 1982).

Zobl (1980b) has pointed out that, while English speakers will place object pronouns post-verbally in their French interlanguage, following English word order but violating French rules, French learners of English do not follow French rules for placement of object pronouns in their English. The explanation for this follows the Transfer to Somewhere Principle: both French and English require post-verbal placement of full NPs, which provides a model for post-verbal placement of pronouns, which happens to match English but violate French rules. Thus, English speakers have a model in the input to transfer to: post-verbal placement of full NP objects in French. But French speakers have no such native English model to cause them to transfer their pre-verbal placement of clitics to English.[8] A similar finding pertains to the acquisition of Spanish by English speakers (Andersen, 1983b). The Spanish data, however, reveal that the Transfer to Somewhere Principle (or any equivalent transfer principle) operates in conjunction with other operating principles (such as the Principle of Formal Determinism discussed previously).

What might such a principle mean in a foreign language classroom context? I will postpone discussion of this until after I outline the next principle.

**Relexification**

In accounting for the special type of second language acquisition which results in a pidgin language, Derek Bickerton argues that the main determinant of the resulting structure of the pidgin is relexification from the pidgin speaker's native language. He offers examples such as the following, from a Japanese speaker of Hawaiian Pidgin English, which shows Japanese-influenced verb-final sentence structure (Bickerton, 1977:53): *as kerosin, plaenteishan, wan mans, fo gaelan* **giv** 'The plantation **gave** us four gallons of kerosene a month.'

A Relexification Principle could be stated as follows: When you cannot perceive the structural pattern used by the language you are trying to acquire, use your native language structure with lexical items from the second language. As stated this principle is still too imprecise. Even in the unique situation of the pidgin speakers who have limited or absolutely no access to native English, such uses of verb-final structures, while as frequent as 60% of all sentences, are usually lower and there is definitely no categorical relexification from Japanese. Somehow we need to explain better this variable use of what is apparently relexification of the native language in the use of the second language.

One may easily argue that the pidgin situation is far too different from the normal SLA situation. The pidgin setting is certainly quite unique, especially with regard to the lack of access to adequate input on which to model acquisition of the second language. Nevertheless, it is not hard to find examples of such apparent relexification in the English of Japanese-speaking immigrants to the continental United States, speakers whose English is far more 'English-like' than that of the Hawaiian Pidgin English speakers. One such example is given below. Most of the time this speaker follows quite clearly an English subject-verb-object pattern. But it appears from this excerpt (and others like it), that a Japanese-based processing preference for final placement of verbs is still at work in this speaker's use of English (example from Kuwahata, 1984; verb is in bold italics, object in square brackets):

| Interviewer: | 1. When you were in Japan, did you ever *study* English? |
| Kei: | 2. I never ***study*** [English]. |
| : | 3. I don't ***like*** [a English], because (*chuckle*) yes. |
| Interviewer: | 4. Why didn't you like English? |
| Kei: | 5. Because . . . I never ***talk*** [to American people], |
| : | 6. I'm never learn. |
| : | 7. Then, I'm (gonna) marry, |
| : | 8. must be [English], ***I am study***. |
| : | 9. Then, I'm not ***marry*** [. . . (the) American people], |

|    |                                                      |
|:--:|------------------------------------------------------|
| :  | 10. I not [English], *take* [the class]. (*laugh*)   |
| :  | 11. I *have* [a Junior high school],                 |
| :  | 12. never [English], *take* [the class].             |
| :  | 13. Never.                                           |
| :  | 14. I don't *like* [a English].                      |

Kei uses both English verb-object word order and an apparent double-object construction: object verb object. It appears that, in utterances like 8, 10, and 12, Kei repairs an 'in-progress' object + verb construction by adding a second object, which fits well into the information flow. That is, I am suggesting that she is initially aiming at 'I not [English class] *take*', but is able to repair such a clearly non-English construction while speaking.

In a setting where the learner has access to native English input, the Transfer to Somewhere Principle would predict that such constructions, based on relexification, would be infrequent and short-lived precisely because there is no 'somewhere' in native English to transfer to, nor do any of the operating principles support a preference for object-verb constructions. In other words, in acquisition-rich environments, the learner would soon realize that the native English input does not contain constructions with the verb after the object. It may be the case that, in settings where pidgin languages develop, there is not enough input from the target language available to promote transfer based on the Transfer to Somewhere Principle and relexification is the only resource the learner has. It should be noted, however, that, whereas Japanese has utterance-final placement of the negator, such a position appears *never* to be used in either Hawaiian Pidgin English nor the English of Japanese immigrants to the continental United States (see the examples with *not* in the excerpt above). This difference somehow has to be accounted for, whether in further specification within the Relexification Principle or in some interaction among several of the operating principles.

Both the Transfer to Somewhere Principle and the Relexification Principle, if they are, indeed, separate 'principles', are potentially relevant to the foreign language classroom context. Research to explore their effects would have to be conducted along the lines of studies like Cancino (1976), who compared the English of a Spanish speaker with that of a Japanese speaker. Since Japanese and Spanish differ in very clear ways, the relative effects of transfer can be readily studied in the learners' English. Cancino's subjects were young children acquiring English through natural contact. It appears that the dramatic type of relexification discussed by Bickerton for pidgin settings does not occur in such naturalistic settings.

At least Cancino and Hakuta (1976), who conducted the study from which the Japanese-English data were taken, do not mention examples.

It would seem, however, that in a foreign language classroom setting where most of the 'input' is in the form of examples, rules and paradigms, with little or no access to natural speech of native speakers, the Relexification Principle would assume a much more important role in governing construction of the interlanguage than the Transfer to Somewhere Principle. Research designed to test these two principles within a classroom context would have to control input carefully in order to determine the source of learner's interlanguage constructions. The hypothesis to be tested would be that, when learners are provided with adequate native speaker input they will follow only the Transfer to Somewhere Principle and not the Relexification Principle, while learners in an acquisition-poor classroom would be more likely to fall back on relexification.

## Strategies of Language Use (By Native and Non-native Speakers)

I have focused most of my discussion on the cognitive processes I believe guide language acquisition in a variety of settings. The particular setting from which I have drawn examples, however, is that of natural non-instructed SLA. In such settings the learner presumably accesses the language being learned through a variety of short as well as more involved interactions with native speakers (and probably other non-native speakers). It is through such interactions that the learner is able to perceive new forms and constructions as well as new form–meaning relations and thus expand his interlanguage system in the direction of the native target.

The communication strategies used by native and non-native speakers during native–non-native interaction have been well documented over the years in such studies as Hatch (1978b); Gass & Varonis (1984; 1985a; 1985b; 1985c); Long (1980a; 1981); Peck (1978); and Tarone (1977; 1980); and in collections such as Day (1986), Hatch (1978a), Larsen-Freeman (1980), Seliger & Long (1983), and Wolfson & Judd (1983). A detailed treatment of the role of such communication strategies in facilitating acquisition of new forms and their meanings, functions and distribution in the second language requires a paper at least as long as this one, if not a book. To underscore the importance of such communication strategies in acquiring new forms, I will draw on an unpublished paper by Barbara Hawkins (1981), a Ph.D. student at UCLA, who has taught me a lot about the value of such interaction.

In a joint study of Hawkins's learning of Papiamentu in an experimental communicative-language teaching course at UCLA, Hawkins and two other students investigated various aspects of Hawkins's communication with a native speaker after ten weeks' instruction in Papiamentu. In her paper Hawkins combined procedures of discourse analysis, following Hatch (1978b; 1983b), with retrospective comments by herself and in an interview (in English now) with the native speaker of Papiamentu, to try to access the communication strategies used by both the native and non-native speaker in communication (see Hawkins, 1985, for further use of these procedures). In the example I will cite here, Hawkins was trying to tell the native speaker that she had a sister who was going to get married, but she didn't know how to say 'going to' in Papiamentu, which is *ta bai*. She tries to use an irrealis marker, *lo*, which also serves as a future marker, but she was aware that it was not appropriate and that she didn't know how to do it right (Hawkins's retrospective comments are in italics):

**H**: Mi tin un ruman muhé ku ta-
No, ku . . . uhm . . . let's see . . .
ku *lo*, *lo* a . . . kas-
ku *lo* a tin kas-
ku *lo* tin kasá . . .
I don't know . . . I just forget.
Na . . . No . . . Okay.

[**H**: I have a sister who is-
No, who . . . uhm . . . let's see. . .
who will, would . . . marr-
who would have hus-
who will have a husband . . .

(*RETROSPECTION: I remember struggling to form the future and not knowing; I wanted him to tell me*)

**NS**: Kon e yama?
Bo ruman ku *ta bai* kasa?

**NS**: What's her name?
Your sister who is going to get married?

(*RETROSPECTION: I knew immediately that this meant 'is going to marry'—from Spanish.*)

**H**: Oh, Ku *ta bai* . . . a kasa . . . a kasa?

**H**: Oh, Who is going to . . . to-marry to to-marry?

*(RETROSPECTION: I wasn't sure if the 'a' was present. I was thinking of Spanish.)*

| | |
|---|---|
| **NS**: Ku **ta bai** kasa. | **NS**: Who is going to marry. |
| **H**: Ah, Sí? | **H**: Oh, yah? |
| **NS**: Sí? | **NS**: Yah?] |

*(RETROSPECTION: I got it! I was really excited.)*

(The two occurrences of *sí?* at the end may be difficult to follow. Hawkins's *Sí?* means, 'Oh, that's how you say it?' The native speaker's *Sí?* means, 'Oh, she's going to get married?') (Hawkins, 1981:83).

Hawkins's (1981:86) comment in her conclusion is relevant here:

> For the student, early speech may be learning to say, 'Huh?', until understanding is achieved. Beyond this, I think it would be worthwhile to teach students to use all of the various mechanisms involved in repair requests. If students know how not to let themselves be overcome by native speech that is too fast or beyond their vocabulary limits, they can, slowly but surely, progress in the target language.

Such repair strategies would form part of the 'interaction' portion of the cognitive-interactionist model I have tried to outline in this paper. In this paper I have focused almost completely on the cognitive side of this model, since I believe that it is here that there is considerable common ground between second and foreign language learning. This is also the area to which I have devoted most of my attention in my research. But in a foreign language classroom environment like the one in which Hawkins learned Papiamentu, the interaction with the language must be planned for and carefully orchestrated, in contrast with the natural acquisition of a second language through interaction with native speakers on their home territory. In many ways the foreign language classroom is a better laboratory for studying the relative roles of cognitive operating principles and interaction strategies than the second language setting, since better controls can be imposed in the classroom setting.

## Summary and Conclusion

What kinds of goal should we have for the future to pursue the factors which govern progress in acquiring a foreign language in a classroom setting and what role can naturalistic second language research play in such research? There is always a tendency for specialized sub-fields, such as the sub-fields of natural SLA versus classroom-based foreign language acquisition, to treat each other as pursuing different questions and producing results only minimally relevant to each other. This has already happened to some degree: those interested in a classroom setting tend to pursue their own paradigms and research procedures quite different from those in what is commonly referred to as 'interlanguage studies', and vice versa. Whether one wants to 'buy' this particular cognitive-interactionist model or not, I believe that much can be gained by exploring both the cognitive principles and the interactional strategies that must be at the core of SLA both in and outside the classroom. Non-classroom-focused SLA research stands to gain much from classroom-centred research and classroom-centred research can benefit considerably from the type of research carried out in settings outside the classroom. And, in order to understand how authentic language texts can form the basis of successful SLA *in a foreign language classroom*, we need to understand the nature of natural SLA. This theoretical framework is intended to be a step in the right direction in arriving at this understanding.

## Notes to Chapter 5

1. I will limit my discussion to this particular model.
2. The term 'nativization' is used for this model because of the origin of the model in an acquisition view of the creation of a creole language: when a creole language is first created, the children creating it are, in effect, creating a new native language. Thus nativization is meant to capture what it takes to create a new native language. As extended to other first and second language acquisition situations, it should suffice to quote from an earlier discussion of the model (Andersen, 1983a:11):

   Creolization, pidginization, and the creation of a unique interlanguage in first and second language acquisition in early stages of acquisition share one attribute—the creation of a linguistic system which is at least partly autonomous from the input used for building that system. This system can then be considered 'native' to the individual in that it is the individual's mental capacity to construct such a linguistic system that makes it possible for a new 'native' language to arise, as in the creation of a creole language. Each individual has the potential for creating his own system. New input then must assimilate to his system. This process of creating an individual autonomous system I call nativization in order to capture what is common to these four cases.

3. I must clarify that I am not prescribing doing away with 'the usual rules, examples, and paradigms for memorization and practice'. Rather I wish to focus attention on the need for new research within a communicative framework which also permits manipulation of input so as to test some of these hypotheses.
4. Earlier SLA research had considered and rejected Slobin's Operating Principles

as an explanatory framework for SLA. Dulay & Burt (1974) and Larsen-Freeman (1975), for example, objected that Slobin's (1973) OPs were difficult to test and were not mutually exclusive. As Bowerman's (1985) critical evaluation of the revised OPs reveals, these limitations are still there. Such criticism would also apply to the principles discussed here for SLA. My position on this criticism is that, rather than rejecting the OPs (with nothing comparable to replace them), we should work with them as they are and improve on them with further research. Besides, the difficulties faced in testing some of the operating principles as well as the interrelatedness of certain OPs with each other are quite possibly the result of the complexity of language and human cognition, not necessarily a weakness in the operating principles.

5. For German (Clahsen, 1984a) and French (Trévise & Noyau, 1984) this needs to be rephrased as 'immediately next to (before or after) the main verb' for propositional negation. But this qualification is probably the result of the Formal Determinism Principle.

6. This hypothesis is similar in many respects to Krashen's Input Hypothesis and his focus on the hypothetical i + 1 stage of development, as well as Pienemann's research on formal instruction that fits the learner's particular stage of development. The major difference is that Krashen's work depends on a view of acquisition in terms of whole target language morphemes being acquired in one fell swoop (such as 'article' or 'copula') and Pienemann's work also depends on discrete target language syntactic rules. A Multifunctionality Principle predicts that there are a number of small changes leading up to so-called 'acquisition' of the target language form or construction and it is these small changes that should be researched.

7. At least one additional variable must be considered in such a design: time between contact with such input and first spontaneous use of the forms in question. This variable must be explored in pilot studies or as a separate dependent variable.

8. This also conforms to Eckman's (1977) Markedness Differential Hypothesis.

# Part II:
# Frameworks and Approaches to Research Issues

While second language acquisition (SLA) and foreign language learning (FLL) are arguably two disciplines, they have generated data bases that fall along Berns's contextual continuum, as evidenced by the papers gathered in Part II. In this section, specific issues in SLA and FLL are explored. These issues are suggestive, not exhaustive, of current concerns in both SLA and FLL and, as mentioned previously, a variety of factors colour each author's perspectives on not just the how and why of a particular phenomenon but just what the phenomenon under investigation is and how it should be investigated. And in each case, certain assumptions and implications about the relationship between SLA and FLL are made explicit.

Like the papers in Part I, these papers are divided into two sub-sections. The first concerns the nature of learner language or interlanguage. What is important about these contributions is that they consider data from both second language (L2) and foreign language (FL) contexts. In so doing, both contributions take the position (and make the assumption) that L2 data and FL data, if apparently different on the surface, must somehow be reconciled at the level of theory and that this reconciliation is indeed possible. Even though the three papers on interlanguage are vastly different in both the phenomenon they investigate and the 'tools' they employ to describe and explain interlanguage, they do serve to illustrate how both L2 and FL data are necessary to a comprehensive account of non-primary language acquisition.

In the first paper, Eubank critically examines two competing explanations for the acquisition of German negation by L2 and FL learners, one cognitive, the other linguistic, concluding that the linguistic explanation is superior. In so doing, Eubank (implicitly) argues that processes and constraints in language acquisition do not change as a result of environmental factors. Rather, differences in output are traceable to the way universal principles interact with differing kinds of input data. Grounded in linguistic theory and current problems in *first* language acquisition, Eubank's account implies a unified theory of language acquisition, one which obliterates the contextual differences between L2s and FLs. It is important to keep in mind, however, that Eubank's immediate motivation is to account for the acquisition of negation in German, not the acquisition of language in general.

In a somewhat different vein, Odlin seeks to explain why the basic word order of a first language is or is not transferred into the second language. Like Eubank, he finds that there are differences in learner output in various contexts, but, unlike Eubank, Odlin does not see universal(ist) accounts as adequate explanations of the observed differences. Instead, Odlin suggests that metalinguistic awareness, derived from form-focused interactions, is a potentially important part of explaining why linguistic outputs may vary according to context of acquisition and therefore that contexts of acquisition may be defined by the degree of metalinguistic awareness involved. Again, the reader is reminded to consider that Odlin is focusing on the specific issue of transfer.

The third paper in this section, VanPatten's case study comparison of the acquisition of Spanish clitic pronouns, offers a detailed look at how learners under two very different conditions of exposure manifest similar and different patterns of clitic pronoun usage. More descriptive than theoretical, VanPatten's study is an attempt to examine detailed aspects of how context impacts upon learner language development and the result of his effort is a list of eight hypotheses concerning classroom/non-classroom impact. Important in VanPatten's discussion, however, is the notion of deep versus superficial differences in the creation of a linguistic system by a learner. Accordingly, a deep difference reflects a change in fundamental processes of language acquisition, altering how a learner interacts with the input; superficial differences are the result of input differences, where context does not alter the fundamental processes guiding acquisition.

Although one may view the perspectives of Eubank, Odlin and VanPatten as vastly different or somewhat similar, it must be kept in mind that specific research questions often lead to different paths of inquiry and the path taken must be appropriate to the question addressed. None the less, as is the case with all three papers, different paths of inquiry can and should attend to both second and foreign language learner data.

The second sub-section of Part II treats issues in how learners use language. The reader will immediately notice a difference between the first sub-section and the second. In the first, pedagogical aspects and implications of research for teaching do not enter into discussion. Instead, learner data are taken as they are and examined for what they reveal about the processes of language acquisition. In a sense, they echo VanPatten's request for including FL data in theory-building. In the second sub-section, the researchers concentrate on how learner language is used and for what purposes it is used with a clear eye towards understanding classroom discourse with stated pedagogical implications. As research, then, these papers respond to Kramsch's call for research which includes a broader agenda involving classroom-*specific* phenomena.

Wildner-Bassett documents and discusses various types of discourse behaviour among language participants. These language behaviours are tied to discourse worlds coexisting during language use. In her example of the use of 'corrections', Wildner-Bassett notes that real-life corrections tend to focus on clarifying content while classroom-based discourse tends to include evaluation of formal accuracy. These and other observations lead Wildner-Bassett to distinguish FL use from L2 use, but what is important to note is that, in her data, the learners of English are in the FL context while the learners of German are in the L2 context.

Following Wildner-Bassett is the research on FL discourse conducted by Brooks. His main argument is that FL learners, when left in groups to 'interact', play out the same social roles that exist at the level of the entire class, i.e. teacher–student roles. Thus, students incorporate into their interactions the same power relationships and evaluative speech behaviours that they witness between teacher and other students. Compared to research conducted in L2 settings where natives and non-natives interact for the real purpose of communicating (e.g. Brock *et al.*, 1986), Brooks's investigation underscores one of the fundamental differences between FL and L2 discourse. However, as Wildner-Bassett demonstrates, the discourse differences noted may be due more to classroom–non-classroom differences rather than FL–L2 differences.

Adding one more piece to this discourse puzzle is Bacon's investigation of learner speech during oral testing. In a nutshell, Bacon finds quantitative and qualitative differences depending on whether learners choose the topic of conversation or not. This observation leads her to conclude that some learners treat oral examinations as what they are intended to be, tests, whereas others apparently treat the examination as an opportunity to engage in real language use. While data elicitation tasks have been the object of scrutiny in SLA before and while there is evidence to link style-shifting to purpose of language use in both L1 and L2 research, Bacon's study underscores the need in both SLA and FLL to be careful of oral data collection procedures.

# 6 Linguistic theory and the acquisition of German negation[1]

LYNN EUBANK

*University of Texas at Austin, USA*

Steven Pinker (1984) has pointed out that an adequate theory of primary language acquisition must account for the intermediate stages as well as for the final state of linguistic knowledge accrued by the learner. He thus divides the problem of explaining acquisition into two parts:

> First, a rule system at a particular stage must have been constructed by an acquisition mechanism that began with no knowledge about the particular target language and that arrived at the current state on the basis of the parental input it received in the interim. Second, the rule system must be convertible by the acquisition mechanism into a rule system adequate to represent adult abilities, also on the basis of parental input (Pinker, 1984:5–6).

Somewhat later, Pinker designates these concerns as the *learnability condition* and the *extendibility condition*.[2] In essence, the first asks how a particular construction could be learned, given parental input. This line of questioning is especially important for transitional constructions which are absent in speech directed at the learner. For example, the data in Brown (1973) indicate that children learning English apparently have rules to generate copuless sentences at early stages. The charge of learnability here is to explain how these rules could be learned from input which does not contain them. The extendibility condition, on the other hand, considers how a particular transitional construction might then be changed into the final-state form. This problem often deals with unlearning: given that a uniquely developmental construction has been learned, how can it be expunged in the absence of negative evidence? Consider, for instance, how the children in Brown (1973) discover that their early copulaless constructions are not permissible in English. They could conceivably spend a lifetime waiting for the one input string which would confirm the optionality of the construction (i.e. a copulaless utterance). In sum, if a mechanism can meet these conditions in a plausible way, then the puzzle of acquisition can be approached.[3]

The dual conditions of learnability and extendibility may be applied to evaluate theories of acquisition. One might, for instance, find that a particular theory is able to meet the learnability condition, but unable to deal with extendibility. Conversely, a theory might handle the extendibility condition while failing learnability. At worst, a theory might fail both learnability and extendibility. Whatever the case, it would be apparent that changes, minor or fundamental, will have to be considered in order to make a theory into a possible one.

In an obvious sense, theories of second language acquisition (SLA) might be evaluated in the same light as theories designed for primary language learning. In doing so, of course, contextually conditioned input differences—primary language (L1) learning, naturalistic non-primary (L2N) learning, formal classroom (L2F) learning—must be taken into account. This done, it may be the case that the same theory which satisfies the two criteria for primary language learning might also account for non-primary learning, especially if that theory is stated within the context of faculty psychology (cf. Fodor, 1983). Alternatively, a particular theory of acquisition might be found to fail one or the other of the criteria. Crucially, any failure to predict what is obvious from observational data must be indicative of architectural flaws in the theory or of possible neurological changes brought about through maturation or of both.

The present contribution seeks to show how the framework of learnability and extendibility might uncover shortcomings in current acquisition theorizing and to suggest how these shortcomings might be handled. To do so, we shall select a theory of acquisition, the processing constraints employed by Clahsen (1984a) and Eubank (1987), and examine its application to a specific area of language development, sentential negation in German, a verb-second language (Thiersch, 1978; see note 5). Analysis under learnability and extendibility will indicate a number of predictive failures. To solve these problems, we will consider supplementing the theory with particular principles and constraints garnered from recent research in linguistic theory, especially Government-Binding (GB) Theory (Chomsky, 1981a; 1981b). The lesson to be learned here is this: if we, as second and foreign language researchers, want to deal honestly with L2 learning in general and with the difference between L2N and L2F in particular, then we must turn our attention to highly specific, perhaps idealized theories of acquisition, theories that constantly run the risk of being falsified.

Pursuant to this goal, the following will be divided into four parts. The first part deals with the nature of the final state of German negation and with developmental data from L1, L2N and L2F studies of German. From this review, specific questions of learnability and extendibility will be formulated as evaluative measures. In the second part, the applicable processing heuristics from Clahsen (1984a) and Eubank (1987) will be evaluated for their ability to predict the problems of extendibility and learnability selected from the developmental sequences. In the third part, certain conditions and principles from linguistic theory will be developed as a supplement to solve the problems of learnability and extendibility. In the final part, the developmental data will be reanalysed in light of these principles and conditions.

## The Final State and Developmental Data

Descriptively, the final state negator, *nicht* ('not'), appears in matrix surface structures after the finite verb and the object toward the end of the sentence. This part of the sentence also contains several other elements in so far as they are present. Non-finite verbal elements (verbs and particles) are generated in final position, and the so-called 'bound' adverb is adjacent to the left. Before these, one finds the object and the 'free' adverb. Example (1) illustrates this order of elements:

(1)     *Ich habe den Wagen gestern nach Worms gefahren.*
        I have the car yesterday to Worms driven.
        I drove the car to Worms yesterday.

The object is *den Wagen*, and the free adverb is *gestern*. These occur before the non-finite verb (*gefahren*) and the bound adverb (*nach Worms*). Sentential *nicht* is realized just before the bound adverb and the non-finite verb. For the present analysis, we shall refer to this final-state construction as FS-NEG.[4]

The facts on the development of sentential negation by learners of German exposed to more or less natural input (L1 and L2N) are available in a variety of studies (e.g. Felix, 1978; Pienemann, 1981; Clahsen, 1982). Initially, the learners utilize a form of *nicht* (occasionally a form of *nein* ('no')) in pre-verbal or post-verbal position:

(2) pre-verbal:              *nicht habe kurve*
                             not have curve
                             (I) don't have a curve.

(3) pre-verbal:              *ich das nicht mach*
                             I that not do
                             I won't (?) do that.

(4) post-verbal:             *ich hab nicht die Zucker-
                             kluntje*
                             I have not the bonbon
                             I don't have the bonbon.

(5) post-verbal:             *geht nicht*
                             goes not
                             It doesn't work (=I'm not
                             successful.)

As a second stage, pre-verbal negation as in examples (2) and (3) becomes
less frequent and finally disappears altogether while post-verbal negation as
in examples (4) and (5) continues. The last stage is the disappearance of
post-verbal negation and the appearance of final-state sentential negation
(FS-NEG).

Sentential negation by formal learners is reviewed in Eubank (1987),
which deals with the early stages of development only. What is of interest
here is that the learners generally do not utilize pre-verbal negation.
(Among the more than 500 negated utterances, only one instance of pre-
verbal negation is indicated.) Instead, the data in that study suggest that
the six learners initially negate utterances, propositions as well as
constituents, with a true sentence-final negator (hereafter S-NEG):

(6)    *Das ist gut Kaffee nicht*
       That is good coffee not
       That isn't good coffee.

(7)    *Sie hat Geld nein*
       She has money no
       She doesn't have the/any money.

Note that the S-NEG position of the negator in example (7) looks very
much like the position of the sentential FS-NEG (given the interpretation
of 'the'). Some weeks later, still during the first of the two semesters
covered by Eubank, most of the subjects appear to learn FS-NEG:

(8)     *Sie geh nicht aus*
        She go not out
        She isn't going out.

For reasons that will become clear later, a review of word order development is also in order.[5] The L1 data in Clahsen (1982) indicate that the learners utilize surface word orders with the verb in either second or final position at a time corresponding to the first stage of negation. The data at this stage suggest that the underlying order of verb-phrase (VP) elements may be either head-initial (yielding VO) or head-final (yielding OV) (cf. DuPlessis *et al.*, 1987, especially note 4; see also Felix, 1984). Subsequently, the acquisition data clearly indicate that the head-final order is selected. This point in time corresponds very closely to the second stage of negation development. The final stage of word order development of interest here concerns embedded clauses. The data in Clahsen indicate no embeddings until a very late stage. Moreover, when they do appear, they exhibit the standard verb-final order. Interestingly, standard sentential negation (FS-NEG) appears at nearly the same time.

The L2N word order data in Felix (1978), Dittmar (1981), Klein & Dittmar (1979), and Clahsen *et al.* (1983a) suggest that L2N learners in early stages of development will often utilize a surface order of elements like that of their first languages (SVX for English, Spanish, and Portuguese; SXV for Turkish). On the other hand, a number of utterances in these data indicate surface orders unlike that of the L1 order. Dittmar (1981), for instance, includes a sample of utterances from eight Turkish-speaking learners of German in which verbs occur in either the second position or the final position. In addition, Klein & Dittmar (1979), drawing on cross-sectional data from speakers of Italian and Spanish learning German (see Heidelberger Forschungsprojekt 'Pidgin Deutsch', 1975), show that the large majority of utterances produced by subjects in their lower proficiency groups range from one to three constituents in length. Significantly, the verbs among these utterances are split almost evenly between the second and third positions. Hence, the L2N data are not simple and provide little independently motivated evidence for the initial existence of some particular underlying order of VP elements, head-initial or head-final. Indeed, they might also be interpreted to mean that VP headedness remains initially undetermined by the L2N learners.[6] As in the L1 data, the possible existence of either of two underlying orders by the L2N learners generally corresponds to the early stage of negation.

Subsequently, the L2N data indicate that the head-final order is selected, a conclusion reached by Jordens (1987), DuPlessis *et al.* (1987), and Schwartz (1988). As in the case of L1 development, this stage roughly corresponds to stage-two negation. In contrast to the L1 learners, the L2N learners utilized embedded clauses in the early stages, and they do not differentiate in the early stages between the word order of main clauses and that of embedded clauses. What thus constitutes the final stage of word order development for the L2N learners is the correct occurrence of the finite verb in final position in embedded clauses. This final stage, occurring rather late, corresponds closely to the appearance of FS-NEG.

In contrast to L1 and L2N, a review of the L2F transcripts on which Eubank (1987) is based has provided no indication whatsoever in the surface data of an underlying head-final order at a time corresponding to the early stage of negation. Moreover, the word order data collected late in that project only equivocally suggest the presence of a particular underlying order of VP elements, although it must be kept in mind that these first-year students were at a rather early stage of development.

The observational data on the development of negation can serve as the basis for a number of questions concerning learnability and extendibility. The learnability questions are the following:

1.  How can pre-verbal negation be learned, given that pre-verbal negation does not exist in German main clauses?
2.  How can the post-verbal negator between the second-position verb and an object be learned, given that German has no sentential negators in this position?
3.  How can clause-final negation (S-NEG) be learned, given that this type of negation is not like standard FS-NEG?

A problem associated with learnability relates to the fact that final-state structures often appear to be avoided in the interlanguage. The negation data thus suggest the following question:

4.  How can FS-NEG be initially avoided by learners when the construction is clearly evident in the input?

Questions of extendibility deal with eliminating grammars for negation after they have been learned:

5.  How can the pre-verbal negator be expunged in the absence of negative evidence?
6.  How can the clause-final negator (S-NEG) be expunged in the absence of negative evidence?

7.   How can the post-verbal negator between the second-position verb and an object be expunged in the absence of negative evidence?

## Predicting Acquisition from Processing Constraints

Clahsen (1984a) proposes three universal processing strategies which appear to predict sequences of word order and negation development. In essence, the processing strategies operate as output constraints on underlying form, the latter apparently a reflection of logical or conceptual structure.

Of Clahsen's three strategies, two are of importance for his analysis of L1 and L2N negation. The Canonical Order Strategy (COS) allows only direct mappings of underlying structure to surface form due to the ease of processing. Hence, the underlying adjacency of subject, verb and object may not be interrupted by permuting other material into positions between them, and the three elements themselves must remain in the same positions relative to one another. The other strategy is his Initialization Finalization Strategy (IFS), which allows sentence-initial and sentence-final permutations of underlying form. In other words, the IFS preserves underlying adjacency, but not in terms of relative positions. For instance, a permutation allowed by the IFS is topicalization of the object noun phrase (NP). In this case, the object is moved from behind the verb to a position in front of the subject, an operation which nevertheless keeps the subject, verb and object adjacent to one another, albeit not in the same order (i.e., object, subject, verb). An operation disallowed by the IFS is movement of a sentence-initial adverbial into any position which would cause any one of the three underlying elements to be separated from any one of the other two (e.g. S V ADV O).[7]

In reference to the development of L1 and L2N negation, Clahsen (1984a) proposes that the initial presence of the negator before and immediately after the finite verb can be traced to the COS. He notes (1984a:239) that 'Regardless of whether the negator is placed pre- or postverbally, it appears adjacent to the element to which it refers, i.e., next to the verb'. Presumably, then, the negator is next to the verb in the underlying grammar. The subsequent disappearance of pre-verbal negation is dealt with as a matter of individual variation. The last stage of development, the appearance of the final-state form (FS-NEG), Clahsen predicts on the basis of the IFS, which allows the negator to be moved from a position adjacent to the finite verb, now always in the second surface position, into one after the NP object (i.e. the adjacency of S, V and O remains undisturbed).

The conclusions one might reach by projecting these strategies onto the development of L2F negation are interesting. Recall that the negator appears in clause-final position during the initial stage of development. At first blush, one might conclude that these learners are in some way able to overcome the restriction imposed by the COS. On the other hand, it may also be the case that these learners begin with an underlying S-NEG, the result of a non-communicative processing strategy, the 'S-NEG strategy', developed for the L2F data by Eubank (1987). In other words, if the negator occurs underlyingly in clause-final position (perceived, as it must be, to have sentence scope), then the COS correctly predicts that pre-verbal negation and immediate post-verbal negation will not exist during the initial stage of learning. The subsequent development of FS-NEG might then be predicted to result from the IFS, which allows non-finite forms of the verb to be permuted to final position after the negator.

While this analysis appears to predict the development of L1 and L2 negation, closer inspection from the perspective of learnability (questions 1–4 above) reveals a number of deficiencies. How is it, for instance, that pre-verbal negation might occur at all in the L2N and L1 data? More specifically, if the negator is adjacent to the verb in the underlying grammar of L1 and L2N learners, how did it get there? Moreover, if the negator is placed either pre-verbally or post-verbally, why is it that the data indicate no post-verbal placements after the final-position verbs? Further, while the negator may be adjacent to the verb underlyingly for the L1 and L2N learners, why is it not there for the L2F learner? Eubank's 'S-NEG strategy' would appear in this case to predict— rather absurdly—that L1 and L2N users might place NEG at the end of a sentence only if they do not attempt to communicate. Or might one then conclude that the L2F learners have sentence scope from an underlying sentence-final NEG because they were given a rule for it in the formal classroom? Finally, why is FS-NEG initially avoided by all learners, particularly given the apparent ease with which the L2F learners use an alternative to an underlying negator near the verb? In these cases, the output-processing constraints clearly need to be supplemented with some sort of specific mechanisms or principles guiding the acquisition of underlying competence.

The questions of extendibility also suggest the necessity of architectural supplements. Recall that the issue concerns knowing—without recourse to negative evidence from the environment—that a particular structure, once learned, is not part of the final-state language. Consider the L1 and L2N learners, who use pre-verbal negation during the initial stage. The IFS strategy, acting as a somewhat less restrictive filter than the COS, simply allows them to permute the negator to a position after the object NP. Note, however, that this strategy does not force them to abandon pre-verbal negation. Indeed, there is nothing in the processing approach which could guarantee that pre-verbal negation will disappear. At best, one might expect the L1 and L2N learners to conclude that German has pre-verbal negation as an optional structure. The same sort of criticism applies to the disappearance of immediate post-verbal negation, since the IFS, while *allowing* the negator to be permuted to final position, does not require that it will *always* appear there. In other words, the strategy does not positively predict that the immediate post-verbal negator will be expunged. Indeed, while the L2F data indicate a switch from S-NEG to FS-NEG, the 'S-NEG strategy' concocted by Eubank does nothing whatsoever to ensure it. Hence, Clahsen's IFS and COS as well as Eubank's 'S-NEG strategy' do not provide the necessary information leading to the demise of the structures (i.e. extendibility) in the absence of negative environmental evidence.[8]

In short, the processing strategies fall short of providing an explanation for the acquisition of underlying competence as established by the observational data. On the other hand, it would be wrong to conclude that constraints of some kind are not involved in linguistic performance. Indeed, the idea that cognitive machinery outside of an autonomous grammar might have an impact on linguistic performance is part and parcel of faculty psychology.

## Learning Underlying Competence

The supplement I am suggesting for the sort of approach adopted in Clahsen (1984a) and Eubank (1987) separates language learning from linguistic performance. The idea rests crucially on recent work in GB theory (see Sells, 1985; van Riemsdijk & Williams, 1986). Under this theory, the syntax (phrase-structure (PS) rules and transformations) is allowed maximal generative power, the over-generated (ungrammatical) results being removed or ignored by the principles and parameters of Universal Grammar (UG). Consider, for instance, PS rules. Under earlier conceptions such as presented in Baker (1978) or Edmondson (1982), these consist of language-particular rules and result in particular trees for particular sentence types. In contrast, one might now consider allowing any one constituent to be connected in any order and at any level to any other constituent. Only where the result of this rather wild operation is allowed by the constraints of UG will phrase structures actually be generated. Likewise, earlier conceptions of transformational rules, as described by Baker and Edmondson, account exhaustively and explicitly for particular cases of movement in particular sentence types of particular languages. More recently, the tendency is to replace this abundance of transformational rules with a single rule, Move Alpha, allowing anything to be moved anywhere. Again, the results of such movement may produce a possible sentence only to the extent that the relevant principles of UG are not violated.

This recent approach to grammar might be clarified more by considering the difference between the initial state and the final state. The former consists of UG along with a set of learning procedures, but no grammar for the particular language to be learned. This is essentially the set-up proposed by Wexler & Culicover (1980). But what of the final state? Does it consist of language-particular PS rules and transformations such as those in Baker or Edmondson? Probably not, certainly not in the explicit form of earlier theory. What it surely does consist of is the principles of UG whereby any open parameters have been set by exposure to positive evidence in the input.[9]

Under this concept of the final state, learning would appear to play a rather trivial role, aside from parameter-setting. Indeed, it would appear that no language-specific grammar rules (in the sense of Baker or Edmondson) need be learned at all. Further reflection reveals, however, that this idea cannot be entirely right, for under certain conditions it over-generously predicts the acquisition of grammar rules which are not demonstrated in acquisition data. For example, before a learner sets the parameters of UG relevant to the structure of NPs, the idea predicts that determiners (a specifier in X-bar theory) might actually occur—in performance data— either before or after the head noun. In English and German acquisition data, however, learners never utilize determiners after the head, to my knowledge. Rather, they follow only what is unambiguously demonstrated in the input, namely that the determiner precedes the noun.

These observations lead to some limited conclusions for learning and learning procedures. For syntax, one might conclude that learners (i.e. the learning procedures) may connect any constituent to any other constituent in any order and at any level, and, further, may move any constituent anywhere. These are exact correlates to the freedom allowed in the syntax of recent GB theorizing: ungrammatical results are ignored or removed through interaction with the (initially unset) parameters of UG. In addition, however, one disallows learners from connecting or moving constituents in ways that they do not perceive (parse) in the input. In a sense, then, both UG and what is picked up from input serve to constrain the hypothesis space of learners.

If this line of reasoning is correct, then one might further conclude that input data (i.e. what is perceived) might crucially limit what one might expect to find as developmental data. This idea, however, is obviously false, for learners often create apparently novel grammars for which there is no obvious model in the input. Rather, one must consider the possibility that whatever grammar is created by the learner may have the side-effect of generating utterances which may not in fact have been perceived in the input at all. By this means, one might account for a range of 'over-generated' forms in developmental data: the regularized irregular verbs in Brown (1973), the over-extended accusative morphemes in Clahsen (1984b), and—as will be argued below—the distribution of stage-one negation in the L1 and L2N data.

These conclusions lead in turn to some interesting predictions for real-time acquisition, predictions that are crucial for the present analysis of negation. Consider the case of the head-initial or head-final VP in German. Koopman (1984) proposes that the principles of UG determining the choice among these two alternatives involve not some parameter directly associated with X-bar theory (which only creates the general configuration of phrase structure, both head-initial and head-final), but the directionality of case assignment (e.g. nominative, accusative, etc.) and thematic-role assignment (e.g. agent, patient, etc.). What might one predict, where it is assumed that the input data suggest both orders to the learner and that the relevant parameters of UG (e.g. the directionality of case assignment and thematic-role assignment) are as yet undetermined? Obviously, the learning procedures will construct two representations of the VP, and for the time being neither will be ignored or expunged by UG. Hence, for real-time acquisition it is possible under certain conditions to predict the transitional existence of multiple underlying orders of elements.

It is important to note that the prediction of multiple underlying orders cannot be made under all conditions. What is crucial here is the initial state of the universal principles in question. For instance, a number of the principles of UG are considered to be parameterized in such a way that the most restrictive option obtains in the initial state. Referred to as the Subset Principle (see, e.g. Wexler & Culicover 1980 (the

'Superset Principle'); Manzini & Wexler, 1985; Berwick, 1985), the idea predicts that the learner will not require negative evidence in order to select the parameter setting which is compatible with the input.

In terms of learnability, of course, the Subset Principle has obvious appeal. Moreover, if it is assumed that this principle obtains for all parameters of UG, then the above prediction of multiple underlying orders in transitional states is obviously false. However, while the Subset Principle seems to work for principles such as the Binding Conditions (Manzini & Wexler, 1985; cf. Finer & Broselow, 1987), it appears less plausible for other parameters of UG. Consider, for instance, how the child learning German determines VP headedness. Clearly, if only the head-initial order is learned from input, then the remaining grammar to be learned will be difficult at best. In particular, selection of the head-initial VP will require rightward movement to final position of an unnatural class of elements (finite verbs, participles, infinitives, and particles). Moreover, in order to create the required subject-verb inversion where some non-subject is initial (e.g. an adverbial or an object), the head-initial VP will require either leftward movement of the finite verb or rightward movement of the subject into the middle of the VP. In other words, selection of the head-initial VP will have secondary consequences which violate UG. On the other hand, this problem does not mean that the selection of a head-final over a head-initial VP is in any way more (or less) set-restrictive than the opposite case. Rather, if one abstracts away from the secondary, interactive problems that might arise, it would appear that these two options for the organization of the VP will lead to essentially equal sets. Hence, in a case such as this one, it might still be maintained that the learner may consider more than one underlying grammar at a time.

Finally, while the grammars of natural languages generally fall within the range of those grammars permitted by the options of UG, one must also deal with the possibility of constructions, perhaps often historical residues, that would require the relaxation of UG in a somewhat less than principled fashion. In this regard, what I would like to suggest is that the modern German FS-NEG described earlier falls out from the configurations allowed by UG. Preliminary evidence to support this idea comes from Dahl's (1979) typology of sentence negation, which suggests that, among languages using what he calls 'syntactic negation', negative particles only rarely occur in positions that are not adjacent to the verb. The idea might also be given a more principled account as well. For example, Harald Clahsen (personal communication) has suggested that NEG is placed adjacent to the verb due to its association with the semantic head of S, namely the verb itself (cf. Abney, 1986). For the present analysis, we will assume that this association is, in fact, a universal principle. Furthermore, we will assume that the principle relates to the interpretation of sentential negation at Logical Form and, therefore, that it applies at S-structure. In particular, we will assume that the principle disallows maximal projections between NEG and the verb. The transitional constructions of examples (2)–(5) do not violate it, for there are no intervening maximal projections. In contrast, FS-NEG does require the intervention of maximal projections between NEG and the verb, as shown in example (9):[10]

(9)     *Ich habe den Wagen gestern nicht nach Worms gefahren*
        I have the car yesterday not to Worms driven
        I didn't drive the car to Worms yesterday.

Hence, what one finds here is a situation where a construction in a particular language appears to require a marked relaxation of an otherwise inflexible principle of UG.[11]

Until now, we have discussed three scenarios for learnability: cases where input may serve to select among hierarchically arranged options of UG under the Subset Principle; cases where input (perhaps only weakly) serves to select among essentially equal options permitted by UG; and cases where input appears to require a marked relaxation of UG. In the first two, learnability from direct positive evidence is possible (although in the second case it may require the interaction of other principles). In neither case would one predict actual resistance to learning. In contrast, where the particular grammar of input appears to require a relaxation of UG, one might with some certainty predict that the structure in question will resist learning even in the face of direct positive evidence.

Translated into real-time acquisition under exposure to input, the idea of resistance to learning yields some interesting predictions. In cases where the learner's perception of the input (that is, whatever is parsed) includes possible configurations which fall within UG, then these will be tried out before those which require a marked relaxation of UG. This is a principal source of problems for extendibility. Where the (perceived) input in fact does not contain any other possible means of learning other than through a relaxation of UG, then relaxed it must be. One might, of course, expect the latter case to be rather rare, since what the input in fact contains and what the learner actually learns are often mediated by parsing and parsing failures.

## Learning German Sentential Negation

Assuming that the learner is antecedently equipped with this sketchy portrait, we turn to the problem of learning German negation. First to be dealt with are the L1 and L2N learners, who will be assumed to receive syntactically similar input.[12] After this, the course of acquisition by the L2F learners will be treated. For these learners, it will be shown that the input to the learning mechanism differs considerably from that of the L1 and L2N learners.

For the L1 and L2N analysis, we begin with two assumptions. First, we will assume that the discontinuous nature of German finite and non-finite verb in main clauses has not been picked up. The L1 data as well as the cross-linguistic L2N data do, in fact, indicate that the discontinuity of the verb system is acquired somewhat later, so the assumption is probably not too strong. The second assumption we will make is that the learner has determined that all movement rules go to the left rather than to the right. In fact, one might conduct the analysis with the assumption that movement may occur in either direction. The results for the analysis of negation, however, are the same. Hence, for simplicity of presentation we will exclude discussion of rightward movement rules.

With the assumption that the discontinuous nature of the German verb system remains (temporarily) unlearned, one can entertain the possibility of constructing two representations of the VP, one head-initial and the other head-final. As noted above, the transitional existence of multiple underlying orders appears in this case to be allowed by UG, so long as the relevant parameters for case assignment and thematic-role assignment remain unset.

What is interesting about the stage of development prior to the acquisition of the discontinuous verb system of German is that the learner has no indication that it is the verb—and not the NP object—that must move in the final-state VP. Given a learning analogue to Move Alpha, in fact, it is entirely possible that the learner at this stage might conclude that NP movement may cause the superficial 'verb shift' in the input. In other words, if the learner considers the head-initial order (VO) and notes the presence of a verb-final string (OV), then the procedure creating movements might move the object to a position before the verb, a position that at this early stage might appear to the learner to be the second position. This kind of movement might, for instance, be handled as VP adjunction, in which the moved NP c-commands its trace. If only leftward movement is accessible, then NP movement is the only option that the learner has. Likewise, consideration of an early head-final underlying order (OV) when presented with a verb-second input string may cause verb movement to a position that would appear at this stage to be the second position. Again, with only leftward movement, this result is the only possible one. In summary, the superficial VO order may arise either from a base-generated head-initial VP or from a head-final VP with leftward movement of the verb; the superficial OV order may arise either from a base-generated head-final VP or from a head-initial VP with leftward NP movement.

It is important to remember that the proposed existence of two underlying VP representations obtains only for a very early stage of acquisition. In particular, at this point the acquisition data indicate for both L1 and L2N that the rules governing 'subject-verb inversion' have not been learned and that no significant aspect of the discontinuity of German verbs (finite verbs versus participles, particles, and infinitives) has been picked up. In other words, this stage does not automatically lead to the possibility of rejecting the head-initial order on the basis of its incompatibility with other principles of UG.

As opposed to word order data for verb and NP complements, it is clear from very early stages of acquisition (not reviewed above) that NEG is positioned to the left of the head. Consider the following utterances, drawn from Clahsen's (1982) L1 study and from Felix's (1978) L2N study of children:

| (10) | *nein da* | no there |
| (11) | *nein kaputt* | no broken |
| (12) | *nein helfen* | no help |
| (13) | *nein bauch harke* | no need(?) rake |
| (14) | *nein essen* | no eat |

The very early data do contain utterances in which the negator is placed to the right (e.g. *da nein* 'there no'), but their number is rather small (Wode, 1981). From this point, the learner may suppose that NEG is generated to the left of projections, i.e. NEG AP, NEG NP, NEG VP.

So far, we have made the twin assumptions that the learner has created two underlying orders for the VP and that NEG is generated to the left. A combination of these two, along with a strict interpretation of the associative principle noted in the previous section, yields the following results:

| *base generated* | *left movement* | *associative principle* |
|------------------|-----------------|-------------------------|
| NEG V O          | O NEG V         | O NEG V                 |
| NEG O V          | V NEG O         | NEG V O                 |
|                  |                 | V NEG O                 |

The last column shows configurations that might actually occur in performance data. Interestingly, with the assumptions made up to now concerning headedness and the position of NEG *vis-à-vis* the VP, one predicts an early stage of development with the negator in no other than those positions demonstrated by the acquisition data themselves.

In the previous section, it was suggested that what is demonstrated in acquisition data might go beyond what actually occurs in input. The analysis of early L1 and L2N negation appears to illustrate this idea. Under this proposal, the only necessary ingredients in constructing the three positions of the negator are the pre-VP position of the NEG, leftward movement of NPs and verbs, and the assumed associative principle. To these one might add that the naturalistic learners' stage-one perception of what constitutes sentential negation in German is likely skewed by the undetermined nature of VP headedness. For instance, German input might be said to include strings which demonstrate both pre-verbal and post-verbal negation, as in examples (15)–(18):

(15)     *ich verstehe nicht*
         I understand not.
         I don't understand.
(16)     *nicht schreien*
         not yell.
         Don't yell.
(17)     *das darfst du nicht machen*
         that can/may you not do.
         You can't do that.
(18)     *ich weiß, daß du nicht essen willst*
         I know that you not eat want.
         I know that you don't want to eat.

Hence, unequipped with some specification for VP headedness, the learner at this stage might conclude that sentential negation includes both pre-verbal and post-verbal placements of the negator.

Subsequent to the first stage, the discontinuous nature of the German verb system is recognized. At this time, we will assume, following DuPlessis *et al.* (1987) and Schwartz (1988), that the head-final order is selected. What this means for the learners at this stage is that leftward NP movement out of an underlying head-final VP is also made impossible.

In other words, at this stage the L1 and L2N learners are essentially in possession of something close to the final-state configuration: a head-final VP with leftward verb movement.

The removal of the head-initial order and, by extension, of NP movement has an important impact on the development of negation. In particular, rather than the three superficial configurations of sentential negation indicated above, only one remains: V NEG O. The other two, NEG V O and O NEG V, derive from the underlying head-initial order and from leftward NP movement, respectively. Expunging these two solves the extendibility problem for pre-verbal sentential negation. What remains is stage-two negation.

At this stage, we continue to assume that the associative principle still disallows the intervention of lexically filled maximal projections between the verb and the negator. Note that this situation will only hold as long as there is verb-second movement, for if the verb remains in final position (as in final-state embedded clauses), then the pre-VP position of NEG in the base will generally result in the intervention of (at least) the object at S-structure:

(19)    *Ich wußte, daß sie nicht den Wagen hatte*
         I knew that she not the car had.
         I knew that she didn't have the car.

In example (19), the negator *nicht* is not adjacent to the verb *hatte*; therefore, the sentence is ungrammatical under the reading of sentential negation. In other words, the appearance of verb-final embedded clauses, the next stage of word-order development, might cause the breakdown and removal of the pre-VP NEG.

This situation puts the learner into a kind of dilemma. Because the finite verb may, in the final stage of word-order development, occur either in 'second' position (main clauses) or in final position (embedded clauses), pre-VP NEG fails due to the associative principle. On the other hand, given FS-NEG in the input along with the head-final VP and leftward verb movement, there appears to be no other place to generate the negator without such a violation. What I would suggest, therefore, is that the assumed associative principle both expunges the pre-VP placement of NEG—resulting in the disappearance of superficial S V NEG O sequences—and causes the late appearance of FS-NEG, which requires relaxation of the principle.[13]

In contrast to L1 and L2N, the L2F learners in Eubank (1987) were exposed to the discontinuity of the German verb system only gradually.

During the first two months of the course, the only indication in the instructional materials of a head-final order is in the form of a small number of verbs with finalized non-finite particles (e.g. *abwischen* (away-wipe) 'erase', and *anziehen* (on-pull) 'put on (clothing)'). This initial period corresponds roughly to the use of S-NEG negation. The introduction of modal auxiliaries (infinitives final) in the fourth chapter of instruction represents the next indication of an underlying head-final order. This point in time occurs during the first semester covered in Eubank (1987), between elicitation sessions three and four. Chapter five of the instructional materials, introducing the perfect tenses (past participles final), represents the last evidence of an SXV underlying order in the first semester. It is only during the second semester (elicitation sessions seven to eleven) that subordinate and relative clauses (finite verbs final), the passive (past participle final), and infinitival clauses (*zu* 'to' + infinitive final) are introduced. Given these facts on available L2F input and the acquisition data reviewed previously, it seems clear that these learners might create only a head-initial order for the VP during initial stages.[14]

The initial L2F negation data in examples (6) and (7) suggest that the L2F learners might use a post-VP position for NEG, a stark contrast to the pre-VP position of NEG proposed for L1 and L2N. Indeed, the very early stage of L2F development in Eubank (1987) (not reviewed above), which is quite similar to that of L1 and L2N, would appear to lead the learners to a pre-VP NEG:

| (20) | *nein hier* | no here | (It's) not here |
|------|-------------|---------|-----------------|
| (21) | *nein fahren* | no drive | (They're) not driving. |

Hence, what appears to be problematic is explaining why the L1 and L2N learners might use pre-VP NEG while L2F learners appear to switch to post-VP NEG. The problem is particularly crucial since post-VP NEG results in an S-structure with the verb separated from the negator as in example (7), a direct violation of the assumed associative principle.

Closer inspection of the L2F input data reveals an explanation of the problem. As a first factor, one can assume that the L2F learners have, at this early stage, only constructed a head-initial representation of the VP (yielding SVO superficial orders). To this one can add certain facts on the input for negation. Of particular interest is what the learner might perceive to constitute sentential negation in German. As noted above, L1 and L2N learners might be said to assume that German has a variety of possible ways to negate propositions. Evidence for this perception derives from negated split-verb constructions as in example (17), from negated embedded clauses like example (18), and from negated impersonal commands such as example (16). In other words, given the possibility of a head-initial as well as a head-final VP and of verb as well as NP movement, it is entirely possible that the naturalistic learners might not know exactly what makes up FS-NEG. Significantly, the impersonal command as in example (16) is simply not included in the L2F German programme Eubank describes, and the split-verb constructions and embeddings like examples (17) and (18) are withheld during initial exposure to the language. As a second factor, then, the L2F learners—as opposed to the naturalistic learners—appear to be presented with much less ambiguous input: The sentential negator may only appear at the end of the sentence after the second-position verb and the object. (Indeed, this superficial regularity is not only what the input supports, but also what the formal instruction described in Eubank (1987) aims for.) It follows from these observations that the L2F learners may only perceive a narrow range of ways in which sentential negation might be accomplished. In fact, the situation is rather similar to that of the naturalistic learners at the final stage: Given the head-initial VP and the clarity of input, the L2F learners have no other option but to relax the associative principle and thus to allow the separation of the negator from the verb.

Of course, in certain ways the switch from pre-VP NEG to post-VP NEG will appear to emulate the effects of FS-NEG, as in example (7). Moreover, if these learners continue with a head-initial representation of the VP, then example (8) can also be predicted (via rightward movement of the particle) without assuming that FS-NEG has actually been learned. Indeed, because FS-NEG is closely bound to the head-final VP, the L2F data in Eubank's (1987) transcripts are insufficient to determine whether or not S-NEG is ever expunged and FS-NEG ever picked up by these learners.

## Conclusion

In sum, what has been shown here is that an adequate account of acquisition must, as Pinker (1984) suggests, deal with specific questions of learnability and extendibility. To this end, a theoretical model must be developed which goes beyond the sorts of descriptive mechanism employed, for instance, by Clahsen (1984a) and Eubank (1987). At the same time, such a theory must be specific enough to be falsified while maintaining independent motivation.

Thus, the present contribution ends with nearly as many questions as answers. Consider, for example, the theoretical status of the assumed associative principle or the supposed peripheral status of FS-NEG in German. In both cases, the strongest support derives from somewhat superficial facts of typology and acquisition. What is needed is more specific, independently motivated evidence. Thus, for the associative principle one might hope for an account as specific as the given, for instance, by May (1985) on the principles involved in the interpretation of constituent negation. Applied to German, such an account will have to deal with the different kinds of verb (i.e. finite, non-finite) and with the location of these verbs, given verb-second movement and the traces left behind. Without such independent evidence, the present analysis is clearly speculative.

### Notes to Chapter 6

1. Thanks are due to Robert Bley-Vroman, Kevin Gregg, Maria Beck, and Harald Clahsen for comments on an earlier draft of this paper. Any errors are, of course, my own.
2. In fact, Pinker (1984) considers a third problem, that of a particular representation's consistency with the learner's language. The consistency problem, which will be dealt with here only in a broad sense, constrains the types of grammar posited for the learner to those generating utterances that are demonstrably a part of the learner's language. In other words, under this condition a grammatical representation must not generate utterances which are systematically absent from learner speech.
3. There are, of course, other criteria for a plausible acquisition mechanism (see Pinker, 1979, for a review of these).
4. It is interesting to note that when *nicht* occurs before a bound adverb as in example (1), it is difficult to know if it is the proposition as a whole or only the adverbial constituent that is being negated. See Stickel (1970) for a more in-depth—if theoretically somewhat dated—review of negation in German.
5. German, like Dutch and several other languages, displays a discontinuity in its verb system. In main clauses, the finite verb always occurs in second position after the subject or a topicalized element. Non-finite verbs, on the other hand, occur only in clause-final position. In embedded clauses, both the finite and the non-finite verb occur in final position. This discontinuity has led to some questions as to the headedness of the German VP. Presently, it is generally assumed that the language is head-final (see, e.g. Koster, 1975; Thiersch, 1978). For principled accounts of the verb-second phenomenon, see Koopman (1984) and the contributions in Haider & Prinzhorn (1986). See Clahsen & Muysken (1986), as well as DuPlessis *et al.* (1987) and Schwartz (1988) for discussion of Universal Grammar and the development of German word order in L2.
6. In a re-examination of the data in Dittmar (1981) as well as Klein & Dittmar (1979), Clahsen & Muysken (1986) attempt to show that the verb-final utterances might also be the result of preposing constituents that occur after the verb underlyingly. In doing so, they attempt to prove their claim that L2

learners invariably begin with a canonical SVO underlying order. Clearly, their analysis does have the capacity to describe the data out of an underlying SVO order. However, what is important to point out about this interpretation of the data is that it has little independently motivated evidence. In other words, they present no evidence that compels their analysis, no means by which their analysis might be falsified. Thus, there is no reason to believe that an analysis which predicts dual underlying orders, head-initial and head-final, must be incorrect in so far as the acquisition data are concerned.

One might, of course, object to this interpretation by pointing out that certain word orders, particularly those unlike the learner's L1 order, are underrepresented in L2 acquisition data. Such questions of balance, however, are more properly accorded to some (as yet undeveloped) theory of performance, a sub-part of which might be language transfer. In other words, that speakers of Romance languages who learn German might only rarely produce verb-final utterances in the initial stages does not count against the existence in principle of such an order of elements underlyingly.

7. The third processing strategy in Clahsen (1984a) is the Subordinate Clause Strategy, which prohibits any sort of permutation in embeddings.

8. One might propose that the L2F learners are, in fact, exposed to the necessary negative evidence (classroom correction) which would allow them to expunge S-NEG. It is, however, my impression that this is not the case. My reasons for this idea are based on the sceptical reactions of classroom teachers to the data in Eubank (1987). Maria Beck (personal communication) suggests that the highly controlled nature of classroom activities in that programme probably excluded the possibility of students producing sentences in which S-NEG resulted in incorrect German.

9. I ignore the problem of negative evidence, especially indirect negative evidence. See Wexler & Culicover (1980) for discussion of this concern.

10. In this regard, it is interesting to note that Old High German as well as Middle High German had pre-verbal negation. Exactly why and how a language might thus go through such a switch (known as 'Jespersen's Cycle') would make for interesting research. See Dahl (1979) and Bach (1970: 177) for descriptive discussion; see Lightfoot (1981) for a general discussion of Universal Grammar and diachronic change.

11. Similar problems have occurred with the Adjacency Requirement on case assignment. In particular, it seems that the requirement must in some way be relaxed in certain languages, especially those in which case is marked morphologically. See Chomsky (1986) for discussion.

12. Clearly, there are certain differences between the input received by L1 and that received by L2N learners. The studies by Freed (1980) and Meisel (1980) suggest, however, that these differences may be minimal as concerns basic word order and negation. On the other hand, if the findings of Jordens (1987) on the distribution of certain semantic features in Dutch motherese could be substantiated more widely, then one might argue convincingly against the assumption of essential equality made here.

13. One might argue that this analysis suffers from 'wanting to have the cake and eat it, too'. However, relaxing a principle of UG should not be considered to lead to widespread violations. Rather, such a process is seen here to extend to specific cases. This is in contrast to parameterized principles of UG, where selection among the options allowed will have far-reaching results.

14. Of course, classroom teachers could have provided the input which is absent from the instructional materials. Such an idea cannot be ignored. However, it might be pointed out that the pedagogical tendency in the programme described in Eubank (1987) was to withhold new material until it was introduced formally (grammar as well as vocabulary).

# 7 Word-order transfer, metalinguistic awareness, and constraints on foreign language learning[1]

TERENCE ODLIN

*Ohio State University, Columbus, USA*

## Introduction

Of the many problems in second language research, the role of language transfer in the acquisition of syntax has been one of the most intractable.[2] In comparison with attitudes in the 1960s and 1970s, there is now less scepticism that knowledge of one language can greatly influence performance in another language, but controversy over the extent of syntactic transfer has by no means disappeared (cf. Dulay *et al.*, 1982; Gass & Selinker, 1983; Meisel, 1983). Much of the ongoing controversy is related to the ever-growing interest in language universals. While some research suggests that transfer and universals can and do interact in the acquisition of syntax (e.g. Zobl, 1980a; Gass, 1979), there is no consensus about how much interaction there is or about the role of transfer and universals (and other factors) as independent influences on acquisition.

The interest in universals has no doubt made clearer the range of questions that research on second language acquisition must answer, but universalist analyses are just as problematic as contrastive analyses. While contrastive analyses often fail in predicting when transfer will occur, there is an obvious pitfall in predicting when transfer will *never* occur. A putatively universal constraint on some kind of transfer cannot be universal if a single clear-cut case of such transfer exists. The literature on language attrition is instructive on that point. With regard to what may be termed *borrowing transfer*, there have been many claims by eminent scholars denying that transfer of bound morphology is possible in any bilingual milieu. However, as Thomason (1981) has observed, there are unambiguous cases of just such transfer; some dialects of Anatolian Greek, for instance, have incorporated many Turkish bound morphemes (Dawkins, 1916). In this type of transfer, speakers' knowledge of a second language (Turkish) influenced their native language (Greek). Such cases suggest that putative constraints on other kinds of transfer may also be illusory.

Counter-examples to any would-be universals might come either from data on borrowing transfer or from data on *substratum transfer*, i.e. the influence of a native language (or some other previously learned language) on the acquisition of another language (cf. Thomason & Kaufman, 1988). In this paper evidence from both substratum and borrowing transfer is relevant to the problem of cross-linguistic influences on word order. Recent studies with a universalist orientation purport that there are structural constraints on the transfer of word order (Rutherford, 1983; 1986; Zobl, 1986a; 1986b). Yet like purported constraints on morphological transfer, the supposed constraints on word-order transfer are dubious on empirical grounds; this paper will cite cases of word-order transfer that violate the constraints. Whatever value universalist analyses may have, there exist other factors relevant to the phenomenon of word-order transfer. Among those factors is *metalinguistic awareness*, i.e. individuals' awareness of language. If such awareness has an effect on the development of second language syntax, the study of syntactic transfer and the study of Foreign Language Learning, i.e. acquisition of a second language influenced by instruction, are interrelated. This paper first considers the universalist positions of Zobl and Rutherford and the counter-examples to their claims, then considers various factors relevant to the issue of word order, and finally considers the relations between transfer, metalinguistic awareness, Foreign Language Learning and Second Language Acquisition.[3]

## The Analyses of Zobl and Rutherford

Although different in some respects, the interpretations of word-order acquisition given by Rutherford and Zobl are similar in two important ways. First, neither denies that word-order transfer plays some role in the acquisition of syntax. Zobl sees transfer as a real influence in, for example, the placement of adverbs in English as documented by

Selinker (1969) and others. Rutherford finds transfer occurring at a rather abstract level involving typological properties or 'parameters'. For instance, the rigidity of word order in some languages (e.g. English) is, Rutherford claims, a transferable parameter.

The other major similarity in the positions of Zobl and Rutherford is that both scholars are sceptical that negative transfer of *basic* word order takes place: i.e. that there are any simple cases of linguistic interference in which the canonical declarative pattern of the syntactic constituents subject, verb phrase (VP), and object in one's native language is anomalously used in lieu of the canonical pattern of the target language. For example, in an examination of syntactic patterns of Japanese ESL students at an American university, Rutherford (1983: 367) emphatically claims that transfer of the subject-object-verb (SOV) pattern of Japanese never occurs: 'Japanese learners of English do not at any time produce writing in which the verb is wrongly placed sentence finally'. Though English uses a subject-verb-object (SVO) pattern, one might expect to find occasional SOV sentences in the speech or writing of Japanese ESL students. Rutherford, however, found no evidence of such transfer. While the quotation just given might suggest that Rutherford's analysis is restricted to one aspect of ESL performance (i.e. writing), the substance of the claim found in his paper is clearly universalist; Japanese and other learners are likely to rely on other native-language 'parameters' but not on the basic SOV pattern. Citing evidence in Rutherford's study as well as other evidence, Zobl (1986a: 178) is sceptical about the occurrence of transfer of word-order traits that are 'central' to the syntactic typology of a language: 'learners are sensitive to the principle that defines the central traits of a word order type and that the L1 does not lead to transfer in the central traits'. Although he sees basic word order as one of those 'central' traits, Zobl does believe that basic word-order transfer is possible in one very restricted case, when a language makes use of more than one basic word order as in Dutch, which uses SOV in subordinate clauses and SVO (as well as other patterns) in main clauses. His analysis thus takes into account some European research, such as a very detailed study of the acquisition of Dutch by speakers of Moroccan Arabic (an SVO language) and Turkish (an SOV language) that shows that transfer was quite common (Jansen *et al.*, 1981). However, it is clear that Zobl regards such cases of typological ambiguity as exceptional and not as ones that call into question his hypothesized universal principle on the non-transferability of basic word order.

Both Zobl and Rutherford thus make claims about the non-transferability of basic word order in *all* 'unambiguous' second language contexts. As both analyses are thus universalist in the strictest sense of the word, both can be falsified if there exists a single 'unambiguous' counter-example of basic word-order transfer. The claims of Zobl and Rutherford are in fact untenable since counter-examples do exist: 11 will be presented in this paper. These counter-examples show that universalist claims about the non-transferability of basic word order cannot be true in any absolute sense although universalist analyses might point to interesting statistical tendencies (cf. Comrie, 1981).

## General Patterns Seen in Basic Word-Order Transfer

Table 7.1 summarizes four attested cases of basic word-order transfer in the acquisition of a second language (i.e. substratum transfer). In Hawaiian Pidgin English, Bamboo English, Andean Spanish, and Pidgin Fijian there are documented cases of the use of an SOV pattern that in all likelihood is due to influence from the native language as discussed below. Table 7.2 summarizes three other cases of word-order transfer that are instances of borrowing transfer in which change in the word order in the native language can be attributed to the acquisition of a second language having a different basic word order. For example, Young People's Dyirbal, the drastically altered form of Traditional Dyirbal, an Australian language, employs a word order that shows the effects of Dyirbal/English bilingualism in an aboriginal community. All of the cases in Tables 7.1 and 7.2 show other influences in addition to transfer. In the case of Andean Spanish, for example, both SOV and SVO patterns are used. While the SOV patterns show an influence from the native language, Quechua, the SVO patterns indicate the effects of exposure to the target language, Spanish.

TABLE 7.1 *Attested cases of basic word-order transfer in second language acquisition*

| Target language | Native language | Interlanguage |
| --- | --- | --- |
| English (SVO) | Japanese/Korean (SOV) | Hawaiian Pidgin English (SOV)* |
| English (SVO) | Korean (SOV) | Bamboo English (SOV)* |
| Spanish (SVO) | Quechua (SOV) | Andean Spanish (SOV)* |
| Fijian (VOS/SVO) | Hindustani (SOV) | Pidgin Fijian (SOV)* |

* SVO order is also used

TABLE 7.2 *Attested cases of basic word-order transfer in language attrition due to bilingualism*

| Traditional language | Second language | Language Shift |
|---|---|---|
| Bhojpuri (SOV) | Mauritian creole (SVO) | Mauritian Bhojpuri (SVO)** |
| Dyirbal (OAV, AOV) | English (SVO) | Young People's Dyirbal (AVO)** |
| Nubian (SOV) | Egyptian Arabic (SVO) | Cairo Nubian (SVO)** |

** SOV order is also used (in Young People's Dyirbal: AOV)
The category A in Dyirbal indicates a subject of a transitive verb.

Table 7.3 indicates four language-contact situations that occurred in earlier times and that show a strong likelihood of basic word-order transfer having taken place. In these cases, however, there are uncertainties about the exact nature of the contact situation, and so the languages involved are simply referred to as Contact Language 1 and Contact Language 2, with the result of that contact listed in the third column.

TABLE 7.3 *Historical cases of basic word-order transfer*

| Contact Language 1 | Contact Language 2 | Result |
|---|---|---|
| Portuguese (SVO) | Tamil (SOV)/ Gujarati (?) (SOV)/ Hindustani (?) (SOV)/ Malayalam | Indo-Portuguese (SOV)* |
| Ethiopic (SVO) | Cushitic (SOV) | Amharic (SOV) |
| Cushitic (SOV) | Bantu (SVO) | Ma'a (SVO) |
| Sinitic (SVO) | Altaic (SOV) | Hui (SOV) |

* SVO order is also used.

## Cases of Substratum Transfer

The cases listed in Table 7.1 warrant extended description since they pertain most directly to syntactic transfer affecting the acquisition of a second language. Two of the cases (Hawaiian Pidgin English and Andean Spanish) have been discussed elsewhere in connection with basic word-order transfer, but there are facts relevant to both that have not received sufficient attention.

### Hawaiian Pidgin English

Hawaiian Pidgin English (HPE) is commonly characterized as having a basic SVO order, but there are attested examples of other word orders and these examples indicate transfer. Nagara (1972) characterized the HPE of Japanese speakers as having both SVO and SOV. The SOV pattern he attributed to Japanese influence, as in example (1) (Nagara, 1972: 300–01):

(1)     *mi: cu: stoa gécc*
        Me two store get
        I got/acquired two stores.

Bickerton and Givón (1976) provide detailed quantitative evidence of transfer-based differences in basic word order in HPE. Their statistics indicate that verb-final utterances are by no means unusual among Japanese speakers of HPE. They found, moreover, that verbs sometimes preceded subjects in the utterances of speakers of verb-initial Philippine languages (e.g. Ilocano) as in example (2) (Bickerton & Givón, 1976: 27):

(2)     *samtaim kam da shak*
        Sometime come the shark.
        Sometimes sharks came.

As in the case of the Japanese speaker, Bickerton & Givón attribute the Philippine English word order employed to the native-language patterns (here VSO).

Both HPE studies make it clear that SVO is an alternative order to the transfer-based pattern. In the case of the Japanese and Filipinos studied by Bickerton & Givón, the evidence indicates that the most proficient speakers of HPE used SVX patterns the most while the least proficient speakers used SVX patterns the least and instead used a sizeable number of SXV or VSX patterns in keeping with word order in their native languages.[4] Similar instances of a relation between word-order transfer and language proficiency will be seen in the discussions of Andean Spanish and Young People's Dyirbal below.

Aside from the SOV and SVO patterns in the HPE syntax of Japanese speakers, another frequent pattern is OV as in example (3) (Nagara, 1972: 303):

(3)     *hawai kám*
        Hawaii come.
        (I) came (to) Hawaii.

While the example just given suggests that OV phrases are reduced variants of the SOV pattern, some scholars who have been sceptical about the existence of basic word-order transfer have suggested that OV patterns may result from other factors besides native language influence. In a critique of transfer cited by Mühlhäusler (1986:125), Meisel claims that OV patterns merely reflect syntactic movement rules that are motivated by a (putatively) universal pragmatic mode.[5] In other words, what seems to be syntactic transfer could be an instance of topicalization or some other language-neutral discourse function. For example, the phrase *hawai kám* does have an OV pattern, but one might still claim that the word order reflects discourse considerations such as a desire on the part of the speaker to introduce Hawaii as the setting for subsequent discourse.

Although the discourse-universal explanation may account for some of the word-order patterns seen in HPE, there are at least three reasons to be sceptical about the value of such an explanation for most of the HPE data. First, that explanation does nothing to account for the existence of SOV sentences such as *mi: cu: stoa gécc*. Second, a language-neutral discourse explanation probably cannot account for such verb-final phrases as example (4) (Bickerton & Givón, 1976: 18):

(4)     *æn luk-laik-punkin-kain get*
        And look-like-pumpkin-kind get.
        And there's the kind that look like pumpkins.

As Bickerton and Givón note, the use of *get* seems to function as an existential marker somewhat like *there is* or as a possessive somewhat like *have*. However, this clause-final position of the existential/possessive marker may be less frequent in some other varieties of HPE. For example, in the HPE of a Hmong refugee described by Huebner (1979; 1983), VO order involving existential/possessive constructions seems to have been more common than OV order (Huebner, 1979:23):

(5)     *bat kaemp nam pong haeva sowjer*
        But there was a soldier at Camp Nam Phong.

In all probability, then, the clause-final position of *get* in *æn luk-laik-punkin-kain get* reflects Japanese influence. A third reason to reject a language-neutral discourse explanation is that it probably cannot account for differences in HPE word order produced by speakers of VSO and SOV languages. Transfer-based differences in the use of OV and VO patterns are in fact evident in a study of discourse functions in the early stages of second language acquisition (Givón, 1984). A speaker of Korean, which like Japanese is SOV, produced many more instances of OV patterns than did a speaker of a VSO Philippine language, as seen in Table 7.4.[6]

TABLE 7.4 *Comparative frequency of VO/OV patterns in two texts in Hawaiian Pidgin English*

| | Definite NP objects | | Indefinite NP objects | |
|---|---|---|---|---|
| | VO | OV | VO | OV |
| Philippine-English text | 26 | 2 | 32 | 0 |
| Korean-English text | 11 | 22 | 17 | 28 |

Figures are adapted from those in Tables I–IV in Givón (1984).

### Korean Bamboo English

Similar instances of transfer are evident in Bamboo English, a trade jargon that developed through contact between American soldiers and Japanese and Korean civilians in the 1940s and 1950s. While there is little written about the use of Bamboo English, one study of Korean Bamboo English (Algeo, 1960) indicates that by the 1950s it showed signs of developing into something quite like a pidgin. Algeo illustrated that development with a few sentences that follow the SOV and OV patterns of Korean, as in example (6):

(6)     *You number one washee-washee catchee, number one presento hava-yes.*
        If you do a fine washing, you'll get a fine tip.

As with HPE, Korean Bamboo English also employed SVO patterns, but the verb *hava-yes* probably occurred more often in clause-final position than in any other environment (John Algeo, personal communication). An instance of semantic transfer in Korean Bamboo English makes all the more plausible the occurrence of basic word-order transfer: the use of *number one* reflects a Korean (and Japanese) tradition of indicating satisfaction through the use of a number. There is also historical evidence suggesting that basic word-order transfer would be likely. American soldiers generally were not in Korea for more than 16 months, and so what norms there were in Bamboo English probably developed more among Koreans who used the jargon frequently than among the American military (John Algeo, p.c.).

### Andean Spanish

Spanish, an SVO language in most dialects, does not normally use an SOV pattern except when the object noun phrase (NP) is a pronoun.

However, in the Spanish spoken in Peru and Ecuador there are verb-final patterns in which the object is a noun. Luján *et al.* (1984) studied the Spanish of several Peruvian children who sometimes used SOV patterns such as

(7)  *Y mi hermano aquí otro paloma hembra había chapado*
and my brother here another dove female had caught
And my brother had caught another female dove here.

Luján *et al.* also found numerous OV patterns such as

(8)  *Volantín antes hacían*
somersault before did
They used to do somersaults.

They claim that the OV as well as the SOV patterns reflect influence from Quechua, an SOV language.

Scepticism about basic word-order transfer in Andean Spanish has, however, been expressed by another investigator (Muysken, 1984). In his study of the variations in the Ecuadorean Spanish of adults of different social classes, Muysken found no examples of SOV sentences although there were some occurrences of SXV sentences (he does not specify the exact number) and frequent occurrences of OV patterns. Using an argument like that of Meisel about HPE, Muysken does not see the OV patterns as evidence of transfer, but rather of movement rules that reflect 'stylistic' (i.e. discourse) considerations. Yet, just as there were in the case of HPE, there are reasons to question the discourse-based explanation of the OV patterns in Andean Spanish. First, although Muysken appeals to 'stylistic' considerations, he provides no discourse analysis (such as that developed by Givón, 1983, and others) which could determine just how often discourse factors encourage the placement of object nouns before verbs. Second, the data in both his study and that of Luján *et al.* suggest that the least proficient speakers of Spanish use OV patterns the most. This statistical tendency is very similar to that seen in the study of HPE by Bickerton and Givón (1976). One explanation for that tendency is obviously transfer. Another explanation—and one that Muysken would presumably favour—is that the least proficient speakers would be the most likely to make use of 'stylistic' OV patterns even if OV patterns are rare in their native language. However, that explanation is dubious in light of the data in Table 7.4 showing that the speaker of basilect Philippine English made almost no use of OV patterns. Another difficulty with Muysken's 'stylistic' explanation is seen in statistics provided by Luján *et al*. The speakers who used OV patterns the most were five-year-old children. If their use of those patterns was primarily 'stylistic', that would contradict other findings indicating that learners around the age of five show a great deal of 'syntactic conservatism', i.e. such learners are not likely to use word-order shifts such as from VO to OV for 'stylistic' reasons (Zobl, 1983).

### Pidgin Fijian

A pidginized variety of Fijian seems to have been spoken from the mid-nineteenth century onwards (Siegel, 1987). First used as a *lingua franca* among Fijians, Europeans and islanders from other parts of the Pacific, it assumed new forms when used by immigrants from India, who started coming to Fiji about a century ago. Some descriptions of Fijian characterize the basic word order in the language as VOS, although Siegel sees word order in Fijian as highly variable. On the other hand, the pidginized form of Fijian spoken by most groups has had, according to Siegel, a rigid SVO order. SVO is probably the order that Indians would most frequently hear (and thus take to be the syntactic target); Siegel claims that Fijians prefer to communicate with Indians in a form of Pidgin Fijian. The Pidgin Fijian of Indians uses SVO, but SOV sentences also occur, such as:

(9)     *koau dua na bisnis sa rawa tiko*
        I one business can have.
        I can have a business.[7]

Siegel attributes the SOV pattern to the influence of the Hindustani spoken in Fiji. The status of both Fijian and Hindustani reflects a rather complex language contact situation, and space does not permit an extended discussion. However, Siegel's description of the contact situation suggests that other types of substratum (and perhaps borrowing) transfer involving word order are not unusual in the languages spoken in Fiji.

## Other Cases of Basic Word-Order Transfer

### Borrowing transfer

The cases of basic word-order transfer listed in Table 7.2 pertain more to issues of language attrition and thus are less directly relevant to transfer in Second Language Acquisition and Foreign Language Learning. Nevertheless, the word-order changes evident in these cases show effects of transfer in bilingual communities and thus have implications for second language research. The case of Dyirbal will serve as a useful illustration of how some changes proceed. Schmidt (1985) presents a very detailed analysis of the changes that have taken place in Dyirbal, and among these shifts is an increasing use of word order that reflects influence from English. In Traditional Dyirbal, subjects of transitive verbs normally are marked with an ergative case inflection, and this case-marking of transitive subjects (such inflected subjects are designated with the letter A in the sentence patterns) is sometimes seen in Young People's Dyirbal. However, while the more proficient Dyirbal children continue to make frequent use of the AOV pattern (example (9)) common in Traditional Dyirbal, the less proficient speakers have come to use AVO much more, as well as to drop the ergative inflection (example (10)).

(10)   *jugumbil-du nyalnga bura-n*
       woman-ERG child see-NONFUT
       The woman sees the child.

(11)   *jugumbil bura-n nyalnga*
       woman see-NONFUT child
       The woman sees the child.

Another sign of word-order change due to influence from English is that young speakers depend much more on AOV and AVO. In Traditional Dyirbal word order was rather flexible, with OAV and AOV being the most common but by no means the only possible word orders (cf. Schmidt, 1985; Dixon, 1972). The dependence on rigid word order that has developed in Young People's Dyirbal may support Rutherford's claim that word-order rigidity is a transferable property.[8]

The use of SVO order in Mauritian Bhojpuri reflects the influence of the creole spoken in Mauritius. Speakers of Bhojpuri who emigrated from India in the nineteenth and twentieth centuries have increasingly come to use the creole, which has a basic SVO order. As a result of bilingualism the traditional SOV pattern of Bhojpuri has weakened (Domingue, 1971). A similar change seems to be taking place in Cairo Nubian, an SOV language, although details provided by Rouchdy (1980) are rather sketchy. Nevertheless, Rouchdy offers evidence that the SVO patterns seen in Cairo Nubian show the influence of Arabic/Nubian bilingualism.

**Other cases of language contact**

The cases in Table 7.3 are also examples of word-order change due to transfer, although the historical circumstances of the language contact leading to transfer are not entirely clear. Indo-Portuguese was a creole that developed on the coasts of India and Sri Lanka during the centuries of contact between Asians and Europeans in several colonial enclaves. In two descriptions of local varieties of Indo-Portuguese, Schuchardt (1883; 1889) noted examples of SOV and other verb-final sentences. In his account of one of these varieties, the Indo-Portuguese spoken in Diu in Gujarat, Schuchardt (1883) was hesitant about attributing to transfer the peculiarities of grammar and pronunciation that he found; nevertheless, his description in that article of the SOV word order in Hindustani indicates that he considered basic word-order transfer a likely explanation for the SOV sentences that he listed. One problem with Schuchardt's data is an uncertainty about who the speakers were. They may have been native speakers of Indo-Portuguese, or Hindustani, or Gujarati, or Malayalam, the latter being a probable source of the SOV examples from Mahé and Cannanore cited by Schuchardt (1889). Other evidence, however, gives much support to Schuchardt's intuitions about transfer. A detailed investigation by Dalgado (1906) of the Indo-Portuguese of Diu and other northern enclaves also turned up SOV sentences. According to Dalgado, such sentences were especially common in spontaneous speech. Other evidence comes from an investigation by Smith (1977) of a dialect of Sri Lankan Portuguese Creole. Although the focus of his study was phonology, Smith cited SOV order as an instance of grammatical transfer occasioned by speakers' knowledge of Tamil (an SOV language). Neither in Smith's investigation nor in the earlier studies is it clear whether the instances of SOV order reflect substratum or borrowing transfer—or both. However, the evidence from as far north as Diu and as far south as Sri Lanka points to the effects of cross-linguistic influence in Indo-Portuguese.

Evidence from Amharic also points to cross-linguistic influence on word order. Most scholars who have worked on Amharic and other Semitic languages of Ethiopia, which are known as Ethiopic languages, believe that the SOV order in those languages reflects a change due to contact centuries ago between speakers of Ethiopic and Cushitic languages (Leslau, 1945). Modern Cushitic languages such as Galla are generally SOV whereas most of the ancient and modern Semitic languages outside Ethiopia have been SVO or VSO. Accordingly, Amharic seems to be a textbook case of structural change due to language contact (cf. Comrie,

1981). Nevertheless, extremely little is known about the people, the specific languages they spoke, or the nature of the language-contact situation that led to the development of Amharic word order (Leslau, 1945). As in the case of Indo-Portuguese, it is not clear whether the instances of SOV order reflect substratum or borrowing transfer. Thomason & Kaufman (1988), however, suggest that the Ethiopian contact situation involved both types of transfer.

Further south in East Africa is a contact zone between Cushitic and Bantu languages. In some areas of this zone, speakers of Cushitic languages have learned Bantu languages, and it appears that some of the ensuing bilingualism led to a hybrid known as Ma'a (and also as Mbugu). Though there has been some controversy over the classification and origins of Ma'a, there is little question that Ma'a shows many characteristics of both Cushitic and Bantu languages (Goodman, 1971). Its basic word order (SVO) is that of neighbouring Bantu languages whereas much of its basic vocabulary is Cushitic. According to Thomason (1983) borrowing transfer can best account for the language mixture. Her argument is essentially that Ma'a is the modern version of an earlier Cushitic language that became increasingly influenced by the word order and morphology of the surrounding Bantu languages as a result of Cushitic/Bantu bilingualism.

Hui is a variety of Chinese spoken by Moslems in several parts of China. A variety of Hui spoken in Gansu province reflects a mixture of Sinitic and Altaic features including SOV order, which Li (1984) considers to be the result of substratum transfer from an Altaic language. Although Mandarin does make use of SOV as well as SVO patterns, SVO is still the predominant order according to Li and also according to Sun and Givón (1985). In contrast, the Gansu variety of Hui relies primarily on SOV and on morphological and phonological devices much more characteristic of Altaic than of Sinitic languages. Little is known, however, about the specific Altaic language(s) involved in the contact situation.

## Explanations for the Infrequency of Word-Order Transfer

The counter-examples presented thus suggest that there is no universal constraint on the transfer of basic word order. In the light of so many counter-examples, there might seem to be little reason for doubting that basic word-order transfer is a very common phenomenon in language contact situations. Nevertheless, the vast amount of research on bilingualism shows relatively few examples of such transfer. There is more than one possible explanation for the apparent scarcity. Metalinguistic awareness seems to be a constraint on the frequency of word-order transfer, as suggested earlier, but there are at least two other possible explanations (and these explanations are not mutually exclusive). Accordingly, before metalinguistic awareness is discussed, the other two possibilities will be considered.

**Language universals**

Universals may indeed play a role similar to what Rutherford and Zobl have hypothesized. Research on language universals contains many instances of 'universal tendencies' where data from most but not all languages corroborate a generalization, e.g. the tendency for SOV languages to employ postpositions (Greenberg, 1966). Refinements of Greenberg's analysis by Hawkins (1983) have proven useful not only for a general understanding of word order but also for an understanding of basic word-order transfer in Andean Spanish (cf. Luján et al., 1984; Zobl, 1986a). It is indeed possible that a similar analysis would be useful for understanding word-order change seen in languages such as Cairo Nubian. Nevertheless, the fact that there is no absolute bar to any kind of word-order transfer indicates that it is desirable to consider other possible explanations for the infrequency of basic word-order transfer. The explanatory value of universalist analyses cannot be ascertained until the merits of other explanations are also understood.

**Observational problems**

In comparison with universalist approaches, a second explanation is far more prosaic but perhaps more important. The seeming infrequency of basic word-order transfer may simply reflect insufficiencies in the data available to linguists. One aspect of this problem is related to language proficiency. In the studies of Bickerton & Givón and of Luján et al., the least proficient speakers showed the greatest use of native-language SOV and OV patterns. If there is a definite relation between proficiency and basic word-order transfer, observers may have to make a special effort to detect the phenomenon: speakers with minimal second-language proficiency are often shy and ashamed of the way they speak. (Schmidt, moreover, notes a similar difficulty in working with speakers of a drastically altered language like Young People's Dyirbal.)

Another aspect of the observational problem is the dearth of research on some important aspects of second language acquisition. In some one hundred years of study of language contact both inside and outside the classroom, adult speakers with extremely little proficiency in a language have only recently received much scholarly attention. Even now the number of studies that have looked at basic word-order transfer in the early stages of acquisition is very small. Researchers often lack access to a large, homogeneous group of individuals who have only minimal proficiency in the target language. Rutherford (1983), for example, seems to have based his claim about the non-transferability of basic word-order on the writing of Japanese college students in California whom he considered to be beginners. However, English is a required subject for all pre-college students in Japan (Conrad & Fishman, 1977); it thus is probable that the Japanese students observed by Rutherford were not really beginners, despite their relative lack of proficiency in English.

Still another observational problem is related to the fact that many languages have relatively flexible word orders. In cases where both the native and target language allow a great deal of flexibility, documenting any transfer might prove difficult even though basic word order in the two languages differs. For example, both Turkish and Serbo-Croatian make use of most of the six permutations of basic word order: VSO, SVO, SOV, OSV, OVS and VOS (Slobin, 1982). While the basic word-order of Turkish is SOV and that of Serbo-Croatian SVO, the extreme flexibility of word order in both languages would make it difficult to document negative transfer in a case, for example, of a Turk learning Serbo-Croatian. A study of differences in the frequency of each of the six permutations or a study of violations of discourse constraints on word order in the target language might show negative transfer, but the difficulties of such a study should not be underestimated: aside from the problems created by the complex relations between syntax and discourse, such a study would require a very large data base. While positive transfer is also possible—indeed likely—it would also be hard to establish since success in acquiring word order could also be attributed simply to exposure to the target language.

## Metalinguistic awareness

Aside from universals and observational problems, metalinguistic awareness may be a very important reason for the apparent scarcity of basic word-order transfer. That is, learners may be somewhat conscious of basic word order both in their native language and in the target language, and that consciousness could aid in the acquisition of the target-language word order, or at least in the avoidance of native-language word order if that order is different. There is some evidence that word order is a structural characteristic rather *accessible* to consciousness. This does not mean that word order, or any other accessible structure, is always automatically available as *explicit knowledge* (Odlin, 1986). In many cases training may be necessary. Many native speakers of English are probably not consciously aware, for example, of the difference often found in the position of the modal auxiliary in declarative and interrogative word-order patterns (e.g. *You can swim* versus *Can you swim?*). Yet while some training would probably be necessary to make native speakers aware of this difference, it seems likely that such training would require less time than, for example, training to make people aware of the differences in the prescriptive usage of *who* and *whom*.

There is a diverse array of evidence pointing to the accessibility of word order under certain conditions. A study of the metalinguistic awareness of children (Hakes, 1980) indicates that children as young as five can reliably judge as ungrammatical sentences that violate English word-order rules; at the same time children of that age have difficulty with sentences that require some awareness of sub-categorization rules and selectional restrictions. In a study of adults in a non-literate society, Heeschen (1978) noted that individuals generally made unreliable judgements about sentences that involved violations of verb morphology but that the same individuals proved quite capable of making reliable judgements about sentences that involved violations of word order. In at least one case, the use of a transfer-based word order has become a marker of negative social prestige: Spanish speakers in Lima sometimes use SOV order to mimic and deride Indians and mestizos in the Quechua-speaking hinterlands of Peru (Carol Klee, p.c.).

The accessibility of word order is also evident in a study of individuals' awareness of transfer-based errors in ESL (Odlin, 1987). Korean/English bilinguals in the study were very successful in identifying English word-order errors characteristic of Korean speakers, and Spanish/English bilinguals were very successful in identifying word-order errors characteristic of Spanish speakers. For example, a stereotypical Korean word-order error might be *She fell in love with a different country man* 'a man from a different country'; a stereotypical Spanish word-order error might be *The car is the transportation system most popular* 'the most popular transportation system.'[9] Significantly, very few Koreans thought that the Spanish errors were characteristically 'Korean' and very few Spanish speakers thought that the Korean errors were characteristically 'Spanish'. Moreover, the judgements that Korean and Spanish speakers made of word-order errors were more consistent than, for example, their judgements of article errors.

While the evidence thus suggests that word order is highly accessible, there are constraints on accessibility. For example, in languages such as Dutch and German the number of word-order rules is large, with some rules involving intricate structural detail. The complications that multiple rules of any kind engender are formidable, and, as Bialystok (1979) has shown, rules involving a substantial amount of structural detail are not very accessible. Not surprisingly, then, studies of the acquisition of Dutch and German show frequent examples of word-order errors with many of the errors attributable to cross-linguistic influence (cf. Jansen *et al.*, 1981; Andersen, 1984a).

There may also be typological constraints, and Zobl's analysis of 'central' and 'peripheral' traits may thus have implications for accessibility. It seems plausible that peripheral traits in a word-order typology (e.g. the placement of adverbs) would be less accessible and that errors involving the placement of adverbs or other peripheral constituents would therefore prove harder for learners to monitor. Yet while there may be some relation between typology and accessibility, word-order accessibility is not simply a function of formal parameters. Empirical work by Bock & Warren (1985) suggests that the accessibility of word order is not rooted in formal principles such as serial order but in the functional role of constituents in basic clause structure. That is, people may easily access patterns such as SOV and SVO because the semantic information in subjects and objects is generally crucial to discourse processing (cf. Odlin, 1986).

Another reason why formal principles alone cannot explain accessibility is the considerable variation in individuals' metalinguistic abilities. Individuals who know two languages are likely to show more awareness than individuals who know only one (Galambos & Goldin-Meadow, 1983). Individuals who can read are likely to show more awareness than individuals who cannot (Scribner & Cole, 1981). And individuals who are in classes where explicit knowledge is often presented will likely know more 'about' language than will individuals acquiring a second language in informal contexts that involve little Foreign Language Learning. No matter what methods are used or how effective the methods are, the pedagogies found in second-language classrooms are likely to involve at least some and often a great deal of 'consciousness-raising' (Sharwood Smith, 1981).

One type of awareness that is especially likely to develop in Foreign

Language Learning settings is the notion of 'negative transfer'. Even when that term is unknown to language teachers, the concept that it represents is often familiar. Whether through overt correction, or through paralanguage functioning as covert correction, or through questions eliciting clarifications, or through other means still, teachers frequently provide negative feedback. Such feedback does not always deem the cause of an error to be transfer—and of course many errors are not due to transfer. Nevertheless, teachers frequently speak or at least know something about the native language of their students and are therefore in a position to identify and warn about transfer errors. In many second language classrooms, then, one important characteristic of the pedagogy is the teacher's effort to warn students about those structures liable to negative transfer. In the light of the evidence presented earlier on the accessibility of word order, it is likely that the pedagogies used in Foreign Language Learning can make basic word order even more accessible.

The consciousness-raising that occurs in formal instruction may thus put constraints on the possibilities for native language influence. A study by Trévise (1986) provides evidence of just such constraints on word order transfer. Trévise notes that while spoken French has quite flexible word order patterns, French students speaking English are rather conservative in the variety of patterns they use. Some patterns do seem to be the result of transfer: e.g. *I think it's very good the analysis between the behaviour of animals and the person*, which has a close translation equivalent in French. However, many of the French patterns that might be transferred did not show up in the conversations recorded by Trévise. The reason why students used only a narrow range of patterns may lie in 'their more or less conscious feeling for the French written standard they were (intensively) taught in school' (Trévise, 1986: 197).

The apparent cautiousness of the students described by Trévise seems related to the formality of linguistic contexts in which standard languages are used. Just as formality may discourage negative transfer, informality may encourage it. Evidence for that possibility is seen in the observation made by Dalgado (1906) that Indo-Portuguese sentences were especially likely to have an OV order in spontaneous language use. Dalgado's observation accords well with the findings of other sociolinguistic analyses of transfer (cf. Odlin, 1988).

## The Social Context of Transfer

The cases of basic word-order transfer discussed earlier offer important evidence for the relation between negative transfer and metalinguistic awareness. Table 7.5, which is a synthesis of the information in Tables 7.1 and 7.2, shows the strong likelihood of basic word-order transfer occurring in language-contact situations in which speakers have relatively little metalinguistic awareness. (Since terms such as 'target language' are not appropriate to all seven cases, the languages in the first two columns are simply labelled 'Contact Language X' and 'Contact Language Y'.) The social contexts in which learners acquired a knowledge of HPE, Bamboo English, Andean Spanish and Pidgin Fijian were generally informal. Although speakers may have had some formal instruction in the target language, the descriptions of those four contact varieties suggest that informal second language acquisition prevailed. In the case of Cairo Nubian, Mauritian Bhojpuri and Young People's Dyirbal, the descriptions indicate that there was virtually no formal instruction in the native language. Thus in all seven cases speakers received little or no formal instruction in Contact Language X, and in all seven cases there is evidence of basic word-order transfer due to knowledge of Contact Language Y.

If basic word-order transfer occurs most in contexts involving relatively little metalinguistic awareness, the distinction between *focused* and *unfocused* systems proposed by Le Page & Tabouret-Keller (1985)

TABLE 7.5 *Attested cases of basic word-order transfer*

| Contact Language X | Contact Language Y | Result |
|---|---|---|
| English (SVO) | Japanese/Korean (SOV) | Hawaiian Pidgin English (SOV)* |
| English (SVO) | Korean (SOV) | Bamboo English (SOV)* |
| Spanish (SVO) | Quechua (SOV) | Andean Spanish (SOV)* |
| Fijian (VOS/SVO) | Hindustani (SOV) | Pidgin Fijian (SOV)* |
| Bhojpuri (SOV) | Mauritian Creole (SVO) | Mauritian Bhojpuri (SVO)** |
| Dyirbal (OAV, AOV) | English (SVO) | Young People's Dyirbal (AVO)** |
| Nubian (SOV) | Egyptian Arabic (SVO) | Cairo Nubian (SVO)** |

\* SVO order is also used.
\*\* SOV order is also used (in Young People's Dyirbal, AOV).

may be relevant to the distinction between Second Language Acquisition and Foreign Language Learning. Le Page and Tabouret-Keller claim that in some communities the notion of what constitutes a language is not very sharply defined. For example, in Belize speakers often mix elements of Spanish, English and creole in varying proportions, with relatively little concern for what is 'grammatical' or 'ungrammatical'. In contrast, the language of some communities—most typically, communities with a standard language—is highly focused, and the notion of what constitutes grammatical utterances can assume considerable importance. It would be mistaken, however, to equate focused languages and standard languages. In multilingual Indian communities of the Vaupés region in South America studied in the 1960s (Sorenson, 1967; Jackson, 1974), there do not seem to have been distinct linguistic varieties corresponding to the standard–non-standard oppositions found in many places; nevertheless, members of the Vaupés communities evinced a considerable effort to speak 'correctly' according to norms that had developed despite the absence of formal schooling. For members of the Vaupés communities, 'correctness' included taking great care to avoid mixing languages. As Jackson (1974) notes, speakers often had a strong aversion to using words from several languages; in formal contexts speakers would object to the employment of forms that were not characteristic of a particular focused variety being used. The aversion that Vaupés Indians had to language mixing was due to the close relation between language, kinship systems, and marriage: Indians may only marry speakers of certain languages. Accordingly, linguistic focusing can occur in contexts besides formal language instruction.

In the analysis of Le Page & Tabouret-Keller, the distinction between focused and unfocused varieties is not a dichotomy: some forms of language behaviour are simply more focused than others. Accordingly, many of the types of language-contact situation discussed in this paper can be distinguished in the following manner:

| *More focus* | *Less focus* |
|---|---|
| Foreign Language Learning | Unstable pidgins |
| Vaupés multilingualism | Language attrition |

In contrast to Foreign Language Learning, Second Language Acquisition is not classified as either focused or unfocused. While the term 'Foreign Language Learning' is applicable only to contexts that involve considerable metalinguistic awareness, the term 'Second Language Acquisition' is applicable to contexts as diverse as unstable pidgins, multilingualism in the Vaupés region, and also to classroom contexts in which learners acquire some mastery of the target language (i.e. foreign language learning). As one process or strategy in Second Language Acquisition, transfer can occur both in focused and unfocused contexts. However, since negative transfer (including transfer of word order) leads to language-mixing, it may occur more in unfocused contexts in which speakers are not as concerned about linguistic variation.[10]

## Summary

Rutherford and Zobl have made strong claims that unambiguous cases of basic word-order transfer do not exist. However, 11 counter-examples suggest that there is no strong universal constraint on the occurrence of basic word-order transfer. Attempts to explain some of the counter-examples as evidence of language-neutral discourse strategies such as topicalization cannot account for all of the data (e.g. SOV sentences in Hawaiian Pidgin English) and such attempts do not even seem to account well for many of the tokens that might have a discourse-based explanation (e.g. OV sentences in HPE). Word order is susceptible both to substratum and to borrowing transfer: that is, transfer of basic word order is possible not only in second language acquisition but also in cases of native-language attrition due to language contact.

Despite the existence of basic word-order transfer, examples of it do seem to be somewhat rare. There are at least three explanations—which are not mutually exclusive—for the scarcity of examples of such transfer: probabilistic effects of universal grammatical constraints; observational problems, including insufficient attention to the speech of individuals with low proficiency; metalinguistic awareness, which makes the basic word order of the native and target languages accessible and which encourages the monitoring of negative transfer. There is evidence suggesting that negative word-order transfer is most likely in situations involving relatively little focusing, i.e. situations in which metalinguistic awareness is relatively low. While Foreign Language Learning involves focused language behaviour, Second Language Acquisition may not be inherently focused or unfocused.

## Further Directions

The dearth of attested cases of basic word-order transfer thus has three possible explanations. Each explanation may account in part for the dearth of cases, but the relative importance of each explanation is not yet clear. Accordingly, the role that universals may play in the observed infrequency of word-order transfer remains uncertain. While the role of universals may be considerable, metalinguistic awareness is a factor that warrants further investigation. The social dimension of metalinguistic awareness especially merits further study since it has implications both for the study of transfer and for the relation between Second Language Acquisition and Foreign Language Learning.

An extended discussion of the social dimension of metalinguistic awareness is beyond the scope of this paper (cf. Odlin, 1988). However, the importance of that dimension for the study of transfer can be illustrated not only in relation to word order but also to lexis. Kellerman (1977; 1983) has argued that there are psycholinguistic constraints on the transferability of lexical items. According to Kellerman (1977), Dutch-speaking university students frequently find it strange that certain English idioms correspond word-for-word with Dutch idioms (e.g. *to have the victory in the bag*). A test that Kellerman devised pointed to the probability of certain semantic constraints on what kinds of lexical knowledge may or may not be transferred, but it may not be that Kellerman's results are generalizable to all second language contexts. Whatever psycholinguistic constraints there may be on lexical transfer, there are known cases of the idioms of one language becoming used in translation form in another language. For example, a Malay idiom *goyang kaki* is now commonly used in Singaporean English and Malaysian English: *to shake legs* (Platt *et al.*, 1984). Interestingly, the meaning of *to shake legs* is 'to be idle' and thus is just the opposite of a well-known English idiom *to shake a leg*. The use of *to shake legs* does not seem to follow from any of the predictions made by Kellerman. Quite possibly, different sociolinguistic norms on transfer obtain in South-East Asia. If so, more lexical transfer may occur among Malaysians than among Dutch university students. In any event, how much variation may exist in the metalinguistic awareness promoted in different educational systems and in less focused social contexts is an empirical question of clear importance for a better understanding of language contact.

## Notes to Chapter 7

1. I would like to thank several people for their valuable comments on the substance and form of this paper in some of its earlier versions. I am especially indebted to Sarah Grey Thomason for her extensive comments. The paper has also benefited from comments and other help from John Algeo, Sara Garnes, Elaine Horwitz, Brian Joseph, Carol Klee, and Bill VanPatten. Naturally, I take full responsibility for any problems that remain in the paper.

2. I define as *transfer* any kind of cross-linguistic influence and believe, as Kellerman (1984) does, that the term is still serviceable despite the discredited behaviourist notions that it suggests to some scholars. While the distinction between *borrowing transfer* and *substratum transfer* given subsequently reflects important differences in language-contact situations, the evidence on word order in this paper indicates a fundamental similarity in all cases of cross-linguistic influence.

3. When the terms *Second Language Acquisition* and *Foreign Language Learning* appear with word-initial capital letters in this paper, they represent a theoretical distinction in which the former term refers to acquisition that may or may not be guided, while the latter term refers only to contexts involving guided instruction. When these terms are not capitalized, there is no theoretical distinction implied. Similarly, the terms *acquire* and *learn*, not capitalized, do not imply any of the theoretical distinctions often found in the literature.

4. The use of X instead of O allows for a description of sentence patterns involving other constituents besides objects. For example, the SVX abbreviation can represent certain sentential complements in English, e.g. *I believe that you're right*.

5. Mühlhäusler's bibliographical citation of the article by Meisel is inaccurate, and I have not been able to determine what paper by Meisel is the source of the long quotation about word order that Mühlhäusler gives.

6. Since no examples of object pronouns occurred in the Korean-English text, Table 7.4 only lists occurrences of nominal objects. Ironically, Givón's analysis downplays the possibility of transfer and instead emphasizes the importance of discourse universals. I do not believe, however, that the data in his tables invalidate any of his claims except for one, namely, that the word order found in basilect pidgins is asyntactic.

7. The special (and complex) functions of *na* within the noun phrase and of *sa* within the verb phrase are not marked since discussion of them is not relevant to the issue of basic word order.

8. There is, however, another possible explanation for the rigid word order, namely, the declining reliance on bound morphology in Young People's Dyirbal. Word-order rigidity may simply be a compensatory strategy that develops as the reliance on morphology dwindles.

9. The two examples given represent the format used in the survey of bilinguals' intuitions. Each sentence with an error was preceded by another sentence to establish a context and each was followed by a correction so that informants would focus on the error in the underlined sentence.

10. Positive transfer may occur just as much in focused as in unfocused contexts since such transfer involves a convergence of the source and target languages.

# 8 The acquisition of clitic pronouns in Spanish: two case studies

BILL VANPATTEN

*University of Illinois at Urbana-Champaign, USA*

## Introduction

In second language (L2) research, the distinction is often made between different types of language acquisition contexts, in particular classroom and naturalistic (or non-classroom). The basis for this distinction lies in the principal source of language input and interaction with the input. In the case of classroom learners, the principal source of language input and interaction is confined to the classroom, and often involves exposure to explicit presentation and explanation of how grammatical features in the language operate; mechanical and 'meaningful' practice of grammar items; sequencing of grammatical items in a structurally orientated syllabus; and a form-before-function approach to language use. In the case of naturalistic learners, the principal source of language input and interaction is the environment in which the learner is living. In this environment, while the learner himself may consciously seek out and obtain grammatical features in the input (see VanPatten, 1985b for discussion), there is no external manipulation of grammatical features and the form-before-function relationship of the classroom does not obtain.

A crucial question in the description and explanation of learner language emerges based on this distinction: How, if at all, does context impact upon the development of learner language? Put in different words, do classroom learners and naturalistic learners exhibit different or similar developmental patterns in learner language production? Such questions eventually lead us to practical concerns: specifically, how does grammatical instruction impact upon a learner's developing communicative system? This question is far from trivial, as will be discussed later, but it should be observed that while related fields such as English as a second language have asked this question (e.g. Fathman, 1978; Long, 1983a; Pica, 1983; 1985; Lightbown, 1983, 1985; Turner, 1979) the foreign language (FL) profession has always *assumed* that grammatical instruction makes a difference (for the better) and has sought better techniques and methodologies to inculcate grammatical competence in the learner (see the introduction in VanPatten *et al.*, 1987, for some discussion).

The purpose of this paper is to generate hypotheses about the impact of instruction on the developing language of early-stage classroom learners. I am limiting the discussion to early-stage learners for, as I have argued elsewhere (VanPatten, in press), only by rigorously examining what happens to learners at every given stage (i.e. early, intermediate, advanced) can we hope to put together a more global picture of learner language development. In order to generate these hypotheses, I will compare and contrast the usage of certain clitic pronouns (see Appendix 8.1) in the speech of two subjects learning Spanish in two distinct contexts. While the study is admittedly limited in that case studies may not always be generalizable to all language learners, it does afford the luxury of examining learner speech in more detail without losing individual differences to cross-sectional studies or large data pools (Rosansky, 1976; Hatch, 1978a).

First, a purely *quantitative* comparison will be made. This will be followed by a discussion of three *qualitative* analyses which serve to elucidate the quantitative comparison. At each point, instruction as a factor in learner performance will be discussed. Two specific questions guide this comparison: Do the two subjects, under different conditions of exposure, manifest similar or different performance patterns with clitics? If there are differences, are they traceable to formal instruction in grammar?

## Subjects

The two subjects come from two different data sources: Andersen (1983b) and VanPatten (1985a). Andersen's subject, Anthony (a pseudonym), is one of several subjects in an ongoing investigation of the acquisition of Spanish in a natural environment; that is, Anthony is not an FL student. Anthony is described as a 14-year-old who lived with his parents in Puerto Rico for four years (the data for this study were collected during his last year there). He lived in a mixed middle-/working-class area where only one other English-speaking family lived. Anthony attended a private school where both English and Spanish were the medium of instruction (although Spanish was not taught as a language course). Andersen notes that while Anthony had access to other English-speaking friends on the island, he normally interacted with the Spanish-speaking children of his neighbourhood. Thus, Anthony can be said to have 'picked up' Spanish via communicative-social interaction in and out of school.

David (also a pseudonym), on the other hand, is an adult language student at the university level (aged 20). He is one of ten subjects who were volunteers in a longitudinal study of the acquisition of Spanish in a purely formal setting (see VanPatten, 1985a). David was selected for the present discussion for two principal reasons: he had never studied any language formally before university so the variable of previous instruction in Spanish or another language was eliminated; he was evaluated by his teacher as an excellent student. His attendance was 100%, his homework was always done, his test scores were always high, he was conscious of grammar when writing compositions, he voluntarily spoke in class, and in the end he received the highest earned percentage of his class. For this study, then, David was purposefully chosen; if instruction has an impact on anyone, it would most likely be on someone like him.

Both subjects were tape-recorded and their speech was later transcribed. Anthony's speech was collected in one data-gathering session during a fairly natural conversation with the interviewer. The data on David, on the other hand, were collected over a period of three months at two-week intervals during the latter part of the spring semester. The reason for admitting three months' worth of data from David is to allow for a better quantitative comparison; David did not produce enough clitics in any one session to permit a meaningful contrast with Anthony's usage. While at first glance, these differences in data-collection point towards possible differential effects on the product being examined, it should be pointed out that there is much evidence that learner language (in terms of grammatical manifestations in spontaneous speech) does not develop significantly in the time span in which David's data were collected. (For discussion of this, see VanPatten, 1985a, as well as Harley and Swain, 1984.) In addition, David did not receive explicit instruction in clitics during this time period. Indeed, David's use of clitics did not seem to develop either quantitatively or qualitatively during the entire spring semester.

TABLE 8.1 *Quantitative analysis of clitic pronouns: Anthony*

|            | OV order |       | VO order |      |
| ---------- | -------- | ----- | -------- | ---- |
| *me*       | 15/17    | 88%   | 1/2      | 50%  |
| *te*       | –        | –     | –        | –    |
| *nos*      | 1/1      | 100%  |          |      |
| *se* (refl)| 5/5      | 100%  | 1/3      | 33%  |
| *lo(s)*    | 0/2      | 0%    | 3/4      | 75%  |
| *la(s)*    | 0/2      | 0%    | 0/1      | 0%   |
| *le(s)*    | 0/2      | 0%    | –        | –    |
| TOTALS     | 21/29    | 72%   | 5/10     | 50%  |

TABLE 8.2 *Quantitative analysis of clitic pronouns: David*

|            | OV order |       | VO order |      |
| ---------- | -------- | ----- | -------- | ---- |
| *me*       | 14/15    | 93%   | 3/3      | 100% |
| *te*       | 3/7      | 43%   | –        | –    |
| *nos*      | 3/3      | 100%  |          |      |
| *se* (refl)| 5/6      | 83%   | 2/4      | 50%  |
| *lo(s)*    | 2/5      | 40%   | 1/2      | 50%  |
| *la(s)*    | 0/5      | 0%    | –        | –    |
| *le(s)*    | 28/29    | 97%   | –        | –    |
| TOTALS     | 58/70    | 79%   | 6/9      | 67%  |

## Quantitative Comparison

Tables 8.1 and 8.2 offer a gross comparison in terms of overall accuracy/ability with clitic pronouns used by the two subjects. Anthony's data appear in Table 8.1 while David's data appear in Table 8.2. As can be seen, both Anthony and David exhibit average performance with clitic pronoun use (72% and 79%, respectively). However, much of David's performance in overall correct clitic use is due to his performance with the pattern *le(s)* + V + NP, e.g. *Juan les da dinero a ellos*, which accounts for 41% of the sentence types. If these 29 utterances are removed from the data, then David's total number of utterances involving clitics is closer to Anthony's and his performance overall is 66%, rather lower than Anthony's score.

The tables suggest that both learners perform worst with third person direct objects than with any other single class, producing fewer instances for obligatory occasions and making more errors when the occasions present themselves. On the other hand, first person *me* is used with much greater accuracy and there is some indication that reflexive *se* is easier for both learners as well.

As Andersen notes, however, quantification of data as in Tables 8.1 and 8.2 may obscure important information about usage and performance. That is, does a 100% score for Anthony in usage of *se* reveal in what contexts he uses the clitic? Does a 93% score for David in use of *me* indicate that he uses the clitic in all of its functions, as well as pre- and post-verbally? Are there patterns of use that reveal strategies or underlying rule systems? It is to these and other questions that we now turn our attention.

## Strategies

Andersen (1983b: 194) notes that Anthony apparently uses 'different strategies to cope with different sorts of pre-verbal clitic pronouns'.[1] The question is whether or not he and David exhibit these same strategies. These data are summarized in Table 8.3. It is apparent from this summary that Anthony and David have only two patterns/strategies in common. Both rely heavily on an SVO word order pattern (to be discussed in detail later) and both sometimes use a stressed pronoun where there should be a clitic; however, the stressed pronoun chosen is not necessarily the same (e.g. Anthony: *Ello va llamar a mí pa'cer . . .* [They will call me to . . . ]; David: *Y si Berkely dijo a yo . . .* [And if Berkely tells me . . . ]).

As can be seen, there are more differences in strategies than similarities. While Anthony on occasion omits a direct object clitic (e.g. *pue ø ponemo en cajas* [First we put them in boxes] and *Ellos ø usaba pa'el compañia* [They use them for the company]), David never does this. His sentences are consistent in that all underlying semantic information regarding agents, objects, datives, patients, are explicitly marked in surface structure by *something*.

Another marked difference between the two sets of strategies is that David does not exhibit any chunked patterns such as Anthony's *se/sa fue*, a strategy which, incidentally, gives Anthony a deceptively better score for use of the reflexive. (The reader will notice in Appendix 8.2 that Anthony has both *se* and *sa* in his speech, the latter being an interlanguage 'allomorph' of the reflexive particle.)

TABLE 8.3 *Comparison of strategies*

|  | Anthony | David |
|---|---|---|
| SVO order | yes | yes |
| Stressed pronoun | yes | yes |
| O$_{PRO}$V pattern | yes | no |
| Omission of direct clitic | yes | no |
| Chunking | yes | no |
| Overgeneralization of reflexive | yes | no |
| Omission of *se* | no | yes |
| Repetition of full NP | no | yes |
| Wrong person | no | yes |

Furthermore, Anthony has SVO$_{PRO}$, SO$_{PRO}$V and O$_{PRO}$V structures in his speech while David never once produced a sentence with O$_{PRO}$V where the subject has been deleted. His sentences consistently begin with an explicitly marked subject, even when the subject has been used in ongoing conversation between him and the interviewer (see Appendix 8.3).

Up to now, the comparison has centred on what Anthony does that David does not. What does David do with clitics that is not evidenced in Anthony's speech? One difference is that David will occasionally omit the reflexive *se* (*y el decidió sentar, sentar en la silla* [and he decided to sit, to sit down in the chair]) but Anthony does not. However, it must be pointed out again that Anthony's speech sample does not contain the range of lexical items requiring *se* that David's does, so the comparison is tentative.

Another non-native usage in David's speech but not evident in Anthony's is to use the wrong person. David, for example, produces sentences such as *Yo quiero le pregunta sobre tus experiencias* [I want to ask you about your experiences] and *tú se, se levantas* [you get up]. These may be evidence for the overgeneralization of the more frequent (in classroom input) third person forms and the cause for the difference between him and Anthony whose natural input would not predispose him toward third person clitics. It is noteworthy that David's misuse of person occurs only with *te*; that is, he never substitutes another person for *me*, nor does he put first or second person forms in third person contexts.

Finally, the most marked of David's strategies which distinguishes him from Anthony is his repetition of full noun-phrase (NP) complements. When presented with a question or even when continuing within his own utterance, David always repeats the NP direct object complement as the following examples demonstrate:

| | |
|---|---|
| **Interviewer:** | *¿Qué hicieron con los zapatos después de que se los quitaron?* [What did they do with the shoes after taking them off?] |
| **David:** | *Ellos pusieron los zapatos cerca de las flores.* [They put the shoes near the flowers.] |
| **Interviewer:** | *¿Qué va a hacer ella con el plátano?* [What is she going to do with the banana?] |
| **David:** | *Ella, oh, ella quiere comer este plátano.* [She, oh, she wants to eat this banana.] |

As mentioned earlier, Anthony's strategy in these contexts is either to omit the pronoun or to use a stressed form in its place when he did not correctly supply a pronoun.

In these differences, then we *may* see *some* of the effects of formal instruction on performance with clitics. It is highly likely that David is aware of the importance of 'complete sentences' as part of formal instruction. While he may not use certain aspects of surface grammar correctly, his formal training may inhibit utterances where required semantic components are not explicitly stated. Thus, David is 'barred' at this point in his learning from leaving ø in a surface structure string.

Regarding the absence of chunked expressions with clitics in David's speech, this is most likely due to limited access to meaningful language in the classroom. In VanPatten (1986a) it was argued that formal learners will chunk high-frequency expressions such as *cómo se dice* [how do you say] early on since they are part of meaningful classroom interaction but will not chunk much else since the relatively non-interactive nature of the classroom precludes the use of many highly frequent routine-like formulas. It is unlikely, for example, that classroom learners hear *se fue* in a meaningful context (much less frequently) during their course of study while, on the other hand, speech addressed to first and second language naturalistic acquirers would contain this and other formulaic speech in abundance (see Wong-Fillmore, 1976, and Krashen, 1981, for discussion on this issue in English L2; and Hernández Piña, 1984, for some discussion on Spanish L1)[2]. Thus, formal instruction *may not* contribute to the acquisition of some structures or functions/contexts of some structures since they may be most readily internalized lexically rather than syntactically.

Turning to David's lack of $O_{PRO}V$ structures, this lack cannot be easily attributed to L1 transfer since Anthony has them in his speech. Again, emphasis on complete sentences in formal language learning may produce early on an underlying belief that sentences should be completely formed and that to be completely formed they must contain subject nouns or pronouns (a belief that may in turn be reinforced by the L1—see VanPatten, 1986a). Furthermore, differences between naturalistic input and teacher talk may again contribute. While there are no data collected on the classroom input to which David was exposed, this author has made notes on word-order frequencies while observing college-level teaching assistants. After observing the teaching of one native speaker of Spanish in a first-year college course, this author pointed out to the teacher that she almost never deleted subject nouns and pronouns during her limited interaction with students. The instructor replied that she had learned while teaching that in order to converse with her students she needed to speak 'clearly' and that repeating subjects improved learner comprehension during interaction. Learner over-use of subject nouns and pronouns itself was never corrected or pointed out, thus giving additional peer input which overwhelmingly favoured SVO sentence patterns. (The author has seen the same phenomenon in the classroom speech of non-natives as well.) As a typical classroom language learner, then, David's explicit marking of a grammatical subject (apart from verb inflection) was more than likely reinforced by classroom input.

## Form

Andersen found that for Anthony the form of the clitic pronoun presented difficulties in addition to its position. More precisely, different pronouns pose different problems. Does David encounter the same problems with individual pronouns? Table 8.4 offers an overview of both Anthony's and David's knowledge of pronoun forms. As per Andersen, a 'yes' means that the form has been used correctly at least once. A 'no' indicates that in all obligatory occasions for a form, none was supplied. A question mark is used to show that no obligatory occasion presented itself and thus no judgement can be made. Finally, 'yes, but' means that the pronoun has been used correctly but that it is sometimes absent or is under partial control, as exemplified by the examples in Appendices 8.2 and 8.3.

Regarding first person *me*, Anthony and David demonstrate almost equal control. Both seem to use it in a full range of grammatical functions, with the one exception being reflexive. There are no sample obligatory

TABLE 8.4 *Knowledge of clitic form*

|                | Anthony  | David    |
|----------------|----------|----------|
| *me*           |          |          |
| indirect       | yes      | yes      |
| direct         | yes      | yes      |
| reflexive      | yes, but | ?        |
|                |          |          |
| *te*           |          |          |
| indirect       | ?        | yes, but |
| direct         | ?        | yes, but |
| reflexive      | ?        | no       |
|                |          |          |
| *nos*          |          |          |
| indirect       | ?        | yes      |
| direct         | ?        | yes      |
| reflexive      | yes      | ?        |
|                |          |          |
| *le(s)*        | yes, but | yes      |
| *lo(s)*        | yes, but | yes, but |
| *la(s)*        | yes, but | no       |
| *se*           | yes, but | yes, but |

occasions in David's speech for first person reflexive constructions whereas Anthony does show it several times. Anthony also shows one over-extension of *me* to a non-reflexive context (*me camino en bicicleta* [I ride my bike]).[3]

Examining the rest of the pronouns, one finds more divergence between the two subjects. Anthony has one instance of *nos* which is grammatically (but not semantically) part of a reflexive verb. Other functions do not appear in his speech. David, on the other hand, uses this pronoun three times, none of which is reflexive. *Te* never occurs in Anthony's data, but there are seven obligatory occasions for this form in David's speech. However, David does not seem to use *te* as a reflexive marker nor does he always produce it when he should. In one instance, he uses a full NP in object position (e.g. *Yo manejo tú* [I drove you]— like English?) and another time using third person instead (e.g. *Yo quiero le pregunta sobre tus experiencias* [I want to ask you about your experiences]).

The third person pronouns for both learners present numerous difficulties. First, Anthony has partial control of reflexive as does David, but their control is qualitatively different. Anthony has the chunk *se fue* [he/she left] (which David does not) but also exhibits over-extension of this clitic to non-reflexive verbs. In post-verbal position, he sometimes omits this clitic. David knows that the clitic exists, but the examples in his speech are limited to highly frequent and prototypical reflexive actions (e.g. sit down, get up). David also omits *se* occasionally, but does not show evidence of using it in non-reflexive contexts.[4]

Neither subject shows any evidence of plural direct object clitics being present, both failing to supply such clitics in obligatory occasions. However, David only shows evidence of knowing the singular *lo* and not its feminine counterpart *la*. Anthony does have both clitics in his speech, albeit the example of *la* is incorrectly placed.

Finally, Anthony's speech sample never offers one obligatory occasion for a third person indirect clitic, while in David's speech these seem to abound and he is as adept with these as he is with the clitic *me*. However, he may have a preference for the singular form and will sometimes use it in plural contexts, e.g. *ella le dijo a ellos* [she told them].

It is difficult with such variation to identify the possible effect of instruction on clitic form. On the one hand, some aspects of the variation seem to be due to small sample size and possibly to topic and content domains which did not trigger obligatory occasions for some clitics, e.g. *te, nos* for both, and for Anthony, *le(s)*. It is clear that for both subjects *me* is an easy pronoun and is probably the first to be fully acquired. This, more than likely, is due to its relatively formal simplicity and perhaps its cognate status with English 'me'. Instruction, then, does not alter its place in the order of acquisition of clitic pronouns.[5]

It is apparent that for both Anthony and David third person clitics present major problems in pronoun acquisition, yet there is some variation in knowledge of these forms. David is definitely on his way toward acquisition of *le(s)*, while we cannot speak for Anthony. However, if we look more closely at David's data we find that almost all occurrences of the third person indirect object pronouns are with just three verbs: *decir* (tell/say), *dar* (give), and *preguntar* (ask). These verbs are suspiciously similar in that they represent actions where the underlying semantic components of agent and objects are clearly and consistently marked in the surface structure in an almost one-to-one mapping. It is worth noting that David does not have any examples of *le(s)* as marking anything other than the semantically (and perceptually) salient dative, i.e. there are no examples of this pronoun used to mark something else as in *Cuando le vi la cara a él* [When I saw his face] and *Se le rompió* [It broke (on him)]. Nor are there examples of this pronoun used to mark what is semantically the 'acted-upon' as in *Siempre le ayudo con el trabajo* [I always help him with his work]. Thus, it is highly likely that David has learned only one function of this pronoun and has confined it to a handful of the more prototypical verbs, e.g. 'give' and 'tell'. Even though we cannot make any explicit comparison to Anthony's speech, David's use of *le(s)* does suggest that he is following so-called 'natural principles' of second language acquisition (e.g. one form, one function—see Andersen, 1984a; Slobin, 1973) and that the effect of instruction is again to limit his exposure to a variety of contexts for the application of this pronoun. As any observer of a first-year Spanish class would notice, the classroom hour abounds in teacher directives, comments and visuals with the actions say, tell and ask, and rarely does the learner get exposure (except, perhaps, for a brief 'peek' in a grammar explanation or drill) to other functions of *le(s)*.

Regarding *se*, Anthony is not as good as David in supplying the form and David does not have any examples of over-extension into non-reflexive categories.[6] However, the data are inflated in David's favour because those instances where he does use *se* are precisely those true reflexives that are taught lexically in most Spanish courses, e.g. *sentarse* (sit down), *levantarse* (get up). Other functions of *se* (e.g. impersonal subject marker, passive, replacement for third person indirect clitic, inchoative marker, reciprocal reflexive) do not appear. Again, David may be applying a one-form, one-function strategy in spite of any instruction and/or formal presentation of other uses. Anthony, on the other hand, may first have to deal with this clitic in chunked expressions (*se fue* [he left], *se acabó* [it's all gone]) just as Spanish L1 children do since his input may be randomly filled with a variety of functions of this one clitic. Thus, one effect of instruction may be to isolate one function of a complex system and aid its acquisition, but not to aid the acquisition of the entire range of functions in the early and intermediate stages.

Finally, in looking at third person direct object clitics, it seems that Anthony may have one more form under control than David—*la*. Neither shows any evidence, even in obligatory occasions, of the morphologically more complex plural forms.[7] Since third person direct object clitics are the most complex of all clitics (i.e. they have the most forms, they contrast morphologically with other third person clitics, and they overlap with other grammatical functions, namely articles) it is no surprise that neither subject performs well with these forms. Instruction here, then, probably does not hinder nor help David, especially when one considers

TABLE 8.5 *Knowledge of placement of clitic pronouns*

| | pre-verbal | | post-verbal | |
| | Anthony | David | Anthony | David |
|---|---|---|---|---|
| *me* | yes | yes | yes | yes |
| *te* | ? | yes | ? | ? |
| *nos* | yes | yes | ? | ? |
| *lo(s)* | yes | yes | yes | ? |
| *la(s)* | no | no | no | ? |
| *le(s)* | yes | yes | ? | ? |
| *se* | yes | yes | yes | yes |

that of all the clitics, third person pronouns received the most explicit treatment in David's class.[8]

## Position

In Table 8.5, the data regarding whether Anthony and David know the correct placement of clitics are summarized. Anthony generally has no pre-verbal placement problems with *me*, and does know that *me* can go at the end of certain kinds of verb forms as well. He also seems to have a fairly good idea that third person object pronouns may also follow certain kinds of verbs (the last example is an error in form, not placement). Where Anthony does have considerable problems is in pre-verbal placement of these third person clitics. According to Andersen (1983b: 199), these data suggest that Anthony follows certain production processing strategies regarding placement: '(1) maintain SVO word order whenever possible, (2) *me* occurs preverbally unless the verb is an infinitive or participle, (3) other clitics are placed postverbally if the verb is an infinitive or participle and in other cases are omitted or placed to maintain SVO order'. Andersen attributes this system to two phenomena: complexity of clitic form may interfere with learning where to place it; Anthony has a preference for SVO word order (similar in concept to the one-form, one-function strategy—perhaps preserving underlying word order in Spanish, which in turn is probably reinforced by English).

David exhibits much the same overall pattern. Like Anthony, he has no problem with placement of *me* but great difficulty with pre-verbal use of third person clitics (except *le* and *les*, but under the conditions specified in the previous section). David's speech also manifests a strong preference for SVO word order, more so than Anthony's since Anthony has at least some token samples of $O_{PRO}V$ sentences (interestingly these tokens involve *me* and not other clitics). David has no such examples of subject deletion. David also exhibits a marked tendency to repeat complete NPs during conversational interaction (e.g. E: *¿Y qué hizo la mamá con la canasta?* [What did the mother do with the basket?] D: *Ella puso la canasta en el suelo.* [She put the basket on the floor]) which is what gives the overall impression that his speech leans more toward the preservation of SVO word order than Anthony's. Has instruction, then, somehow differentiated David's ability in correct clitic placement compared to Anthony's? Not really. David and Anthony are fairly well matched in their ability to produce and place *me* and both are struggling to produce third person clitics in pre-verbal position. David's only advantage from instruction, it seems, is to have had the true reflexive *se* isolated for him since he was able to correctly place this clitic pre-verbally five times out of six. Whether or not this will aid David in the acquisition of other uses of *se* is a question that cannot be answered here. The one-form, one-function principle is a powerful factor in language acquisition and early success with one function of *se* might actually retard the acquisition of other functions. On the other hand, the fact that the morpheme has been isolated and is correctly placed in at least one context (function) may be half the battle; David's acquisitional 'devices' may turn their attention to the acquisition of other functions at this point. However, it is important to recall the limited input that most classroom learners receive. It is unlikely that David will encounter many meaningful uses of *se* in classroom talk. Anthony, on the other hand, will encounter a wide variety of uses of this clitic in natural input and might catch up and then surpass David's (tentative) early superior performance with these.

One thing that seems evident is that classroom instruction did not have any impact on David's preference for SVO word order. Just like Anthony, David evidences a marked tendency to preserve this word order. In spite of numerous drills, in spite of early introduction to direct and indirect clitics, in spite of lessons on 'unnecessary repetition' (see note 8), David parallels Anthony's use in this regard.

## General Discussion and Conclusion

The foregoing discussion has looked in detail at two learners' use of clitics in spontaneous speech. Keeping in mind the different methods of data collection and that case studies may not be completely generalizable to large populations, some tentative concluding remarks can be made.

TABLE 8.6 *A summary of the hypotheses generated by this study: Early stage use of clitics*

H1.  Instruction does not impact on overall difficulty of learning nor order of acquisition.

H2.  Regardless of context, *me* is the easiest pronoun to acquire while third person directs are the most difficult.

H3.  SVO word order is somehow maintained.

H4.  A one-form, one-function strategy obtains in all learning contexts.

H5.  Instruction impacts upon omission. Classroom learners tend not to omit surface realizations of underlying verbal arguments.

H6.  Naturalistic learners begin the acquisition of reflexive *se* through the process of chunking phrases. Classroom learners begin the acquisition of reflexive *se* through its association with a set of marked lexical items.

H7.  Classroom learners begin the acquisition of third person indirect object pronouns via lexical items, i.e. verbs that are prototypical three-argument verbs and are frequent in classroom discourse.

H8.  Differences in performance patterns between classroom and naturalistic learners are not due to a change in underlying processes which govern the creation of a linguistic system. Differences are attributable to quantity and quality of input received by the learner.

The hypotheses generated by the comparison of Anthony and David's use of clitics are summarized in Table 8.6.

The effect of instruction was not always readily apparent, and only in several instances did it seem to benefit David. In other instances, the classroom context, coupled with instruction, may work to retard the acquisition of clitics due to the limited range of language experiences that the typical learner is exposed to. One fact which emerges is that what is easy in acquisition is easy and what is difficult in acquisition is difficult, i.e. regardless of learning context, there are things that emerge early in speech and there are things that emerge late. While it may seem tautological or trivial to point this out, this is the paradox for grammatical instruction, for what is instruction if not an attempt to make acquisition 'easier'? This author recalls a conversation with one colleague many years ago who was forcibly arguing against 'communicative approaches' since they encourage learners to make errors and rely on their own devices for internalizing rules. In the case of the present study, it can hardly be claimed that instruction circumvented certain natural processes in acquisition such as preference for certain word orders, over-extension of certain forms, and whatever processes are responsible for the order of emergence of grammatical forms in speech.[9] Thus, acquisition was not made any 'easier' for David. It is probably worth recalling at this point that David was an excellent student, who by all definitions should have received maximum benefit from instruction in grammar.[10]

It is important to point out that this study cannot speak to rate of acquisition. While it seems clear that instruction in grammar did not alter relative difficulty or order of acquisition, the data cannot be organized in a manner which reveals whether or not David's acquisition of clitics was 'speeded up' by instruction. This is quite possible, of course, but since Andersen offers no clues as to the relative fluidity of Anthony's speech for purposes of comparison with David's, the possibility is left for future investigation. Also left for future investigation is whether or not early instruction in grammar has any 'hidden' or 'delayed' effects, a claim made by some (e.g. Higgs & Clifford, 1982) but, is as yet, completely untested.

What other questions concerning the acquisition of clitics surface which need investigation? The following are some:

1.  Does the acquisition of one function pave the way for the acquisition of other functions, or does the learner need a rich input base in which he or she sees various functions of one form?

2.  Is there an ordering of clitics within the paradigm for direct objects? Lee (1987a) suggests that for processing input there is an ordered relationship of grammatical features, e.g. plurality and gender. Is this same ordering reflected in production? Why/ why not?

3.  Should all clitics even be taught during the early stages? If *me* is easily acquirable from the input data, but third person forms are not, is it worth instructional time in the early stage classroom to devote explicit attention to these forms and their functions?

Clearly, these questions merit research not only involving case studies such as this one, but cross-sectional ones as well.[11] Also, it would be illuminating to see how clitics continue to develop after the initial stages of acquisition. Preliminary evidence (Elisa Molano, personal communication) indicates that third person direct object clitics do not really 'show up' with any regularity, frequency or accuracy until learners are at a level where they can effectively monologue, e.g. FSI level 2 and the ACTFL Proficiency rating of Advanced. This makes sense if one considers that *me*, *te* and *nos* and reflexives are non-anaphoric and are bound by sentence-level syntax. That is, it is possible to say *Mis padres me llamaron anoche* [My parents called me last night] without previous discourse. *Me* is inserted because the sentence requires it, not because the discourse requires it.

On the other hand, third person direct object clitics are not obligatorily assigned by sentential syntax but rather by discourse convention. Thus, it is not possible to say *Mis padres lo llamaron anoche* [My parents called him last night] without previous discourse. Furthermore, it is possible *not* to use these particular clitics in ongoing discourse, e.g. *¿Visitas a tus padres con frecuencia? No. Generalmente llamo a mis padres por teléfono* [Do you visit your parents frequently? No. Generally I call my parents on the phone], while *me, te, se* and *nos* are impossible to avoid, e.g. *¿Tus padres visitaron a ti?* [Did your parents visit you?] Clearly, research on sentential versus discoursal syntax with clitics would lead to answers to question 3 above about the utility of presenting and (especially) practising all clitics in the early stages of instruction where students' discourse abilities are severely limited.

Any discussion of classroom–non-classroom distinctions would be incomplete without consideration of what can be termed 'deep' differences and 'superficial' differences. That is, which differences are due to instruction having caused a real *underlying change* in the manner in which a learner processes incoming linguistic data and which are due to environmental circumstances (beyond the control of the learner) which results in only idiosyncratic features of learner speech? Indeed, can instruction even alter underlying processes involved in language acquisition, and should it try? Conversely, is the primary role of instruction to manipulate input? Or to mirror, to the best of its possibilities, natural input and interaction with that input?

In this paper, no real changes in the way in which one learner processed language during acquisition could be found, i.e. no 'deep' differences seemed evident. Of the differences noted, almost all could be considered superficial in that they are a result of the quantity and quality of classroom input and not the quality of learning and not all could be considered positive differences. The question which now surfaces, and is also left for future discussion, is what the long-term positive and negative effects are of such superficial differences on the communicative performance of language learners.[12]

## Notes to Chapter 8

1. Andersen's use of 'strategy' involves the description of verbal output. At other times in L2 research, 'strategy' is used to define or describe processes

rather than product. For the sake of comparison with Andersen's work, however, 'strategy' will be used here as he uses it in his 1983 study.

2. Interestingly, Hernández Piña notes that her L1 subject first evidenced the proclitic use of *se* as an 'assimilated element' as in *saió* and *saido* for *se ha ido*.

3. It can, of course, be argued that this is not over-extension but rather Anthony's evolving hypothesis about the use of reflexive forms in the so-called 'personal' or 'extra effort' constructions which are well documented in Latin American Spanish, e.g. *y luego me subí la escalera* [and then I went up the stairs]; *Me senté y me comí toda la torta* [I sat down and I ate up all the cake].

4. Hernández Piña observes that in L1 acquisition, reflexive constructions and the particle *se* are easily acquired and then are generalized to non-reflexive contexts. She cites examples such as *la nena se llora* [the baby is crying] and *se ha quitado papá la tele* [Dad turned off the TV]. The over-extension of *se*, then, may be a standard feature of naturalistic learning (both L1 and L2) since this clitic appears with high frequency and in many contexts.

5. Again, making reference to L1 acquisition, Hernández Piña demonstrates that *me* was the earliest clitic to emerge in her subject's speech. We may have, then, a universal in the acquisition of clitics: *me* precedes all other clitics in both form and function.

6. Any teacher would argue at this point that once reflexives are introduced, students start using them everywhere. However, it should be recalled that the data in this study are different from those that most teachers are exposed to: the data here are gathered in contexts outside the classroom, that, while sometimes elicited, are much closer to language used meaningfully than what occurs in the classroom or in formal written assignments. Do students during classtime and on homework over-use some items because these structures are in focus and over-emphasized? From the student's point of view, 'Aren't you supposed to practise in class what you are currently learning?'

7. See Lee (1987a) for some discussion of the role of gender and number in the processing of written forms of these clitics.

8. In David's program of instruction, third person direct object clitics were introduced the second week of instruction, after learners had been exposed to a variety of transitive verbs of the first conjugation, e.g. *mirar* [to look at], *buscar* [to look for], *llamar* [to call]. An entire week was devoted to handouts and explicit instruction in the concept of 'unnecessary repetition' whereby object NPs are replaced by clitics once mentioned. This grammatical point was reviewed holistically at various intervals and was encouraged in compositions, i.e. instructions included directions to 'avoid unnecessary repetition of nouns'. This early introduction and reviewed practice seemingly did not alter the order of emergence in David's speech nor the inherent difficulty of these clitics.

9. In at least one research report comparing the learning of English as a second language and the learning of English as a foreign language, Pica (1985) argues that there are certain grammatical forms which should not be taught explicitly but should be left to 'natural' acquisitional devices. She argues that students are better off when not instructed in the progressive *-ing* or in articles but are better off when instructed in third person *-s* (but see also VanPatten, 1988, for some counter-argument and a review of Pica's study).

10. Recalling VanPatten's (1985a) study on *ser* and *estar*, David's performance with the Spanish copulas was hardly any better (i.e. more accurate) than those learners who were identified as worse students. David merely talked more and produced more words per minute.
11. Research is currently underway both by Andersen and VanPatten involving more naturalistic and classroom (respectively) case studies of the emergence of clitics in learner speech.
12. 'Deep' and 'superficial' should not be confused with 'important' and 'unimportant', respectively. Certain deep differences could be important, others trivial. Likewise, there are probably certain superficial differences which have important communicative or affective effects and others that are not significant in the long run.

## Appendix 8.1: An Overview of Spanish Clitic Pronouns

|                     | Direct object | Indirect object | Reflexive |
|---------------------|:-------------:|:---------------:|:---------:|
| 1st sing.           |               | *me*            |           |
| 2nd sing.           |               | *te*            |           |
| 3rd sing/2nd formal | *lo/la*       | *le/se**        | *se*      |
| 1st plural          |               | *nos*           |           |
| 2nd plural          |               | *os***          |           |
| 3rd plural/2nd formal | *los/las*   | *les/se**       | *se*      |

*se* is used for double clitic constructions such as *se lo* and *se las* (not **le lo* nor **les las*)

**os* is the plural 'informal' second person used in Spain, but was not a feature either of the two learners in this study were exposed to, both learning Latin American variants of Spanish where 3rd plural serves double function of both formal and informal 2nd plural

Position: clitics immediately precede finite verb forms:
   *lo veo* (I see it)
   *lo doy* (I give it)
   *se lo digo* (I tell it to her)

but they follow and are attached to infinitives and present participles:

*viéndolo* (seeing it/him)
*dándolo* (giving it)
*diciéndoselo* (saying it to her)


## Appendix 8.2: Anthony's Utterances

Grammatical use of clitics

1. . . .*con otro amigo ayundándome*
2. *Y (ellos) no puedo hacerlo pa* . . .
3. . . .*ahí dentro ayundándolo.*
4. . . .*si puedamo cogerlo bien.*
5. . . .*no está listo casarse.*
6. *Yla, ell(as) sa fueron.*
7. *Pue, todo sa fue* (= *todos se fueron*).
8. *Ella sa fue.*
9. . . .*que sa fue pa buscar* . . .
10. *Ella sa fue solo a S.F.* . . .
11. *No me gusta ni* . . .
12. *No me gustaba.*
13. *Ella* . . . *que no me gustaba ella.*
14. *Depués cuando nos aguantamos por el manos.*
15. *Pero porque me mudó aquí.* (= *me mudé*)
16. *Yo no me acuerdo.*
17. *Ya no me acuerdo.*
18. *Yo no me acuerdo del otro.*
19. *No me acuerdo.*
20. *El maestro que me ensañaba español* . . .
21. . . . *el me contesta en inglés.*
22. *Pue él, ello me cambió* . . .
23. *No, ello todavía me llamaron.*
24. *Cuando me llaman.*
25. *A ver si me llaman pa pelota.*


Ungrammatical uses of clitics

26. *Ello va a llamar a mí pa'cer* . . .
27. . . . *que sa fue pa buscar él.*

28. *Pero yo no vi él mucho.*
29. *Yo solo viste la dos veces.*
30. *El no gustaba los americanos.*
31. *Yo gusta todo . . .*
32. *El no gusta mucho problema.*
33. *. . . así pa vender cosas* (*cosas* should have been a clitic)
34. *. . . pregunta a casar con ella.*
35. *Y ella tenía que quedar en el lobby.*
36. *Pue yo quedo con él.*
37. *. . . pue ponemos en cajas.*
38. *Ello(s) usaba pa el compañía.*
39. *. . . si la mamá no lo dejó Raymond salir.*
40. *Yo creo que yo me gusta menos.*
41. *El no le gustaba mucho.*
42. *O camina-, o me camino en bicicleta.*
43. *Se vivía en Palmas.*
44. *esquedar y esquedar* (= *se quedaba y se quedaba*)

## Appendix 8.3: David's Utterances

Grammatical use of clitics

1. *. . . una carta. Me escribo una carta de acceptance.* (= *me escriben*)
2. *. . . si, si Berkely me dijo que . . .* (= *dice*)
3. *. . . quieres aceptar, quieres aceptarme . . .* (= *quieren*)
4. *. . . porque tú quieres testarme.* (*examinarme*)
5. *. . . y Trisha me da . . .*
6. *Tú me miras en este foto.*
7. *Tú me miraste.*
8. *Tú me das el diccionario.*
9. *Tú me preguntas si . . .*
10. *. . . y tú me dices ciao . . .*
11. *. . . él, él me mira a mí . . .*
12. *Tú quieres o no quieres contestarme?*
13. *. . . porque mi profesor me dio un* project *. . .*
14. *Es necesario que yo hacerlo . . .*
15. *El hombre le pregunta a su hermana . . .*
16. *. . . y su hermana le dice . . .*
17. *Es posible que el profesor nos, nos da a nosotros un* report.

18. *Trisha me pedí a mi* . . .
19. *. . . saco el periódico y él lo lee.*
20. *. . . y ella, ella,* the verb to get up, *ella se levanto.*
21. *Ella le dice a este secretaria* . . .
22. *. . . como se dice* . . .
23. *. . . Pedro lo miró* . . .
24. *El le dijo a Pedro que* . . .
25. *El hombre le dijo a Pedro que* . . .
26. *Pedro le dijo al hombre que* . . .
27. *El hombre no, no quiere él le da a Pedro dinero.*
28. *Probablemente le doy a Pedro 25 centavos* (= *daría*)
29. *Yo nunca le pregunte a este hombre para el dinero* (= *nunca le pediría*)
30. *Pedro le dio a la hombre que trabajar en el bar el dinero.*
31. *El le da el dinero.*
32. (*es necesario*) *que Pedro le da a el hombre la moneda.*
33. *El le pregunta a él, '¿Qué es un animal?'*
34. *El le dijo a él- que- es necesario* . . .
35. *El le dijo a ella* . . .
36. *Los pájaros les dan a ellos la comida.*
37. *Tú me dices porque* . . .
38. *También ella se sienta.*
39. *. . . y le dio a la mujer un, la café.*
40. *También él se siento en la silla* (= *se sentó*)
41. *Las dos personas se levantarsan.*
42. *Y también el hombre le pone la chaqueta a la mujer.*


Ungrammatical uses of clitics

1. *Y si, si, si Berkely dijo a yo.*
2. *Yo me gusta.*
3. *Yo me gusta.*
4. *Yo me gusta este* tape recorder.
5. *Yo manejo tú a la Kennedy Airport* . . .
6. *Yo me gusta los* special effects.
7. *Yo me gusta* sledding *en la montaña.*
8. *Y yo, yo me gusta* ice skating.
9. *Yo no conozco tú* (= *conocía*)
10. *Tú se, se levantas.*
11. *Tú vestirse* . . .
12. *Tú sientas en mi silla.*

13. . . . *y tú se vestir, vestirse su ropa.*
14. . . . *un* person, *da una cosa a un otro persona.*
15. . . . *y el decidió sentar, sentar en la silla.*
16. . . . *cuando ella siente en el silla.*
17. *Algun profesores no quieren los estudiantes le dan los papeles.*
18. *El le dijo a Pedro que que si Pedro quiere ayuda el hombre es posible.*
19. *Ellos dicen que . . .* (= *ellos les dicen*)
20. *Ella le dijo a ellos . . .*
21. *Ella le dice a ellos . . .*
22. *Yo quiero le pregunta sobre tus experiencias.*

Instances where David could have (should have?) used clitics

1. (*¿Qué van a hacer los pájaros con las semillas?*)
   *Los pájaros querían comer- querían comer los sem-semillas.*
2. (*¿Qué hicieron ellos con la canasta?*)
   *Ellos no- no sacaron este cosa cuando ellos fueron a- a la agua.*
3. (*¿Qué hicieron con los zapatos después de que se los quitaron?*)
   *Ellos pusieron los zapatos cerca de las flores.*
4. (*¿Qué le hubiera pasado a la rana si no hubiera brincado?*)
   *Este animal- come el- cómo se dice éste (points)?*
5. (*¿Por qué está tan asustado el conejo?*)
   *Porque este animal también quiere comer este conejo.*
6. (*¿Qué pasó con la canasta?*)
   *La familia malo- mala tienen esta cosa . . . tienen la canasta en otra parte de los árboles.*
7. (*¿y esta familia le dio la canasta?*)
   *No. Ellos roben- roban esta canasta.*
8. (*¿Qué va a hacer ella con el plátano?*)
   *Ella, oh, ella quiere comer este plátano.*
9. (*¿Qué les hubiera hecho ella a los pájaros si los hubiera visto?*)
   *Ella (mumbles) querían matar este- estas- estos pájaros*
10. (*¿Cómo consiguieron la comida?*)
    *Los pájaros les dan a ellos la comida.*
11. (*¿Qué crees tú que pasó con la comida?*)
    *Yo creo que- yo SE que los pájaros saquen la comida de la canasta y les dan a la familia bueno.*

# 9 Coexisting discourse worlds: the development of pragmatic competence inside and outside the classroom

MARY E. WILDNER-BASSETT

*University of Arizona, Tucson, USA*

## Introduction

Several recent studies in contrastive pragmatics (e.g. Littlewood, 1983; Richards & Sukiwat, 1983; Thomas, 1983; 1984; House, 1984; 1986; Kasper, 1986) have pointed out that a language learner is faced with countless sociocultural conventions for managing conversation within the target language, and that these conventions may often be in contrast to or in conflict with comparable conventions of the learner's native language culture. As Kramsch (1985:170) summarizes, language learners 'underestimate the difficulty of managing and controlling their own and others' discourse in a context which has other personal and cultural norms of interaction'. While the studies just mentioned and others have greatly expanded our view of pragmalinguistic difficulties facing learners and of possible ways of helping learners avoid these difficulties (e.g. by differentiating between sociopragmatic and pragmalinguistic failure— Thomas, 1983; 1984), there are still many open questions which confront the field of contrastive pragmatics which focuses on foreign language learning (FLL) and second language acquisition (SLA), interlanguage pragmatics. The goal of this paper is to discuss methodological and analytical issues which may have a bearing on the results of our analyses of pragmatic aspects of learners' interlanguage. A closely related goal is to show differences in these aspects of learner language use as dependent on the general learning/acquisition environment as well as on the specific environment of data collection.

## The Situational Frame, Discourse Worlds and Learner Data

A great deal of the data used for contrastive pragmatic analyses, especially those concerned with some aspect of SLA/FLL, is collected by recording face-to-face interactions between native speakers and learners of the language, and/or classroom interaction. While such data are naturally a very fertile source for relevant and exciting findings, their analysis is subject to many of the same complexities which make the data themselves interesting in the first place. When data are collected for the purpose of studying various aspects of the sociocultural conventions for managing conversations, the conclusions drawn about the data by the researcher are in turn subject to the interpretations which are filtered through the particular researcher's own sociocultural orientations. Less apparent are the manifold interpretations which are necessary when the aspects of the situational frame of an interaction, as well as the probable coexistence of discourse worlds, are taken into consideration. The more specific goal of this discussion is to examine the concepts of the situational frame and the coexistence of discourse worlds as applied to analyses of learners' interlanguage. By applying these concepts, I will show that any single interpretation of a particular isolated situational frame for an isolated discourse world does not necessarily lead to valid conclusions about the nature of the interaction. Interpreting data on multiple levels is very important for drawing conclusions about pragmatic aspects of non-native speakers' interlanguage, whether acquired or learned.

The concept of the situational frame, which is one of many models that have been developed for the analysis of communication (see, e.g., Faerch et al., 1984, for an overview) was suggested by Coulmas (1981) under special consideration of routine formulas as conventions for managing conversation. Coulmas asserts that the situational frame associated with any particular interaction makes up the factors which contribute to the disposition to make particular pragmatic choices within that interaction. He maintains that situational frames should therefore be regarded as devices for integrating language data with the other relevant components involved in language use on a descriptive level. Kramsch (1985:181) has offered related suggestions for helping learners to reflect on discourse processes and 'to give the learners greater control over the interactional structures of discourse'. According to Coulmas (1981:246–48), then, there are five elements which are essential for the adequate description of (or for the interactants themselves, the awareness of) the situational frame:

(1) *participants*: sex, age, social role, hierarchical status, authority, and familiarity;
(2) *setting*: when and where the interaction occurs;
(3) *the why and the wherefore*: the reason for the interaction;
(4) *contextual restrictions*: those of sequentialization and stylistic homogeneity;
(5) *concomitant activity*: e.g. gestures, facial expressions

Obviously, the comparison or contrast of data collected within an FLL or an SLA context is greatly facilitated by clear delineations of the above elements of the situational frame. While such a description is relatively straightforward, the complexity is raised exponentially by the concept of what Edmondson (1981; 1985) refers to as 'coexisting discourse worlds'. Edmondson (1985:162) states that:

A discourse world is formally a set of elements whereby a unit of talk acquires a particular negotiated communicative value in the ongoing discourse. The set of elements includes an intended recipient . . . a shared set of presuppositions, an intended speaker meaning (or illocutionary value) and an interactional function.

Edmondson (1985:201) has also introduced the notions of 'coexisting discourse worlds' and 'world switching', such that an individual or groups of participants can operate in two or more discourse worlds, often simultaneously. I would like to add the concept (developed with Edmondson, private communication) to these ideas that any one discourse world may be dominantly operant during any part of a particular interaction or of a particular utterance, while simultaneously coexisting with other worlds that are in turn dominant earlier or later in the interaction.

In the present synthesis of the concepts offered by Coulmas and Edmondson, the elements of the situational frame can be used as a tool to delineate more closely coexisting discourse worlds within one and the same interaction. Whereas certain elements of the frame will naturally remain constant for all discourse worlds of any particular interaction (e.g. participants' sex and age or the setting), the other elements vary within an interaction depending on the nature of the particular discourse world which is dominantly operant for any given utterance.

## World Switching in Role Enactments

Evidence for the concept of the coexistence of discourse worlds, as well as the very important effect of this coexistence on learner interactions and interpretations of data from them, can of course be found in natural discourse of widely varying situational frames (see Edmondson, 1981:156, 201–03, for examples).

In order to illustrate the use of these concepts for data analytical purposes and to show the differences among coexisting discourse worlds as a function of acquisition versus classroom environments, I would like to give some examples from role-enactment data collected within the framework of two larger studies.[1]

The studies, one dealing with English and one with German as foreign languages, were concerned with improving pragmatic aspects of learners' interlanguage. Certain elements of the situational frame will be examined in terms of evidence for coexisting discourse worlds and world switching. The goal of this part of the discussion is to point out the manifold interpretations that must be considered in order to draw conclusions about learner language, especially in relation to its interactional aspects. The essential similarities and differences between FLL in the classroom and SLA, in this case within the target culture, will become evident as we look at the specific data samples.

The first element of the situational frame concerns the participants and their respective roles. This example is taken from the EFL data, which were collected by video-taping role enactments, within the larger context of adult classroom learning in an intensive immersion course. The native speaker participants were the teachers/supervisors of the course. The data sample is as follows:[2]

**(1)**
**L:** good Evening
**N:** good Evening sir + i wish i could say it wEre a good evening
**L:** yes + uh+ i have reserved a + rOOm for this night in this hotel
**O:** L slight bow, puts hands in pockets


**N:** for this Evening sir
**L:** yes + for this night
**O:** L nods

The N's first utterance shows an attempt to establish a kind of familiarity within the role play. The L, though he acknowledges the N's utterance with 'yes', does not proceed with the usual, perhaps expected small talk in any way, and thus rebuffs N's attempt at interactional familiarity within the discourse world of the role enactment (booking a room at a hotel). Since the macro-framework for this interaction is the classroom and its goal-orientated structure, we can also assume that the L's operant discourse world is that of the classroom, and that he is trying to get on with his assigned task rather than seeing himself as a participant in a simulated social situation requiring or at least permitting small talk. The next set of utterances shows a switch of role on the part of the N. He implicitly corrects the L, as shown by the emphasis placed on 'evening', and by doing so moves into the teacher role. However, he retains the formal address term 'sir', which emphasizes his played role as a hotel clerk. Not only does the L not respond to this short-lived switch of social role on the part of the N, but he also does not respond to the lexical correction, only to the content of the statement. He in fact repeats his mistake, with emphasis, in order to reiterate the correctness of the message content of his utterance. Without introspective data, we cannot ultimately determine whether the L did not process the implicit correction at all or whether he had again switched discourse worlds back to the role enactment, with the support of the N's 'sir'. The implicit correction would not likely have occurred had the discourse world of the classroom not been implicitly operant, as supported by Seliger (1980:41) when he maintains that 'a characteristic of L2 learner speech behavior under "natural" conditions is that there is no external intervention. The interlocutor does not correct the speaker or supply the appropriate term.' Our N's correction could thus be based in the interactants' 'world switching' to the situational frame concerning them as teacher–learner rather than the certainly different constellation of clerk–customer within their role descriptions.

The German data were collected under identical circumstances (video tapes of role enactments, one native and one learner participant), but there was no operant macro-world of the classroom. The participants, American students, had been living in the target culture for about two months, had volunteered, and were not involved in classroom instruction that was in any way related to the data collection. As a result, the participant element of the situational frame shows no evidence of a classroom discourse world, even though similarly implied corrections and world switching take place. One example is as follows:

**(2)**

(*Two students, acquainted with each other, meet outside their rooms*):
N:    . . . mensch was hast dU gemacht
L:                     jA ich war im krankenhaus seit
L:    zwei monAten ich bin <u>off</u> mein fAhrrad gefallen
N:                     ja AUf dein fahrrad oder
L:          von meine fAhrrad gefallen
N:                     mhm rUntergefallen


(English translation: N: man, what did you do (to yourself)    L: well,
I've been in the hospital for 2 months I fell <u>on</u> my bicycle N: yeah <u>on</u>
your bicycle or . . .    L: I fell <u>off</u> my bicycle    N: mhm fell down). Here
we have a similar case of implied correction, but one based on a more
crucial communicative detail: exactly how the fall took place. Even though
in any interaction between a native speaker of a language and a learner
the participant roles have an essentially asymmetrical element, namely
mastery of the language being used to communicate, the asymmetrical
power relationship of the classroom is not present: switching completely
to that world is not an option for these participants. As Breen (1985:145)
summarizes:

> One of the features of the culture of the classroom is 'the
> establishment of overt and covert criteria against which its members
> are continually judged. . . . the language class is a highly normative
> and evaluative environment which engages teacher and taught in
> continual judgement of each other, less as persons, but as members
> who are supposed to learn and a member who is supposed to teach.'

The N in this interaction has successfully switched roles from an unmarked
fellow student for the L (as the role descriptions imply) to a native
speaker who implicitly elicits a self-correction from the learner. In contrast
to Extract (1), this elicitation was not carried out for the purposes of
accuracy as such, nor was it normative or evaluative, but had to do with
the information being exchanged. Understanding was negotiated by the
two participants, one with a knowledge of the facts, the other with a
knowledge of how to express these facts. The N then summarizes the
negotiated meaning in her final utterance. Extract (2) shows a major
difference from Extract (1): the implied correction there was to elicit
accuracy rather than message content, and the learner missed both the
world-switch and the correction. They were irrelevant to him for the
negotiation of understanding. In Extract (2), even though the learner was
not apparently aware of her mischoice of preposition, the elicitation–

self-correction–summary sequence proceeded smoothly and the interaction continued, despite the temporary world-switch by the N. In Extract (1), the classroom discourse world, with its evaluatively asymmetrical power relationships for the participants, is dominant to the role-enactment world and to the attempted mirroring of an SLA environment, as realized by an intensive immersion course. In Extract (2), any past FLL experience of the learner takes a background role to the immediate needs of the interaction and the negotiation of understanding. The asymmetrical relationship is one of a knowledge gap rather than a teacher–learner power gap. World switching between coexistent discourse worlds takes place in both examples, but the participant element of the situational frame causes the effects of the world switch on the interactions to be quite different. These differences are ultimately reflected in the language use of the two learners.

Further data samples which reveal the interplay of various discourse worlds in an exchange will be discussed in terms of the contextual restrictions and concomitant activity elements of the situational frame.[3] Extract (3) involves a case of a learner cursing in the foreign language, but the effect of the curse is cancelled by discourse world-switching. Most interesting, perhaps, is that the L himself both notices and reveals the inherent humour of the interaction and of his own utterance, as well as his awareness of the coexistence of discourse worlds.

**(3)**
(*L has just complained about the poor organization of the 'airport' where he is trying to rearrange a booking.*)
N:   all you germans come acrOss here with all your foreign idEas
       +      trying
O:                   N frowns, broad gestures r. hand
N:   to tell us how to run our cOUntry
L:                   oh this bloody England
O:                   L smiles

First, to discuss the utterances within the isolated discourse world of the role play, the L's curse 'this bloody England' does not add a *completely* new dimension to the interaction. The N had already set a fairly hostile and direct tone with his tirade as a reaction to L's original complaint. Therefore L's next utterance is not a disruption of the conversation but rather a redirection. By the use of the more hostile and aggressive 'bloody', as well as the general curse on the entire country, the conversation is redirected to an outright quarrelsome level, and in this sense the utterance contributes an additional dimension of hostility to the interaction. If, however, the coexisting discourse worlds are also taken into account, as well as the L's concomitant smile, other dimensions of the interaction come into play. Within the interactant's discourse world of co-workers in different sections of the same company (centred in West Germany), the N is, of course, explicitly and ironically bringing this setting into the interaction and parodying the role-play discourse setting by calling German ideas foreign. The L's curse is, on this level, actually a response in kind, but at the same time the smile makes the overall effect that of a deviant utterance because L curses but does not follow the N's lead with his gestures and facial expressions. The N's frown and gesticulations remain homogeneous with the lexical content and pragmatic force of the utterance. The L smiles directly after his utterance, and it is precisely his smile which produces the overall effect of this portion of the interaction. This complex of the L's utterance and its accompanying facial expression is specifically the type of phenomenon to which learners might be susceptible both inside and outside the classroom. While the learner's utterance can be viewed as (only somewhat) divergent and certainly intentional, complete with predictable changes in speech rate, stress and pitch, the concomitant facial expression is rather a deviant one, considering the expectations of the interactant and the overall situational frame of the discourse world of the role enactment.[4] Within this discourse world, the smile results in the pragmatic failure (Thomas, 1983) of the utterance. Rather than redirecting the interaction toward even more dominance/hostility, as could the utterance 'this bloody England' alone, the concomitant smile redefines the otherwise hostile interaction in the direction of affection/humour, thus counteracting the purely verbal portion of the utterance. Therefore concomitant activity is a potential source of pragmatic failure and thus a very important aspect of language use for the learner.

A final discourse world involved here and in fact implicitly in all interactions of this type is the separate world of the learner involved in an interaction with a native speaker of the target language. The fact that the native speaker–learner discourse world is now operant and coexistent to the other worlds is in this case potentially disadvantageous for the learner. Perhaps the best treatment of this phenomenon is found in Harder's (1980) discussion of the 'reduced personality' of the foreign language learner. According to Harder (1980:268):

> A foreigner is not permitted to go beyond a certain limited repertoire; if he starts swearing fluently, for instance, he is unlikely to achieve the conventional communicative effect, i.e. underlining the serious objections he has against the situation in question.

It would seem that our learner had precisely this reaction to his *own* utterance. Not only is the learner apparently aware of the disparity between the discourse worlds of the role enactment and the real-life situation; he is also aware of a third discourse world where he as a learner is not expected to (nor apparently expects *himself* to) express an opinion using this type of language. The N has, as previously mentioned, set the tone of this portion of the interaction with his tirade, which can only be viewed as ironic or offered in a sense of self-parody.[5] The learner attempts a further step, in terms of his own role enactment, toward bringing even more parodied 'hostility' into the interaction. The L cannot resist smiling, however, most likely at the sound of such a (relatively) vehement curse coming from his own mouth. Obviously, the entire potential effect is counteracted by the smile. Thomas (1983:96) has stated that the 'non-native speaker who says anything other than what is expected often finds it difficult to get her/his views taken seriously'. Based on the present evidence, it could be added that learners themselves may have difficulty in taking their own utterances in the foreign language seriously, or in articulating them at all, when the utterances are of this type. This effect is not due to any divergent propositional content of the utterance, but rather to its pragmatic force, which goes beyond the limited repertoire of possibilities with which a classroom learner has been confronted and which he has himself apparently accepted or internalized, at least in this case. Thus a learner's utterance could be doomed to pragmatic failure because of a disparity in the norms and expectations bound to coexisting discourse worlds. Furthermore, the learner may himself or herself contribute to this disparity by an awareness of the discourse world involving him or her as a learner, especially when interacting with a native speaker, such that the normative and asymmetrical elements are present in the participant elements of the situational frame. If that native speaker happens to be the learner's teacher in a classroom setting, the evaluative element is also added to the complex. The comparatively complex nature of this utterance, its concomitant facial expression, and four of the discourse worlds involved in its realization, are summarized in Table 9.1.

As could be expected, there are very few instances of comparable samples in the German data. It is my hypothesis that Harder's reduced personality syndrome was in full effect for the non-native participants in the German interactions. There were cases where potential conflict, differences of opinion, or the like could have been expected by virtue of the role descriptions. They were, however, either avoided completely or the non-native speaker seemed to change the course of the interaction

‑

TABLE 9.1 *Discourse worlds of the 'this bloody England' utterance*

| WORLD I<br>Role-play | WORLD II<br>'Real life' | WORLD III<br>Native<br>speaker–learner | WORLD IV<br>Teacher–student |
|---|---|---|---|
| **Participants**<br>N=airline clerk, L=himself. L socially dominant, otherwise neutral for dominance at outset. Previously unfamiliar with each other. N sets hostile tone with his utterance. | N and L co-workers in a large company; familiar with each other professionally; neutral dominance; friendly and non-hostile. | N dominant to L in language ability; friendly and jovial; normative relationship | N dominant to L in language and in evaluation. Normative and evaluative relationship |
| **Setting**<br>Airline desk; evening | Educational centre of firm—classroom with video equipment; afternoon | Same as World II | Same as World II |
| **Why and Wherefore**<br>Response by L in kind to N's tirade; L hopes to regain dominant role. | N's utterance= parody of Worlds I and II; L's response in kind=parody | Same as World II | Tendency toward self-parody strongest here for both L and N |
| **Contextual restrictions**<br>Tone hostile from N; cursing redefines restrictions. | N maintains coexistent World I by frown and gestures | Limited repertoire expected of a learner speaking target language | More risk-taking by L in parody frame; goes beyond limited repertoire. |
| **Concomitant activity**<br>Smile counteracts curse; leads to pragmatic failure of L's utterance | Smile shows L's inability to maintain World I as coexistent to World II; World II dominant for L. | Smile shows L's awareness that he has stepped beyond learner norm restrictions; L surprised (pleasantly?) | Same as World III; less surprise than delight at the parody |

to avoid a necessity for redefining the parameters of the situational frame
in terms of the contextual restrictions which indicate conflict or even
hostility. One exception is a case where the L refused to lend his car to
the N during the role enactment, but he did this so well that the N finally
apologized to the L for trying to persuade the learner to lend him the car.
The L's interaction was pragmatically very successful, even though he did
not do or say the expected. It was more often the case that the pragmatic
failure of a learner utterance could potentially have led to a breakdown
in the interaction, but the N usually saved the day by a complete change
of topic within the given discourse world or by ignoring the failure and
continuing to talk. One example follows:

(4)
N:   geht's gut   ich bin ein bisschen erkÄltet aber sonst
L:       ja                                                                        oh ja
L:   schwEine kalt
N:           jo jo     woher kOmmst du eigentlich aus den
O:               both laugh
L:   new yOrk

(English translation: N: everything fine?   L: yeah   N: I have a little
cold, but otherwise . . .   L: oh yeah, pig's cold (the German routine is
'Saukalt' or sow's cold, and is a derogatory statement about the weather,
not about someone's health)   N: uhuh. Where do you come from in
the . . .   L: New York). The laugh here was by both participants, and
there is no evidence to suggest that the learner was aware of his
pragmalinguistic failure nor of the change in topic that it manifested. This
laugh may even have been one of delight on the learner's part for
managing to use a routine from colloquial speech in what he thought of
as an appropriate way, though this must remain conjecture. The N's
laugh could have been purely social in nature, one of embarrassment,
one of delight or fun concerning the strange ways of the non-native, or
resulting from any number of other impulses.

At this point, I would suggest two conclusions that can be drawn
from a comparison of the classroom and the non-classroom data. In an
FLL environment in the classroom, and in data collected within such a
setting, a learner can be willing to risk more within the classroom
interaction discourse world than within other coexistent worlds. Just as
teachers self-parody, so can and do learners by going beyond their
otherwise reduced learner personality when given the chance. This chance
consists of a temporary suspension of the evaluative mode associated with
the classroom, and is perhaps also initiated by teacher irony or self-

parody. At the same time, the learner in the classroom cannot completely escape the 'real' discourse world which often limits the expected pragmatic force of any utterance a learner makes.

In the SLA environment, especially in the target culture, a learner does not have the luxury of self-parody in most cases. He or she is at the mercy of the usually native speaker interactant who may be willing to accept some pragmalinguistic failures, but who is also often prone to make negative, though inaccurate, personal judgements about the learner based on sociopragmatic failure (Thomas, 1983). Learners interacting in the target culture are aware of this possibility on some level, and are not willing to go beyond the reduced personality of what they perceive to be normative native speaker expectations of them. Even though the fact that they are learners is often thematized in an interaction, it is much more difficult for them to let their learner status become dominant in defining a discourse world. Of course this can happen by direct elicitation of help from the native, but a switch back to the discourse world of the main interaction usually follows immediately.

## Conclusion

I have tried to show that no single interpretation of pragmatic aspects of learner language use can be valid unless the many coexisting discourse worlds are taken into consideration. Some of the salient discourse worlds that are potentially operant in an SLA setting, especially for data collected in role enactments, are: that defined by the role descriptions; that of a native speaker conversing with a learner (a normative, asymmetrical relationship); and the 'real world' of the two individuals and their lives. Any instance of language use, especially on the pragmatic dimension but also in relation to accuracy and content, must be looked at in relation to each of these coexisting worlds. Data collected and language used in the foreign language classroom includes all of the above discourse worlds as well as: the normative and evaluative asymmetrical relationship of teacher to learner; the potential for self-parody on the part of the teacher and the learner which can lead to increased risk-taking by the learner; and a view towards formal accuracy which is not usually explicitly present in any of the worlds in the SLA context, at least not to the same extent. Again, any interpretation of learner language use should only be accomplished after considering the elements of the situational frame of each of these coexistent discourse worlds.

Much has been said and written about the implications of the social context of language learning for improving pragmatic aspects of learners' language in the classroom. I would like to use my data analyses to lend support to what has been said about teaching discourse management. I agree fully with Coulmas (1981), Kramsch (1985) and others (see also Wildner-Bassett, 1984) that routine formulas should be taught explicitly as invaluable tools for managing conversation. I have developed pilot courses to teach these formulas for English and German (Wildner-Bassett, 1984; 1986), and those that have been implemented have been very well received by teachers and learners. This shows that the need is present and the tools are available for sensitizing learners to discourse processes. I also believe that a sensitization to the coexistence of discourse worlds is a valuable tool for any learner, and that this can be accomplished by metapragmatic instruction for adult learners, using examples from their own interactions whenever possible. The requirements for such instruction include access to video-recording equipment and a schooling and sensitization of teachers to be able to look at discourse inside and outside the classroom with an eye to coexisting discourse worlds and the effects of them on language use. A willingness to see and work with the participant element of the situational frame which involves them as teachers and their learners as the taught is also essential. By raising learners' awareness and giving them the pragmalinguistic tools they need, we are also giving them a means to continue learning and gradually to enhance their otherwise 'reduced' learner personalities 'out there' in the target culture as well as 'in here' in the classroom culture.

## Notes to Chapter 9

1. Some of the data and their analyses have been reported in Wildner-Bassett (1984) in a somewhat different context. The analysis of the German data is discussed in even more detail in Wildner-Bassett (in preparation).
2. For this and all following data samples: N = native speaker (of the target language), L = learner; O = observations. The transcriptions norms follow the 'Partitur' system described in Henne & Rehbock (1979).
3. The EFL portion of the data has also been discussed in a different context in Wildner-Bassett (in press).
4. See Wildner-Bassett (in press) and the reference therein for more thorough definitions and discussion of deviant and divergent utterances.
5. As Edmondson (1985) has pointed out, this tendency toward parody or self-parody is quite common in teacher behaviour in the classroom. He characterized self-parodying behaviour as 'the playing of a particular role, while at the same time seeking to play some other observing or distancing role more closely identified with one's own self' (Edmondson, 1985: 161).

# 10 Foreign language learning: a social interaction perspective[1]

## FRANK B. BROOKS

*Longwood College, Farmville, Virginia, USA*

Most foreign language learning in the United States takes place in a classroom setting. Millions of students must take a required number of years of a foreign language as a prerequisite for entering and graduating from both high schools and universities. That languages are learned in classrooms makes it incumbent upon the language teaching profession to come to understand the process of learning languages in the academic setting (Kramsch, this volume; van Lier, 1988).

Most foreign language classroom orientated research has been of three major kinds: interaction analysis (cf. Breen, 1985; Chaudron, 1988; Ellis, 1985; Long, 1983b; van Lier, 1988); the study of teacher talk (Chaudron, 1983; Gaies, 1977; 1979; Henzl, 1973; 1979; Long, 1983b; Long & Sato, 1983; Schinke-Llano, 1983; Wesche & Ready, 1983); and discourse analysis (Gremmo *et al.*, 1978; Kramsch, 1981; Riley, 1977). These approaches to studying foreign language classrooms have produced descriptions of the classroom climate of phonetic, lexical and syntactic features of classroom language, and have been limited to surface-level descriptions through frequency, type and length of interactions in the classroom. Although these descriptions are valuable in allowing us to understand certain features of life in classrooms, we still know very little about the *processes* through which language learners come to learn a foreign language in a classroom setting.

The purpose of this paper is to present and discuss classroom data that have been collected and analysed from a social interaction perspective (Green, 1983a; 1983b; Green & Weade, 1987) that recognizes the classroom as an active social environment in which many things become learned and shared, including both social and academic information (Green & Weade, 1985; Hamilton, 1982). While language learning is the object of foreign language instruction, language learning is embedded in the instructional conversations that take place during lessons. Therefore, by exploring the instructional talk between teachers and students in a principled and systematic manner one is able to extract recurring patterns of action and interaction during lessons to 'be able to explain how classroom instruction influences and interacts with learning' (Breen, 1985: 135). Exploration of the instructional dialogue in foreign language classrooms can illuminate how the process of language learning and teaching takes place and what is learned by means of it.

## Background of the Study

The rationale and theoretical frame for the study are grounded in the social interaction perspective on classrooms, which holds that the classroom is a complex setting where communication takes place between and among participants. Some have considered the classroom an emerging culture (Breen, 1985), a place where people come together to learn, where people conduct their lives through the use of language. As students and teachers work together they mutually construct a pattern of life in their classroom that has its own meanings. In the process, teachers and their students develop and share ways of communicating with one another. Moreover, they develop together and establish expectations for what is appropriate and inappropriate for any given context (Green, 1983a; 1983b). The classroom, then, is an active social environment in which many things become learned and shared, including both social and academic information (Green & Weade, 1985; Hamilton, 1982). Of primary importance to the social perspective is the view that classrooms are active and dynamic communicative environments in which both social and academic goals are pursued (Green, 1983a; 1983b; Green & Smith, 1983).

The task in investigating the processes that take place in foreign language classrooms is first to come to terms with these complexities, and understand and accept them as a fact of life (van Lier, 1988). Reducing classroom interactions to check marks made on a checksheet every three seconds or so by an outsider researcher who is alien to the classroom setting and its participants is paying lip-service to coming to know more about these settings. What is needed, then, is a way of conceptualizing the classroom as a complex social environment in order to begin to investigate in a serious manner the processes of teaching and learning other languages in a formal classroom setting.

The approach used in this study was ethnographic in nature. Using video tape as the means to freeze the naturally-occurring events of the lesson under investigation, detailed observations were made of the unfolding lesson in order to extract recurring action and interaction. While not to be confused with doing an ethnography of this class (Green & Bloome, 1983), the ethnographic approach was used to uncover patterns of social interaction that took place in the classroom between the teacher and students as they came together to teach and to learn academic materials, in this case, Spanish language. The ethnographic approach focuses primarily on the study of classroom processes from a social interaction perspective, which allows for the exploration, investigation, and identification of patterns of behaviour as they are developed over time (i.e. language learning events that occur day after day, year after year). It is during the instructional talk between teacher and students that the goals of instruction as well as the rules for social behaviour within the classroom setting are transmitted (Green & Harker, 1982; Green & Weade, 1985).

Underlying the teaching/learning process when viewed as a communicative process are numerous propositions that, when considered collectively, provide the basis for in-depth descriptions of complex social and instructional processes. These propositions form the conceptual basis for the study of teaching and learning from a social interaction perspective (Green, 1983a; 1983b). There are 24 propositions that fall under five interrelated themes: (1) classrooms are communicative environments; (2) contexts are constructed during interactions; (3) meaning is context-specific; (4) inferencing is required for conversational comprehension; and (5) teachers orchestrate different participation levels. (The complete list of propositions is provided in Appendix 10.1.) From this perspective, lessons are defined by what people are doing, how they are doing it, when they are doing it, as well as with whom they are doing it. The knowledge of what takes place during the interaction is not assumed a priori. With this kind of focus it is possible to 'zero in' on the participants' perspectives of what is going on.

The teaching/learning process as described above is based on two major assumptions. The first assumption is that classrooms are dynamic communicative environments in which interactions between and among the participants have multiple outcomes and meanings and have both social and academic consequences. The assumption of dual outcomes of instruction means that students are simultaneously engaged in acquiring an understanding about how to conduct themselves socially as they acquire and demonstrate knowledge about the academic content of instruction.

The second assumption of the social interaction perspective is that instruction is a goal-orientated process. The goal-directed nature of instruction can be observed through exploring the instructional conversation between and among teacher and students as well as the non-verbal actions of the participants. Observing both verbal and non-verbal actions allows for the description of the social and academic content of lessons from which both teachers' and students' patterned ways of interacting can be described both within a particular lesson as well as across many different lessons.

The purpose of classroom-orientated research from a social interaction perspective is to understand the teaching-learning process from the perspective of the participants and to identify those factors that support and constrain academic achievement. This purpose is accomplished by examining a particular lesson closely and in great detail and comparing it with other lessons examined in equally great detail. Such an analysis involves the extraction of recurring patterns of action and interaction within the language classroom. In this way, variables of interest that are grounded in the observed patterns are constructed and then tested across other lessons.

## Analytical Procedures

The analytical approach used was that of a modified type case analysis (Erickson & Schultz, 1981). A video tape of one day's entire lesson was subjected to limited analysis in order to obtain a working model of the content management procedures used by the teacher (Green & Weade, 1985). This model might be considered a preliminary form of inventory that consists of representative patterns of interaction between teacher and students. The approach described here allows for the identification of patterns of behaviour that are consistent across time, setting and content, as well as allowing for the exploration of these management procedures during subsequent interactions. The instructional conversation is first transcribed and then segmented so that analysis and hypothesis-generation may proceed. Because of the exploratory nature of this study, the degree of descriptive detail Green & Wallat (1981) call for is not provided. The analysis is, however, sufficiently detailed for the purposes of the present study.[2]

## The Sample

The focus of this research project was what transpired between two students during a speaking activity that took place as part of the regular classroom routine on the day video-taping took place. This instructional episode took place as the seventh phase of a nine-phase review lesson in an elementary Spanish class at university level. At the end of that class period, students were given a quiz. For the purposes of this investigation, a lesson is seen as being composed of different parts or phases, each having a distinct instructional purpose (Green & Wallat, 1981). The speaking activity that became the focus for closer analysis occurred as the third part of the seventh phase of the lesson. (A complete breakdown of each of the nine phases of this lesson is provided in Appendix 10.2.) During this activity students were to work in pairs using adjectives to describe in Spanish several fictitious people whose names and descriptions appeared on cue cards that the teacher handed out to the students just prior to the activity. The two students whose performance was video-taped were singled out by the teacher because they were already acquaintances and had carried out similar paired activities together in the regular classroom. In conducting the research, established classroom routines were not altered.

## Discussion

In order to facilitate the discussion, extract (1) provides a complete transcript of the simulated communication activity carried out by these two students. In this episode, Student A began the questioning (line 111). At the end of the first question (line 113), Student B begins to respond while looking at his cue card for a possible response (lines 114–117). Student A, however, appears to have difficulty discerning whether or not Student B used the correct ending on the adjective possibly because of the mispronounced vowel *a* in *rubias*. Student A's manner of indicating his confusion is to repeat the word in which the error was noted (lines 118–121), and more or less indirectly letting Student B know that there was something grammatically wrong with his response. This particular kind of correction behaviour is continued when Student B questions the correct adjectival ending (lines 122–124). Another instance of this error correction behaviour occurs while Student A is questioning Student B as part of the activity. Student B makes an error in noun–adjective agreement (lines 145–147). This prompts Student B not only to correct his error, but also to recognize it (lines 148–149). This behaviour continues after

(1) *Rough Transcript of Students Working in Pairs*

| 101 | **B:** | You're answering the question I'm answering |
|-----|--------|---------------------------------------------|
| 102 |        | Right |
| 103 | **A:** | Correct |
| 104 | **B:** | Okay where's the (inaudible)? |
| 105 |        | Okay go ahead |
| 106 | **A:** | Hold on let's go |

| 107 | **A:** | Cómo estás? |
|-----|--------|-------------|
| 108 | **B:** | Muy bien |
| 109 |        | Gracias |
| 110 |        | Señor |

| 111 | **A:** | Ah |
|-----|--------|----|
| 112 |        | Cómo son |
| 113 |        | Carolina y Luz? |
| 114 | **B:** | Carolina y Luz |
| 115 |        | es |
| 116 |        | no |
| 117 |        | son rubias (final vowel schwaed) |
| 118 | **A:** | Son (voice in holding tone) |
| 119 |        | Rubi . . . |
| 120 |        | a |
| 121 |        | Rubias |
| 122 | **B:** | a |
| 123 |        | o (or) |
| 124 |        | as (question tone) |
| 125 | **A:** | as |
| 126 | **B:** | as |
| 127 |        | Sí |
| 128 |        | Rubias (prosodic stress on 'as'). |

| 129 | **A:** | Ahhh |
|-----|--------|------|
| 130 |        | Cómo es Rodolfo? |
| 131 | **B:** | Rodolfo es |
| 132 |        | OOOO |
| 133 |        | antipático |
| 134 | **A:** | Muy bien |

| 135 | **A:** | Cómo son Alberto y Antonio |
|-----|--------|----------------------------|
| 136 | **B:** | Alberto y Antonio son buenos |
| 137 | **A:** | Muy bien |

| 138 | **A:** | Cómo es Luisa? |
| 139 | **B:** | Luisa |
| 140 | | Ahhhh |
| 141 | | es |
| 142 | | Luisa. |
| 143 | | lindas (prosodic stress on 'as') |
| 144 | | lindas (prosodic stress on 'as') |
| 145 | **A:** | lindas (prosodic stress on 'as') |
| 146 | | o |
| 147 | | linda (prosodic stress on 'a') |
| 148 | **B:** | linda (prosodic stress on 'a') |
| 149 | | You're right |
| 150 | **A:** | Muy bien |
| 151 | | It's not plural |
| 152 | | Okay |

| 153 | **B:** | Switch? |
| 154 | **A:** | Switch |

| 155 | **B:** | Ahhh |
| 156 | | Cómo es Rodolfo? |
| 157 | **A:** | Ohhh |
| 158 | | Rodolfo es |
| 159 | | tacaño |
| 160 | **B:** | tacaño |

| 161 | **B:** | MMMMMM |
| 162 | | Por favor, señor |
| 163 | | Cómo son Luisa? |
| 164 | **A:** | Cómo son o cómo es? |
| 165 | **B:** | Would that be *cómo es* wouldn't it be? |
| 166 | | Cómo es Luisa? |
| 167 | **A:** | Luisa es muy simpática (prosodic stress, muy) |
| 168 | **B:** | MMMMM |
| 169 | | Muy simpática |
| 170 | | OOOOOO |

| 171 | **B:** | Cómo son Carolina y Luz? |
| 172 | **A:** | Ahhh |
| 173 | | Carolina y Luz son |
| 174 | | muy muy muy ricas. |
| 175 | **B:** | OOOOOOOOO |

| 176 | **B:** | Cómo son |
| 177 | | No wait a minute |
| 178 | | Cómo son Alberto y Antonio? |
| 179 | **A:** | Alberto y Antonio son |
| 180 | | siempre activo |
| 181 | **B:** | OOOOO |
| 182 | **A:** | activos (student self corrects error). |
| 183 | **B:** | Does that mean 'always active' right |
| 184 | **A:** | Sí |
| 185 | **B:** | Activos right? |
| 186 | **A:** | Activos |
| 187 | **B:** | Didn't hear that |
| 188 | **T:** | All right! |

the students switch roles (lines 153–154), that is, Student B became the question-asker and Student A the answerer. In lines 162–163, Student B asks Student A a question in which his verb does not agree with the noun. Student A, again by indirectly highlighting the error, corrects Student B's mistake (line 164). Student B is aware of his error (line 165), and corrects it (line 166).

In the examples above, it is easy to see that these two students were not only practising nouns, verbs and adjectives in a contextualized fashion, they were also demonstrating knowledge of a mutually acceptable manner for correcting each other's errors. Based on what had taken place between the students the following research questions were generated: Where did this correction behaviour come from? Why did it occur during an activity that ostensibly was a simulated interview in which one person was to find out something about other people through a second person? In order to find a plausible explanation of the origin and rationale for this behaviour, it is necessary to go back into the entire lesson.

What appears to be happening during this episode is that the students were imitating the teacher's way of correcting pronunciation and adjective–noun agreement errors, that is, by repeating the word in which the error was located. The teacher corrected students in the third and fourth phases of the lesson. Note the teacher's response in eliciting a description of an elderly woman. The class had already established her as being old and generous.

**(2)**

| | |
|---|---|
| **Teacher:** | ¿Es antipática? |
| **Students:** | (several together): No |
| **Teacher:** | No es antipática. |
| **Student:** | Es muy simpático. |
| **Teacher:** | ¿Simpático? (said loudly with rising intonation) |
| **Student:** | Simpática. |
| **Teacher:** | Sí, es muy simpática. |

During the fourth phase of this lesson, in which students were using adjectives to describe President Reagan, the teacher uses this same type of correction behaviour.

**(3)**

| | |
|---|---|
| **Teacher:** | ¿Cómo es el presidente Reagan? En su opinión, ¿cómo es nuestro presidente? |
| **Student 1:** | Es aburrido. (followed by general laughter) |
| **Teacher:** | Dice que es aburrido. Muy bien. ¿Es un señor muy aburrido? ¿Hay otras palabras para describir a nuestro presidente de los Estados Unidos? |
| **Student 2:** | Es rica. |
| **Teacher:** | ¿Rica? (said loudly with rising intonation) |
| **Student 2:** | Rico. |
| **Teacher:** | Rico. Sí, este señor es muy rico. |

Since this behaviour, by teacher and students, also took place during phases of lessons on other days of the class, it is safe to hypothesize that this error correction activity is an extension of teacher–student verbal interaction. In this case, Student A, the academically better student, appears to have taken the role of the teacher by correcting Student B's errors. Student B appears to have maintained his role of student by self-correcting the errors as highlighted by Student A. More importantly, the students knew that at the end of the lesson period they were going to be quizzed on these same discrete elements of Spanish grammar, that is, noun–adjective agreement and subject–verb agreement in Spanish. Therefore, rather than use the exercise to participate in a communication simulation activity, as originally intended by the teacher, the students seem to have turned the activity into another chance to reinforce the rules of Spanish grammar, thereby getting ready for the subsequent quiz.

In this way the students demonstrated their knowledge of what they felt was important to know and did so in a manner consistent with the rules of classroom conduct established by the teacher's interactional patterns. It appears as though the two students have learned through imitation and inference, rather than explicit instruction, an acceptable manner for doing this type of activity.

Internal validity for this finding was established by re-entering the complete set of transcripts from the video-taped lesson. In this much larger corpus of conversational data, several other examples of the same correction behaviour on the part of the teacher were available. External validity was established during a follow-up interview with Student A the following academic quarter. Upon viewing the video tape several weeks later, he reported that one of the things he felt the students had learned in the class, besides Spanish grammar and pronunciation, was a manner for correcting each other's errors in pronunciation and in grammar, in this case noun–adjective agreement. Student A was also asked whether his current Spanish instructor provided opportunities for the students to work in pairs. He answered 'yes' and that they seemed to correct each other in a way consistent with the new teacher's way of doing things.

Another teacher behaviour that these two students inferred and imitated is what can be called 'topic-shift signals'. Topic-shift signals have been identified in the literature as conforming to the initiation–response–feedback pattern of classroom interaction, the major kind of teacher–student talk. This pattern follows a basic three-part structure consisting of an elicitation by the teacher, a response by a student, followed by an evaluative statement by the teacher. Following this cycle of interaction, the teacher typically moves to or continues with the next elicitation (Bellack, *et al.*, 1966; Mehan, 1979; Sinclair & Coulthard, 1975).

Topic-shift signals can be seen in extract (1). In lines 129–134 Student A asks *¿Cómo es Rodolfo?* Student B responds in a manner that is grammatically correct. Student A, interestingly enough, responds with a terse *muy bien* and with a corresponding head nod seemingly indicates his approval of Student B's response. Thus he has signalled a shift of topic because the students then move on to the next question. Another instance of this same topic-shift behaviour is provided in lines 135–137. Student A asks *¿Cómo son Alberto y Antonio?* Student B responds *Alberto y Antonio son buenos*, which is again followed by Student A's slight pause and terse *muy bien*, once again indicating his approval of Student B's response. Still another example of this behaviour is noted in line 150. It is as though Student A is praising B for doing good work. Again, the question of the origin of this behaviour and why it has taken place during the communication simulation activity was raised. During the follow-up interview with Student A, he was asked why he thought he had done the activity in this way. He responded by saying that he had not been aware that he had done it so until he saw himself on video tape. He was mildly shocked, and even laughed.

This topic-shift behaviour manifested by these two students took on meaning when entering the larger corpus of transcript data. Following are selected transcript lines of the second phase of this lesson during which the students and teacher were practising adjectival opposites. The students were to respond with the opposite of the adjective given by the teacher.

**(4)**

**Teacher:** ¿Okay? Bien. ¿Cuál es el opuesto de bonita?
**Students:** Fea.
**Teacher:** Fea. Muy bien. (indicating approval)
Bonita. Fea. (repetition/reinforcement of pair)
Bien. (closes interactional unit)

. . .

**Teacher:** Gorda.
**Students:** Flaca.
**Teacher:** Flaca. Bien. (closes interactional unit)
Eh, muy guapo.
**Students:** Feo.
**Teacher:** Feo.
Muy bien. (closes interactional unit)
Y, ay, pobre.
**Students:** Rico.
**Teacher:** Rico.
Muy bien. (said louder; terminates Phase II)

The instructor begins the actual activity by saying *bien* as though he were indicating to the students 'Ready, Get set, Go!' Then, the instructor verbally marks the end of each interaction unit by saying either *bien* or *muy bien*. This response simultaneously indicates his approval of the students' responses and terminates the interaction unit. Re-entering the larger corpus of transcript data showed that this was a consistent pattern of interaction on the part of the teacher.

Students, too, understood this behaviour. All interviewed students recognized and were able to describe how the teacher moved between phases of lessons as well as between sub-phases of lessons. One student made a particularly interesting comment when asked about what these words meant to him. He stated: 'I never was really sure what those meant, but I always knew that we were going on to something different every time [the teacher] said them'. Moreover, because of teacher voice intonation one student was even able to distinguish between a *muy bien* that meant 'going-on-to-something different' and a *muy bien* that signalled positive feedback.

## Summary and Conclusions

The intent of this paper has been to discuss classroom conversational data from a social interaction perspective the purpose of which is to locate and investigate ongoing classroom instructional and social processes. Several student behaviours that emerged during a student–student communication simulation activity that took place as part of the regular classroom routine were identified and investigated. The two students whose dialogue appears in extract (1) seem to be carrying out social and academic norms for proper behaviour during this kind of activity, norms that appear to have been created across the duration of the course.

Constructing social norms is a process of building expectations for how to behave and what to do.

> Rules are signalled by what people say and do; therefore, rules are more than a list posted on the board. Rules exist as a set of expectations for what to do and how to be that are signalled, re-signalled, and reinforced over time as part of the everyday inter-actions between teachers and students (Green & Weade, 1985: 6).

During the seventh phase of this day's lesson, Student A and Student B seem to be behaving in a manner consistent with what the teacher had signalled as appropriate behaviour. Student A corrected Student B in a way consistent with the way in which the teacher corrected. Moreover, Student A also demonstrated the topic-shift behaviour the teacher used consistently throughout instruction.

Traditional means of observing and studying foreign language instruction have primarily taken a process-product or teacher effectiveness approach whose focus is on locating student and teacher behaviours that are statistically associated with such things as student gain scores on outcome measures such as achievement tests and specifically-designed end-of-instruction product measures. In this way language is more often than not viewed as simply an object to be measured in terms of gain scores. Throughout instruction, however, teachers and students continuously use language in order to teach and to learn language. The interpersonal and conversational nature of foreign language learning in the classroom has largely been ignored, especially by classroom research in foreign language learning. The instructional and communicative processes that take place across time during classroom foreign language teaching and learning influence not only what occurs in the classroom and how it occurs, but also what is eventually learned. That is, as students are learning the pieces and parts of language, they are simultaneously learning how to be competent members of the classroom in order to participate in language learning activities.

From a social interaction perspective it is possible to begin to build on surface-level descriptions of classroom events and to explore more indepth the moment-by-moment, day-by-day teaching and learning processes that take place within the foreign language classroom context. Then we can begin to address questions such as:

(1) How do teachers provide opportunities for speaking/writing/ reading/listening to the target language in the classroom setting?

(2) How do opportunities for, say, speaking the target language get played out? In other words, how do students talk during these activities and how does the structure of this talk compare with what is known about talk and conversation from conversational analysis (Kramsch, 1981; McHoul, 1978; Sacks *et al.*, 1974; Schegloff, 1968; Schegloff & Sacks, 1973; van Lier, 1988)?

(3) How does the instructional process influence what takes place during so-called communicative activities (Green & Weade, 1985; 1987)?

(4) What communicative and academic demands are placed upon students during these activities (Green, 1983a; 1983b; van Lier, 1988)?

(5) What is it about communicating in the target language that students learn by participating in these activities?

(6) What model of conversation/reading/writing are students learning in the language classroom?

Classroom teachers of foreign languages as well as those interested in investigating foreign language learning need to keep in perspective that the classroom is a communicative environment. Students are learning more than pieces and parts of language. As in learning a native language, learning a foreign language is also a tacit process of socialization that comes about through social interaction. We need to ask continuously, what is it that the students are learning in the classroom setting as they progress through the academic year?

### Notes to Chapter 10

1. I would like to thank Elizabeth B. Bernhardt of the Ohio State University and Judith L. Shrum of Virginia Polytechnic Institute and State University for comments and editorial remarks on earlier drafts of this paper.
2. Step one of the analysis involves the development of detailed transcriptions of the instructional talk, including paralinguistic information concerning student–teacher interactions. Step two requires the construction of detailed 'maps' of the lesson structure. Although the construction of these maps requires both linguistic and paralinguistic features, maps based on the talk during this lesson were limited. None the less, the maps are the raw data for analysis. Step three requires the systematic exploration of the maps for recurring patterns of linguistic and paralinguistic events. The investigation of the maps allows for the identification of patterns of behaviour that become developed and maintained over time. Once the patterns of interest are identified, the maps are reanalysed for their occurrence both within and across lessons.

## Appendix 10.1: Theoretical propositions underlying studies of teaching from a social interaction perspective

### Classrooms are communicative environments

Differentiation of roles exist between teachers and students
Relationships between teachers and students are asymmetrical
Differential perceptions of events exist between teachers and students
Classrooms are differentiated communicative environments
Lessons are differentiated communicative contexts
Communicative participation affects student achievement

### Contexts are constructed during interactions

Activities have participation structures
Contextualization cues signal meaning
Rules for participation are implicit
Behaviour expectations are constructed as part of interaction

**Meaning is context-specific**

All instances of a behaviour are not equal
Meaning is signalled verbally and non-verbally
Contexts constrain meaning
Meaning is determined by and extracted from observed sequences of behaviour
Communicative competence is reflected in appropriate behaviour

**Inferencing is required for conversational comprehension**

Frames of reference guide participation
Frame clashes result from differences in perception
Communication is a rule-governed activity
Frames of reference are developed over time
Form and function in speech used in conversation do not always match

**Teachers orchestrate different participation levels**

Teachers evaluate student ability by observing performance during interactions
Demands for participation co-occur with academic demands
Teachers signal their theory of pedagogy by their behaviours
Teachers' goals can be inferred from behaviours

(Developed from Green, 1983a; 1983b; and Green & Weade, 1987)

# Appendix 10.2: Macro-structure of video-taped Spanish lesson

I.  **Numbers**

   a) what we're going to do
   b) 0–50 × tens
   c) 0–50 × ones
   d) 60–100 × tens
   e) 60–100 × ones
   f) 0–50 × ones
   g) 0–100 × tens

## II.   Work with adjectival opposites

  a) intro: What we're going to do
  b) how to do activity
  c) *bonita-fea*
  d) *tacaña-generosa*
  e) *rubia-morena*
  f) *gorda-flaca*
  g) *guapo-feo*
  h) *pobre-rico*

## III.   Adjectives: Describe pictures

  a) intro: What we're going to do
  b) 2 women (*mujeres*)
  c) 2 children
  d) famous couple
  e) grandmother
  f) man
  g) girl-model

## IV.   Describe President Reagan

## V.   Estar

  a) intro: What we're going to do
  b) *yo*
  c) *nosotros*
  d) *usted*
  e) *los señores*

## VI.   Estar: Questions with cue cards

  a) intro: What we're going to do
  b) park
  c) hotel
  d) theatre
  e) plaza
  f) restaurant
  g) movies
  h) library
  i) department store

      j) museum
      k) bookstore
      l) church
      m) stadium
      n) hospital
      o) store
      p) bank

## VII. Simulated communication

      a) intro: What we're going to do
      b) review: *Cómo* vs *Qué es/son?*
      c) students in pairs

## VIII. Quiz

## IX. Dialogue practice

      a) intro: What we're going to do
      b) set stage
      c) acting out dialogue
      d) questions to students
      e) students repeating
      f) comprehension questions in English

# 11 On topic choice in oral proficiency assessment[1]

SUSAN CAMERON BACON

*University of Cincinnati, Ohio, USA*

Recent trends in foreign language (FL) education have highlighted the need to define and describe effective oral communication. The *ACTFL Proficiency Guidelines*, for example, provide categories of information that an individual can be expected to understand and produce at each level of proficiency. These expectations, however, may not take into account previous research in factors that contribute to learning, and some categories of the ACTFL *Guidelines*, particularly at lower levels, do not account for differences in curriculum or, more importantly, differences in learner interest and experience.

Extensive research has supported the hypothesis that learning must be meaningful if it is to be subsumed into the learner's cognitive structure. Research also suggests that learning is greatly influenced by learner variables, especially a learner's previous knowledge, experience and interest (Ausubel *et al.*, 1978).

The *second* language literature of the past 20 years documents a subtle change from having communication as merely the goal of instruction to communication as the means of instruction (Acton, 1983). Although this statement appears to be a truism, the elements that contribute to the definition of 'communication' have been variously interpreted depending on the context in which the word is employed. For Hymes (1972: 277), it means knowing 'when to speak, when not, and . . . what to talk about with whom, when, where, [and] in what manner'. In the typical FL classroom, however, these decisions have been predetermined by the instructor and the curriculum. Even communication-orientated classrooms (e.g. Omaggio, 1984; Savignon, 1983) may fail to account for the many elements that contribute to effective oral communication. Guided oral composition, structured role-play, and even personalized questions produce rather predictable results within the constraints of the classroom.[2] As Rivers (1972) pointed out, when students leave the classroom and must perform, either in an oral proficiency test or in real life, the strategies they have developed often do not transfer. The individuals who have 'nothing' to talk about in the oral test may not have the tools they need to produce the language they are most anxious to produce. Whether this lack of preparation is because educators are unaware of students' interests, or unable to provide the necessary forum to allow students to express themselves, the fact remains that the goal of oral proficiency after a few college-level courses seems almost unattainable.

The present study sought to identify the relationship between what was judged to be effective communication, and other elements that accompanied the communication, that is, both the choice and development of topic. The research question which guided the study was the following: What is the relationship between individuals' previous experience and interest and the quantity and quality of speech produced during an oral interview?

## Population and Sample

The population consisted of undergraduate students who had completed between 90 and 100 hours' formal classroom instruction in Spanish at either the Ohio State University or the College of Wooster. At the time of the study, all students were enrolled in Spanish classes that used the same core materials and included oral testing as part of the regular curriculum. Permission to conduct the research in 24 classes at both institutions was granted by the respective administrators.

The sample consisted of 187 volunteers who expressed an interest in practising speaking Spanish. Each candidate was assigned a number in order to ensure anonymity. No grade or other incentive was given so that the sample would hopefully represent the population of students at the two institutions who were interested in learning to speak (as opposed to read or write) Spanish.

## Criteria

The following five variables were taken into consideration: quality of speech; quantity of speech; development of topic; proportion of structured versus unstructured topics; and the development of structured versus unstructured topics. Operational definitions are given below for each variable.

First, effective communication or *quality of speech* was defined as overall communicative effectiveness (Yorozuya & Oller, 1980), a global score assigned by two independent raters who judged a ten-minute speech sample of each candidate. (See Appendix 11.1 for the rating instrument.) The mean of the two scores comprised the score for the speech sample. The raters had been trained previously to listen to how well the candidate addressed each topic. Appropriate grammar, vocabulary, pronunciation and overall fluency were components of the criterion.[3] Inter-rater reliability was established at 0.845.

Second, the *quantity of speech* was considered an important aspect of the study and was defined as the total number of Spanish words produced during the 10-minute speech sample.[4] Fillers that are considered English words were not counted (e.g. 'umm'), but those considered Spanish were counted (e.g. *este*). Non-Spanish words that were pronounced with Spanish phonology were accepted only if the word had no reasonable translation (e.g. 'Cincinnati'). (See Appendix 11.2 for an analysis of two sample responses.) In examining quantity of speech produced, the question was whether or not the amount of speech had a significant relationship with the quality-of-speech rating.

Third, the *development of topic* was an analysis based on the quantity of speech produced. It was defined as the mean number of words produced in Spanish per topic. The higher the mean number of words, the greater the development of topic.

Fourth, the *proportion of structured* versus *unstructured* topics was also determined. A structured topic was defined as one that gave guidance in the way that the candidate could respond to it whereas an unstructured topic provided no such guidance. (See Appendix 11.3 for examples of topics used.) Since candidates were allowed to speak on original topics as well, those were recorded as unstructured.[5] The *proportion of structured topics* was defined as the total number of structured topics chosen by a candidate divided by the total number of topics chosen. The complement constituted the *proportion of unstructured topics*. These proportions were calculated in order to determine the relationship between topic choice and the quantity and quality of speech.

Fifth, the *development of structured* versus *unstructured topics* was determined. This was defined as the proportion of the total number of

TABLE 11.1 *Summary of criterion variables*

| | | |
|---|---|---|
| QUALITY of speech | = | Mean global score assigned by two independent raters |
| QUANTITY of speech | = | Total number of words produced in Spanish |
| DEVELOPMENT of topic | = | Mean number of words per topic |
| PROPORTION STRUCTURED versus UNSTRUCTURED topics | = | Total number of structured or unstructured topics/total number of topics |
| DEVELOPMENT of STRUCTURED versus UNSTRUCTURED topics | = | Total number of structured or unstructured words/structured or unstructured topics |

words that were produced in response to structured versus unstructured topics.

A summary of the criteria is provided in Table 11.1.

## Procedures

Each candidate scheduled a 20-minute appointment with the researcher. Each was read a prepared script explaining that the researcher was interested in how much Spanish he or she could produce in ten minutes. During the timed interval, the researcher would not provide any vocabulary or structures. Candidates were therefore encouraged to circumlocute if they were unable to think of a word. The topics, which reflected the curriculum of each institution, were printed in English on three-by-five index cards. English was used in order to avoid confounding the study by the listening or reading-comprehension factor. The cards were shuffled before each interview and candidates were allowed five minutes to read through them. They were told to choose any topics, including original ones, and speak as long as they wanted on each topic. All speech samples were audio-recorded for later analysis. After the test, each candidate was encouraged to continue practising speaking Spanish.

## Results

The *quality of speech* variable was determined as the average score assigned to each speech sample by the two independent raters. A 20% random sample of the tapes was rated a second time, which revealed an acceptable inter-rater reliability of 0.86 from the first to the second rating.

TABLE 11.2 *Ranges, means, and standard deviations of criterion variables*

|               | Range   | Mean  | S.D.   |
|---------------|---------|-------|--------|
| Quality       | 1.1–4.5 | 2.73  | 0.54   |
| Quantity      | 52–779  | 269.0 | 120.0  |
| Development   | 12–331  | 49.0  | 13.7   |
| Prop/Struc    | 0–1     | 0.52  | 0.22   |
| Prop/Unstr    | 0–1     | 0.48  | 0.21   |
| Develop/Struc | 0–648   | 48.5  | 41.01  |
| Develop/Unstr | 0–442   | 48.0  | 47.0   |

The *quantity of speech* variable, or total number of Spanish words produced in ten minutes, was collected by the researcher from the audio tape. The reliability of the count was established by a random recount of 5% of the tapes. The variation between count and recount was no more than 3% of the total number of words per tape.

The criterion variables, *development of topic, proportion of structured versus unstructured topics*, and the *development of structured versus unstructured topics*, were computed using an SAS sub-program on the IBM 3081 computer at the Ohio State University. The range, mean, and standard deviation for each criterion are reported in Table 11.2.

All criterion variables displayed wide variance. Even among a group that previously described itself as interested in learning how to speak Spanish, the contrast between the individuals who produced more and better Spanish and those who produced less and poorer Spanish is striking. Table 11.3 displays a significant positive correlation between the quality and quantity of speech; quality and development of topic; quality and proportion of unstructured topics; and quality and development of unstructured topics. The quantity variable significantly correlated with development of topic, proportion of unstructured topics, and development of unstructured topics. The development of topic, or mean number of words per topic, was positively correlated with the proportion of unstructured topics, and the development of unstructured topics. The proportion of unstructured topics was positively correlated with the development of unstructured topics. Candidates who received a higher rating, then, produced more words in Spanish, chose to speak on unstructured or original topics, and spoke longer on the unstructured or original topics.

The relationship between oral communication and unstructured topics is illustrated further in Table 11.4 and in Figure 11.1. The top 8%

TABLE 11.3 *Matrix of intercorrelations of criterion variables*

|   | 1 | 2 | 3 | 4 | 5 | 6 | 7 |
|---|---|---|---|---|---|---|---|
| 1 |   |   |   |   |   |   |   |
| 2 | 0.54*** |   |   |   |   |   |   |
| 3 | 0.30** | 0.52*** |   |   |   |   |   |
| 4 | −0.06 | −0.01 | −0.06 |   |   |   |   |
| 5 | 0.60*** | 0.31** | 0.51*** | −0.99[a] |   |   |   |
| 6 | −0.10 | 0.05 | −0.14 | −0.09 | −0.08 |   |   |
| 7 | 0.21** | 0.31*** | 0.73*** | −0.14 | 0.40*** | 0.10 |   |

$**p<0.01$   $***p<0.001$
1 Quality
2 Quantity
3 Development of topic
4 Proportion of structured topics
5 Proportion of unstructured topics
6 Development of structured topics
7 Development of unstructured topics

[a]The proportion of unstructured topics should be inversely related to the proportion of structured topics. The *r* reported here is less than 1.00 due to rounding error.

($n$ = 15) and bottom 8% ($n$ = 15), as judged by the independent raters, were compared according to the mean number of words per topic (development-of-topic variable), and the mean number of words per structured versus unstructured topic. The difference between the high and the low groups was significant not only in the development of topic variable, but also in the development of structured versus unstructured topic variables. Figure 11.1 illustrates a statistically significant ordinal interaction.

## Discussion

The significant interaction illustrated in Figure 11.1 suggests that those who are less proficient relied on structured rather than unstructured topics. The inverse is true of the high group, where analysis reveals that unstructured topics were developed more fully than the structured topics. Where it was hypothesized that students would profit from the structured topics in order to produce more language, it was found that the more able students preferred to structure the topics for themselves.[6]

TABLE 11.4 *Variance in the Development topic and the Development of Structured versus Unstructured topics*

| Sample | $n=30$ | |
|---|---|---|
| Total words/topic | $\bar{\chi}=46.6$ | |
| Words/structured topic | $\bar{\chi}=42.35$ | |
| Words/unstructured topic | $\bar{\chi}=50.64$ | |
| *Low Group* | $n=15$ | |
| Total words/topic | $\bar{\chi}=32.37$ | |
| Words/structured topic | $\bar{\chi}=39.48$ | $s=22.57$ |
| Words/unstructured topic | $\bar{\chi}=25.25$ | $s=14.49$ |
| *High Group* | $n=15$ | |
| Total words/topic | $\bar{\chi}=60.63$ | |
| Words/structured topic | $\bar{\chi}=45.22$ | $s=36.26$ |
| Words/unstructured topic | $\bar{\chi}=76.03$ | $s=47.09$ |

| | df | MS | F |
|---|---|---|---|
| Topic | 1 | 1,057 | 1 |
| High/Low | 1 | 12,018 | 11.32*** |
| Interaction | 1 | 7,566 | 7.12** |
| Error | 56 | 1,062 | |

**$p<0.01$        ***$p<0.001$

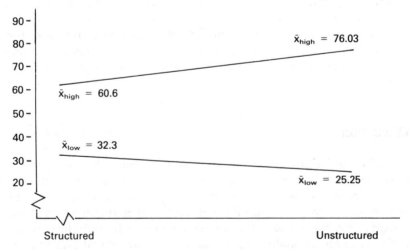

FIGURE 11.1 *Development of Structured versus Unstructured topics*

The difference in achievement may be due to the difference between those who considered the interview experience an opportunity to communicate new information and those who considered the interview simply another test (see Wildner-Bassett, this volume). Those who performed better may have discovered the communicative nature of language, whereas the low group mechanically plodded through each topic. Note the differences between the following examples.

Subject 1 is responding to the structured topic of how he spent summer vacations as a child. Twice he indicates his knowledge of the interview format; he acknowledges that the interviewer can not supply him with words and then abandons the topic with reference to the interview format.

> En el verano . . . en el verano, cuando joven . . . let's see. How do you say 'summer camp' Oh, O.K., you can't tell me any words. Hmm. En el verano cuando joven, nado y . . . con mis amigos, y duermo mucho, sí, duermo muy mucho . . . y, darn! Next card.
> [In the summer . . . in the summer, when young . . . let's see. How do you say 'summer camp' Oh, O.K., you can't tell me any words. Hmm. In the summer when young, I swim and . . . with my friends, and I sleep a lot, yes, I sleep very much . . . and, darn! Next card.]

Subject 2 is responding to the unstructured topic of what it would be like to be an animal for 24 hours. In contrast to the example above, when vocabulary became an issue, this subject circumlocutes. She does not refer to the interviewer's role nor does she abandon the topic by calling for the next card.

> Si tengo la oportunidad de ser un animal por veinticuatro horas, voy a ser un gato. Yo quiero un gato que me quiere mucho. Siempre quiere sentarse en mi . . . *lap*? uh, en mi . . . Cuando estoy sentada siempre quiere estar conmigo. Le gusta comer de la mesa y por eso es muy gordo. Lo llamo Puff. Creo que . . . weighs . . . Creo que tiene más de veinte 'pounds', kilos, no, diez kilos. Quiero ser un gato porque los gatos reciben mucha atención y cariño de sus . . . de su familia.
> [If I have the opportunity to be an animal for twenty-four hours, I am going to be a cat. I want a cat that loves me a lot. He always wants to sit on my . . . lap? uh, on my . . . When I sit he always wants to be with me. He likes to eat from the table and therefore is very fat. I call him Puff. I think . . . weighs . . . I think he is more than twenty 'pounds', kilos, no, ten kilos. I want to be a cat

because cats get a lot of attention and affection from their . . . from their family.]

These findings also suggest that the beginning-level classroom may not be providing students with enough opportunity to express themselves in a communicative way, or to develop a topic beyond a simple, albeit complete, sentence. Whether oral communication is a question of verbal ability or second-language ability, students must be given an opportunity to develop topics that are meaningful to themselves.

The data also have implications for oral proficiency testing. The topics that were given to the students represented those found in the usual elementary FL curriculum. These topics also closely resemble the novice-level description of the *ACTFL Proficiency Guidelines* for speaking. The fact that the more proficient candidates abandoned the structured topics suggests that the interviewer may not be able to predict areas of strength in every candidate. Whereas the *Guidelines* suggest that oral proficiency is not context-bound, the data in this study suggest that the context, or previous knowledge, is of prime importance in effective communication.

## Conclusions

The present study supports previous research that concludes that the learner's background knowledge and previous experience have an important role in an individual's learning and performance. As a descriptive study, however, it shows only the *relationship* between effective oral communication and choice of topic and not the *causes* of effective communication. Since the individual's experience and choice of topic appear so closely related to effective communication, students must be encouraged to express themselves in an extended way on subjects that are of interest to them. In assessing oral proficiency via an oral interview, the interviewer must allow candidates to express themselves, while at the same time avoiding prescribing the level of proficiency from a list of predetermined or expected behaviours at each level.

## Notes to Chapter 11

1. Data for this paper were collected under the direction of Professor Gilbert A. Jarvis of the Ohio State University as part of the author's doctoral dissertation (Bacon, 1985).
2. The following examples illustrate how teachers and testers may forget the

communicative purpose of language: (1) Candidates in the ACTFL/ETS oral interview are advised to respond in an appropriate, though not necessarily truthful, manner; (2) Ethnographic data collected by J. Welch at the Ohio State University suggest that the instructor's perception of the length of time that it takes a student to respond is longer than the 3–4 seconds that actually pass (personal communication). Teachers appear to dread the silence that a student may need to respond, not only in an appropriate way, but also in a truthful way.

3. Because of the nature of the data collection (audio tape rather than video tape), non-verbal aspects of effective communication were not considered.
4. A word was defined as a 'speech sound or series of them, serving to communicate meaning and consisting of one base morpheme with or without prefixes but with a superfix' (*Webster's New World Dictionary*, 2nd College edn. New York: The New York World Publishing Company, 1970).
5. The topics were validated as structured or unstructured by 17 senior or graduate-level students enrolled in a foreign language methods course at Ohio State University. In order to accept a topic for use in the study, at least 80% of those raters had to agree that the topic was indeed structured or unstructured. It was expected that the structured topics would help students in producing more, if not better speech per topic.
6. Since the sample represented a large number of classes with a similar curriculum, the effect of intact classes should not have been a factor in the differences in achievement.

## Appendix 11.1: Scale for Rating Speech Samples

At the extremes of the scale a candidate may be rated as communicating effectively (5) or failing to communicate (1). When evaluating the response to a topic, consider the following:

The subject communicates effectively on this topic:

| 1 | 2 | 3 | 4 | 5 |
|---|---|---|---|---|
| Not at all | Minimally | Sometimes | Often | Usually |

## Appendix 11.2: Sample Responses

The following response to Topic 2 received ratings of 1.70 and 1.60 from the independent raters.

Word count: 25

8   En el verano . . . en el verano, cuando joven . . .let's see
0   How do you say 'summer camp' Oh, ok, you can't tell me
7   any words. Hmm. En el verano cuando joven, nado y
10  . . . con mis amigos, y duermo mucho, sí, duermo muy mucho
    . . . y, darn! Next card.

The following response to Topic 15 received ratings of 4.6 and 4.7
from the independent raters.

Word count: 80

9   Si tengo la oportunidad de ser un animal por
10  veinticuatro horas, voy a ser un gato. Yo quiero un
9   gato que me quiere mucho. Siempre quiere sentarse en
7   mi . . . *lap?* uh, en mi . . . Cuando estoy sentada siempre
10  quiere estar conmigo. Le gusta comer de la mesa y por
8   eso es muy gordo. Lo llamo Puff. Creo que . . .
7   weighs . . . Creo que tiene más de veinte 'pounds', kilos,
10  no, diez kilos. Quiero ser un gato porque los gatos
9   reciben mucha atención y cariño de sus . . . de su
1   familia.

## Appendix 11.3: Sample Topics

*Structured topics*
Topic 2   When you were young, how did you spend your summer
          vacations?
          Swimming?
          Sleeping?
          Playing with friends?
          Attending summer school?
          Reading?
Topic 5   What time did you go to bed last night?
          Did you fall asleep immediately?
          How long did you sleep?
          Did you dream?
          When did you wake up?
          Were you tired this morning?
*Unstructured topics*
Topic 21 You were on your way to class one day and . . .
Topic 15 You have the opportunity to be an animal for 24 hours . . .

# Part III:
# From Research and Theory to Practice

In this section, we turn our attention to specific instances of how second language (L2) research impacts on language teaching and curriculum development. The papers gathered in this section do not present formulas for day-to-day teacher–student interactions. Instead, the authors each discuss broader perspectives on what language teaching might look like. Rather than seek a particular methodology or set of techniques from second language research, these papers show that the real impact of language acquisition research is on approaches to and philosophies of classroom teaching.

Savignon's paper was one of the original keynotes of the SLA/FLL conference and we open Part III with it. Charged with addressing the question, 'Is SLA research relevant to foreign language teaching?' Savignon responds with a resounding 'yes' and mentions the impact of specific research trends, e.g. error analysis as opposed to contrastive analysis. More importantly, she demonstrates through her criticism of proficiency guidelines how an ignorance of second language research and an impatience with theory has led some FL professionals into solutions founded on shaky premises and false assumptions, or, as she states, to 'accept simple solutions to complex problems'. The papers that follow are characterized by a knowledge of the research and a respect for the contribution of theory to practice.

Nattinger demonstrates how L2 research can have a specific impact on teaching, namely, the *what* of a curriculum. Arguing against linguistic rules as a basis for syllabus construction, Nattinger calls for a curriculum based on the research findings of the importance of routines and patterns in SLA. He notes that routines and patterns play two important roles in language learning. First, they serve as an important means by which learners can interact with others in the L2. Second, they serve as the 'meat' of acquisition, being subject to subsequent segmentation by the language processing mechanism of the learner. The reader will want to pay close attention to the procedural aspects of the curriculum that Nattinger outlines, however, in order to assess the methodology used.

Kiraly delves into an often ignored realm of language teaching: translator training. Like Nattinger, he argues that the development of translator skills cannot derive solely from the day-to-day practice of mechanical classroom exercises based on language rules. Calling on Krashen's acquisition–learning distinction, and the expanded definition of language found in L2 communicative competence, Kiraly critically examines current translation programmes and then outlines what he envisions as the core to a programme in translation. The result is a view of the translator as a 'co-creator' of the L2 written text. Imbued with communicative competence derived from a rich acquisitional environment, Kiraly's translator-learner may be able to avoid the pitfalls of word-for-word translation so often documented in the media.

Shifting our attention away from adult language acquisition to examine foreign language learning in childhood, Schinke-Llano asks whether or not FLL can be like SLA. However, her definitions of SLA and FLL are product-orientated rather than process-orientated, i.e. SLA results in more native-like language abilities, FLL less so. In asking the question, Schinke-Llano's bias is clear; that SLA is qualitatively superior to FLL. She proceeds to argue for immersion as the best language acquisition environment for children, but reminds us that immersion courses still do not produce the kind of native-like speakers we would hope. She counters, however, that effective research on classroom interactional patterns will help reveal the weaknesses in immersion courses such that adjustments can be made which will foster more successful language acquisition in the classroom.

The next paper in this section at first seems out of place. Concerned with how minority languages are treated by American 'language policy', Campbell & Lindholm explore the efficacy of bilingual immersion courses. The stated goals of such courses are to provide for the development of English language skills while at the same time providing a means by which the L1 minority language skills can be developed. Finding preliminary positive evidence for such courses, Campbell & Lindholm believe that such programs are a crucial step toward solving what has been termed the 'resource deficit' in FL abilities in the United States and that SLA researchers should turn their attention more to the population of learners on these courses. Different from Nattinger, Kiraly and Schinke-Llano who view SLA research as impacting on curriculum development, Campbell & Lindholm see a particular curriculum as a challenge to SLA research. More importantly, however, Campbell & Lindholm's focus on minority language students brings us full circle to Berns' comments on the contexts of language learning. In the United States a population exists which, if allowed to develop full bilingual abilities as described by Campbell & Lindholm, would be important *foreign* language resources for this country. What, then, is a foreign language in the United States? As Berns points out, there is a continuum of possibilities.

# 12 In second language acquisition/foreign language learning, nothing is more practical than a good theory

SANDRA J. SAVIGNON

*University of Illinois at Urbana-Champaign, USA*

## Introduction

In addressing the relationship between the fields of second language acquisition (SLA) and foreign language learning (FLL), three fundamental questions come to mind from the foreign language learning perspective. How does the foreign language (FL) profession benefit from SLA research? What impact can/does FLL research have on SL perspectives? Is FL classroom learning similar to or different from non-classroom learning?

Of course the FL profession benefits from SLA research. Discussions of classroom teaching increasingly include reference to data on learner strategies and the nature of learner language. And error analysis has replaced contrastive analysis as the perspective from which to make judgements regarding learner difficulties. Teachers today look to research, both inside and outside the classroom, for insights regarding their role in the language learning process.

Conversely, classroom learning brings a needed dimension to SLA research. Whether in immersion, intensive, or more conventional core academic courses, whether in host (i.e. L2), bilingual, or primary language

(L1) environments, classrooms constitute contexts of learning the world over. As such, they present a challenge to the SLA researcher. A comprehensive theory of second language learning is one that will account for individual and group differences in rate and outcome of learning, regardless of where it occurs. No easy task, to be sure, and one that has intrigued scholars and philosophers for centuries.

Granted, not everyone holds this view. Not all so-called 'foreign' language teachers are interested in SLA research findings. Some see the classroom as so different from what have been termed 'natural' learning environments that they are reluctant to consider findings related to the latter. Rather than seek ways to manage classroom learning environments to make them more conducive to L2 acquisition, they shut the door, so to speak, on acquisition data. In so doing, they often shun theory—be it linguistic, sociolinguistic, psycholinguistic, psychometric—in favour of what they see as more 'practical' matters. In place of theory, or research data to support their claims as to what 'works' in language teaching and evaluation, they appeal to logic and/or experience, that is to say, tradition. 'Experientially-based' is the term they sometimes use to suggest that a practice is valid.

To give an example, in his book, *An Integrated Theory of Language Teaching*, subtitled *and Its Practical Consequences*, Hammerly (1985: 15) has the following to say:

> One condition absolutely essential to natural language acquisition, being surrounded by, and constantly interacting with, native speakers, will never exist in second language classrooms. The impossibility of recreating natural language conditions in the classroom means that any claims to success by naturalistic methods should be viewed with great caution.

He goes on to advocate a surface structure to meaning, or 'skill-getting to skill-using', sequence in language teaching, justifying his stance with 'It seems only logical that a language form should come under some degree of control before it is used' (Hammerly, 1985: 25).

## Impatience with Theory

While SLA research has brought new interest in teaching materials and methodologies to many in the FL profession, still others, impatient with efforts to define constructs, to elaborate theories, and to build a research base, seem ready to accept simple solutions to complex problems.

The current debate within the American FL profession regarding the appropriateness of the *Proficiency Guidelines* being promoted by the American Council on the Teaching of Foreign Languages (ACTFL, 1986) is a case in point.

At conferences held recently in Dallas (ACTFL/American Association for Applied Linguistics co-sponsored workshop on the ACTFL Proficiency Guidelines, 24 November 1986) and in Bloomington, Indiana (Indiana University Symposium on the Evaluation of Foreign Language Proficiency, 4–6 March 1987), discussion focused on the need to define communicative competence and to demonstrate the construct validity of tests that purport to measure communicative language ability (Savignon, 1985; Bachman & Savignon, 1986).

The inadequacy of ACTFL (1986) as a basis for methods and materials development has been signalled repeatedly (e.g. Savignon, 1985; Bernhardt, 1986; Lantolf & Frawley, 1986; VanPatten, 1986b; Lange, 1987; Lee, 1987b; and Lee & Musumeci, 1988). Kramsch (1986: 367) has summarized the inappropriateness of their neo-behaviouristic perspective for American school courses:

> The oversimplified view on human interactions taken by the proficiency movement can impair and even prevent the attainment of true interactional competence within a cross-cultural framework and jeopardize our chances of contributing to international understanding. The suggested proficiency-oriented ACTFL/ETS goals differ from interactional goals on three accounts: (1) they focus on behavioral functions rather than on conceptual notional development; (2) they have a static rather than dynamic view of content; (3) they emphasize accuracy to the detriment of discourse aptitude.

Yet ACTFL (1986) continues to be promoted by its publishers as a universally valid measure of L2 ability:

> The 1986 proficiency guidelines represent a hierarchy of global characterizations of integrated performance in speaking, listening, reading, and writing. . . each level subsumes all previous levels, moving from simple to complex in an 'all-before-and more' fashion.
>
> Because these guidelines identify stages of proficiency, as opposed to achievement, they are not intended to measure what an individual has achieved through specific classroom instruction but rather to allow assessment of what an individual can and cannot do,

*regardless of where, when, or how the language has been learned or acquired* (ACTFL, 1986, emphasis added).

The accompanying claim that the guidelines are 'not based on a particular linguistic theory or pedagogical method', is clearly misleading; and persons who have been involved in writing the guidelines are indeed prescribing methods and materials for 'proficiency', e.g. Omaggio (1986).

Another example of an apparent impatience for theory and research within the FL profession can be seen in the current promotion of an equally neo-behaviourist claim: the early encouragement of communication without strict 'error correction'—that is, consistent teacher highlighting of differences between learner language and a selected adult native norm—results in the formation of undesirable and permanent L2 'habits'. Among the terms used to characterize the end result of this undocumented phenomenon are 'fossilization', 'pidginization', and a 'terminal 2 profile'. The term 'undocumented' seems warranted because, in fact, there is no research evidence to support the purported link between teacher correction practice and formal features of learner language. Debate on this issue has become so heated, however, that the claims being made merit more careful examination.

Since no one would presumably wish on another the fate of a terminal anything, much less a 'terminal 2', and since classroom teachers are understandably concerned about the futures of their students, the spectre of 'terminal 2' is indeed a frightening one. The reference most frequently given by those who wish to emphasize morpho-syntactic 'accuracy'—that is, adult native sentence-level grammar—in the oral expression of beginning L2 learners is Higgs & Clifford (1982). (For examples of such references, see VanPatten, in press b.) The following observations by Higgs & Clifford (1982: 57–68) are often cited:

> The most recent buzz word to hypnotize the profession. . . is communicative competence. . . [There is] the widespread impression that communicative competence is a term for communication in spite of language, rather than communication through language. As a result, the role of grammatical precision has been downplayed, particularly by some who carry the banner of communicative competence.
>
> With an eye to identifying terminal 2's and otherwise analyzing the constituent component of student's language abilities, the CIA Language School has developed the Performance Profile reporting form. . . The explanation for the terminal profiles appears to lie in

what cognitive psychology calls proactive interference, in which the prior learning of task A interferes with the current learning of task B.

. . .

If proactive interference underlies the learning disabilities of the terminal 1+ and 2+ students, then there should be identifiable features in the background of each that inhibit their continued language development. Fossilized or terminal language development has been found to be the most commonly shared feature in the language-learning of these students. . . The terminal cases whose foreign language background had included only an academic environment all came from language programs that either were taught by instructors who themselves had not attained grammatical mastery of the target language—and hence were unable to guide their students into correct usage—or by instructors who had chosen not to correct their students' mistakes for philosophical, methodological, or personal reasons.

The authors' failure to offer rigorous experimental data in support of claims that have appeared in a major foreign language publication has not gone unnoticed. In an autumn 1986 graduate seminar on the psycholinguistic foundations of L2 teaching, my students and I looked at this and other reports related to claims bearing on teacher error-correction and the development of learner language ability. What follow are excerpts from assessments by two participants that together rather effectively summarize our conclusions:

(1) Higgs and Clifford inextricably tangle the data, pseudo-data and forensic language meant in support of their arguments about structure and grammar in FL teaching. I will try to sort the lot into main categories of anecdotal opinion and hearsay, citation and quotation, and formal data from review and experiments. . . Is an opinion a datum? Higgs and Clifford assert that their anecdotes and reflections, based on their 'vast experience', constitute 'experiential. . .data'. Such data are in nature unquantifiable and unverifiable. As used here they are also fanciful. . . From them are formed aggregate battalions such as 'most of us', 'the profession at large', 'we and our student clients', 'the typical university-level foreign language major,' which are marshalled against battalions of 'those who would carry the banner of communicative competence'.

(2) Higgs and Clifford seem to have come to the conclusion that the phenomenon of the 'terminal 2' can be directly attributed to

(i.e. blamed on) those who 'carry the banner of communicative competence'. The authors have concluded that the communicative approach has 'an early emphasis on unstructured communicative activities—minimizing or excluding entirely, considerations of grammatical accuracy' (1982: 73) and that its 'undesirable side effect' is irreversible fossilization. Thus it is hypothesized that the problem, as they see it, can be remedied by early and intense emphasis on grammatical accuracy—the 'accuracy-first' approach.

What are the data on which these findings are reported? Let's see. . . we have 'the data', and 'data reported elsewhere in the literature'; and we have lots of experience: 'vast experience', 'practical experience', 'experience in government language schools', and the authors' 'encounters' and 'more than passing acquaintances'. Let us not forget the ever-impressive evidence cited by the authors: 'evidence suggests', and 'evidence abounds'. In short, Higgs and Clifford base their arguments primarily on experiential data. Were I to submit an academic paper full of as many unsubstantiated claims, I would most certainly be laughed out of graduate school. Such a report would never be tolerated, let alone taken seriously enough to serve as a major source of support for a movement in second and foreign language teaching. The obvious question is why has this report been taken so seriously, given its numerous oversights, shortcomings, and sweeping generalizations?

Why indeed? And yet this report currently provides the major support for claims regarding methodological focus, including error-correction policy, in so-called 'proficiency-orientated' methods and materials (e.g. Omaggio, 1986). The attendent disregard for scholarship does much to undermine efforts to encourage dispassionate consideration of SLA research data. Rather, it promotes a persistent parochialism with the foreign language teaching profession that leaves it prey to what Maley (1984), in an affectionate spoof of language teaching ideologies, has called '"I got religion"—Evangelism in second language teaching'! Methods are promoted, their virtues extolled, with a fervour that discourages critical examination, or even explanation. One is asked simply to believe.

## Responsible Theory-Building

But such is by no means the whole story of the SLA/FLL issue. On a much more positive note, there are many widespread efforts today to modify and expand existing courses to make them more reflective of current L2 learning theory. To cite examples from only North America, there are established immersion courses in Canada and the United States (Stern, 1984a; Anderson & Rhodes, 1984). The State of New York recently has mandated L2 experience for all learners, not only the college-bound. State curricula have been revised to emphasize functional goals accessible to all learners, with appropriate changes in teaching methodology. Even in college and university FL departments, bastions of tradition when it comes to language teaching, reassessment of goals, diversification of offerings, and increased student participation in study-abroad programmes have led in some cases to more communicatively orientated teaching (see, for example, Freed, 1984).

Within the American FL profession, hopes are presently high for the National Foreign Language Center, to be established on the campus of the Johns Hopkins University School of Advanced International Studies, Washington, DC. In his statement of goals for the proposed Center, Lambert (1987) includes the development of prototypical teaching and learning systems that would integrate classroom and informal learning; prepared and authentic source materials for both overseas and domestic instruction; and intensive and non-intensive courses of study. The proposal includes plans for establishing a 'number of experimental classrooms and other research settings to evaluate the effectiveness of the new procedures and materials' (Lambert, 1987: 4–5). Throughout his proposal, Lambert (1987: 2) stresses the need for cumulative empirical research in foreign language teaching methodologies. There is a

> surprisingly weak tradition of empiricism in the search for what works and what does not work. In place of solidly grounded practice, we have wildly exaggerated claims for one or another way to teach a foreign language. In place of theory linked firmly to applied study, we have staunchly asserted opinions on how students learn. In place of carefully formulated relationships among practice, theory, research, and curriculum and materials development, we have teachers, theorists, researchers, and pedagogues each going their separate way.

Researchers, for their part, are looking increasingly at the classroom as a language learning environment; and responsible methodologies are careful not to make sweeping claims based on limited data. Thanks to the longitudinal data that have been collected in Canadian immersion courses, we now have a better understanding of the nature of learner classroom L2 interaction in that particular setting and of the communicative ability that develops. This interaction is seen in the broad context of communicative competence, in terms not only of sentence-level morphosyntactic features, i.e. grammatical competence, but in terms of sociolinguistic, discourse and strategic competence (Lapkin & Swain, 1984; Stern, 1984b). Through the work of Breen & Candlin (1980), Long (1983a), Felix (1981), Krashen (1982), Lightbown (1983), Beretta (1987), and others, we are gaining a better understanding of what goes on in immersion and other classroom learning environments and how they can be modified in the interest of promoting SLA. A new collection of research papers devoted exclusively to classroom FL learning (VanPatten *et al.*, 1987), the first such volume published in the United States, to my knowledge, marks perhaps best of all the coming of age of FL classroom learning as a worthy research focus.

Some of the earliest classroom FL research was conducted on the University of Illinois campus (Savignon, 1971). The now well-known study of adult acquisition of French as a second language focused on the distinction between grammatical competence and a much broader communicative competence, assessing the value for adult learners of an opportunity to use French for communication from the very beginning of their study. The results have been widely cited and have become part of an ever-widening research effort directed at defining and promoting the development of communicative competence (see also Savignon, 1983; Savignon & Berns, 1984; 1987).

One of the first references to this research data appeared in a paper by a widely respected FL methodologist, Wilga Rivers (1972). The gist of her remarks was consonant with experimental findings, namely that learners who are not encouraged to go beyond repetition of memorized phrases, to take communicative risks, may never develop the negotiation skills necessary for L2 competence.

At the time, this appeared a startling revision of prevailing language learning theory, which cautioned against early learner self-expression. The fact, however, that Rivers found support for her revised views in classroom research data provided an example that other responsible methodologists would follow: recommendations for improving classroom learning are best based, not on extrapolations from linguistic or psychological theory, but on systematic observation of classroom learners. The significance of this example for the FL profession becomes clear when we recall that just a few years earlier we were giving almost unanimous support to the promotion of a language teaching method with no basis whatsoever in observed language learner behaviour. Nelson Brooks (1966: 359) himself has acknowledged that acceptance of audiolingual theory required by and large 'an act of faith; research to prove the validity of its basic principles is scanty'.

In the intervening years a new research perspective has developed. To meet its demands, a new generation of FL researchers and methodologists has pursued advanced study that includes not only 'foreign' language and culture, but the linguistic, social and psychometric concepts related to language and language learning. They do so often with great difficulty. To understand the effort this involves, one has only to compare the master-level courses of graduate students in ESL with those in FL courses. While the former emphasize theory and research, courses in psycholinguistics, psychometrics and SLA must compete in the latter with required advanced-level courses in literature and civilization. Moreover, the multidisciplinary nature of these courses, while intellectually challenging, often places upon the degree candidates the additional burden of course co-ordination.

Support for research-orientated programmes in FL learning/teaching is increasing, however. Our University of Illinois multidisciplinary Second Language Acquisition and Teacher Education (SLATE) doctoral programme, for example, has brought together teachers, methodologists and researchers from departments of Spanish, Italian, and Portuguese, French, English as an International Language, Linguistics, Psychology, and the College of Education. Graduates of this and similar courses now occupy positions of responsibility for FL and ESL language course direction at major research institutions (Teschner, 1987).

Opportunities for publishing research findings are also increasing. In addition to the major journals of applied linguistics, several language-specific journals now include discussions of SLA theory and research findings, e.g. *Unterrichtspraxis* and *Hispania*. Most important, perhaps, FL departments around the country advertise openings for methodologists with a research interest in SLA. Conferences such as the one held recently at the University of Illinois (SLA/FLL: On the Relationship between Second Language Acquisition and Foreign Language Learning, 3–4 April 1987), moreover, are further evidence of the support within the FL profession for SLA research. The support is welcome, for the research agenda is challenging.

## Nothing is More Practical than a Good Theory

While the field of SLA research is expanding, classroom learning has not been a significant focus of this research. To illustrate, Chaudron

(1986) reports that of all the articles published in two major applied linguistics journals during a seven-year period, fewer than 7% involved either qualitative or quantitative measures of classroom learning. A major barrier in such research, he points out, is the lack of well-defined classroom processes to serve as variables. Both qualitative and quantitative approaches are needed to identify and describe classroom processes; relate these processes to learning outcomes; and discover the nature of the relationships that are revealed.

Failure adequately to identify and describe classroom teaching methods was a major weakness of the methods comparison studies conducted in the 1960s, e.g. the Colorado Project (Scherer & Wertheimer, 1964), and the Pennsylvania Project (Smith, 1970). The blurring of distinctions in classroom practice has been cited as a contributing cause in the outcome of 'no significant difference' between audiolingual and cognitive code methods.

More recently, analysis of classroom processes has taken two related and complementary perspectives. The first of these is that of social patterns of participation, or interactional analysis, following Flanders (1970) and Cazden et al. (1972). The second perspective is that of discourse analysis, teacher talk, and the nature of linguistic input, e.g. Allwright (1980), Gaies (1977), Wells (1981) and Guthrie (1984). But for each of these perspectives, the development and validation of adequate descriptive models of classroom processes are far from complete.

Another major barrier to discovering relationships between classroom processes and learning outcomes is the lack of agreement on what constitutes learning 'success'. The large-scale Pennsylvania Project (Smith, 1970) included no measures of communicative competence. In some of the early Gardner & Lambert (1972) studies of attitudinal variables in classroom language learning, final grades in French literature courses served as achievement criteria. More recently, Hammerly (1985) has termed the Canadian French immersion courses 'a linguistic failure', citing non-native morphosyntactic features of learner language. Stern (1984b), on the other hand, looking at the academic achievement *cum* functional L2 competence of immersion students, has called the course 'highly successful' and Krashen (1984: 61) has termed it '[perhaps] the most successful programme ever recorded in the language teaching literature'. To look at yet another indication of success, community support for immersion has shown impressive growth. About 165,000 Canadian students are currently enrolled in French immersion alternatives, and the number is increasing by about 20% per year (Canadian Parents for French, 1986).

That the majority of these children are no longer the high achievers once typical of such courses reflects their parents' view that immersion is a viable educational alternative for *all* learners, not just the academically talented (Wiss, 1987).

In his evaluation of the activity- or task-orientated Bangalore Communicational Teaching Project (CTP) in South India, Beretta (1987: 93–94) summarizes the quandary he faced in assessing learning outcomes:

> A search through the literature reveals that basically three procedures are used by evaluators in a bid to make their instruments program-fair: (1) a standardized test (2) a specific test for each program and (3) a test of common-unique elements. The appeal to standardized tests is based on their supposed neutrality, or their independence of either program. Their principal shortcoming lies in their considerable potential for insensitivity. Standardized tests are likely to be unresponsive to features of either program, and consequently, to contribute to an outcome of no difference. 'No difference' on a standardized test may quite simply mean that distinct program characteristics have been obscured. On the other hand, specific tests for each program reflect their particular contents and objectives, but preclude direct comparison. The alternative is to identify common areas of content or common objectives, or both, in competing programs and to test these elements proportionately with elements that are unique to each program. Difficulties arise here when there is little apparent commonality.
>
> . . .
>
> All pupils taking part in the evaluation [of communicational and structural methods] were at fairly elementary stages of language study. Pupils taught by the structural method are expected to achieve mastery of a limited set of structures prescribed by the syllabus for each year. Students in communicational programs are not expected to achieve mastery level until, presumably, nature has taken its course, a process that must extend beyond the elementary level. A conventional grammar test measures attainment or nonattainment of mastery. That is to say, it measures a prescribed quota of structures at the level of a fully formed competence. The CTP makes no claim of uniformity concerning which structures will be assimilated or what stage of development learners will have attained at each level. Therefore, at an elementary level, to compare both groups on a conventional grammar test would be perverse. It would mean counting the CTP chickens before they have hatched.

On the other hand, if the evaluation were taking place with advanced level students, then the notion of mastery would be applicable to both groups, because by that stage payoff in such terms could be plausibly demanded. Otherwise, 'incubation' would have to be dismissed as a luxury schools cannot afford.

Learning success must be viewed in a broad framework that takes into account the nature of communicative competence. Much has been written about the importance of a sociolinguistic perspective in developing L2 teaching methods and materials. Interest in communicative competence and in communicative language teaching as a means to that goal has been strengthened by the understanding of language and language behaviour that comes from sociolinguistic research, research with which we associate the terms *varieties, use, norms, appropriacy*. Judging from current methods and materials, however, the message has yet to reach the wider American FL profession. Communication is talked about, but most often as something learners 'practise' after grammatical structures have been presented and drilled.

Goodlad (1984: 27) offers a broader perspective on what is going on in American FL classrooms:

> Tests at both [junior and senior high school] levels stressed recall of specific information—for example, memorized grammatical rules in the junior highs and word and phrase recognition in both groups of schools. At the senior high level, there was considerable stress on technical mastery as demonstrated in short-answer tests and in taking dictation in the foreign language or translating from one language to another. Tests rarely called for writing original paragraphs or short essays.

Berns (1987) has eloquently summarized the relevance of sociolinguistic insight for language teaching, echoing many of the concerns highlighted by Kramsch (cited above). We need

> to promote teaching that is communication oriented in practice and well grounded in theory. A sound basis for language teaching needs to be developed, troublesome shortcomings in existing frameworks for communicative language teaching need to be dealt with, and language teaching in general needs to reflect the realities of language use. In short, language teaching needs the sociolinguist.

## Conclusion

I return to the questions posed at the outset of this paper. Yes, the FL profession can and has benefited from SLA research. Much evidence attests to the awakened interest of FL teachers/researchers in SLA research. Many graduate teaching assistants on large-scale university FL courses today seek teacher *education* not training. They want to know the underlying theory behind the materials and methods they are being asked to use. And they want to know how that theory fits into a more general theory of SLA.

SLA research, on the other hand, cannot ignore the classroom learning context. Theories of SLA developed without serious reference to data from classroom settings provide inadequate explanation of the language acquisition process. Neglect of this context, characterized as it is by limited L2 exposure and interaction primarily with other non-native L2 speakers, would be detrimental to further theory development. Yes, classroom contexts *are* different from other learning environments; and they constitute the most important, if not the sole, L2 access for countless learners. If the goal of classroom learning is, in fact, some measure of communicative competence, then good theory-building is the route to good teaching practice.

There will remain those who disparage research. Frustrated by our inability to date to offer more than a general perspective on the language acquisition process, they call for practical solutions to immediate instructional and curricular problems. Tentative responses to immediate needs are fine, but they should not be viewed as solutions in and of themselves. Respect for a discipline must be earned through careful research, reporting of findings, and reasoned discussion of the implications. Above all, in the absence of compelling evidence, the temptation to make recommendations for classroom teaching must be resisted. When recommendations appear warranted, they should be stated dispassionately, and any reservations clearly noted. Such is and always has been the rule of scientific inquiry. Circuitous though the route may be, in the end, nothing is more practical than a good theory.

# 13 Prefabricated speech for language learning

## JAMES R. NATTINGER

*Portland State University, Portland, USA*

Teachers usually turn to linguistic theory for grammars of what to teach in their language classes, but these grammars are not the best source for ideas for practical application in the classroom. Conventional grammars present language as either definitions of terms and lists of structures, as social prescriptions about what is 'correct' language form, or as descriptions of the abstract language system, which linguists term 'competence', stated in highly general and parsimonious terms. The first two kinds of grammar have already lost much of their former appeal; ever since the waning of audiolingualism and prescriptivism, teachers no longer feel it effective to teach language as simply an arrangement of 'meaningless' parts, nor do they feel it serves their purpose to teach only to external measures of correctness. The third sort of grammar, though, remains a powerful influence and continues to shape classroom activity. Many feel that the subject of language teaching is indeed this abstract language 'competence', or at least some notion of 'formal correctness', and they look to theoretical grammars of linguistic competence for ideas about what to teach. However, the goal of language teaching is not to teach abstract rules of competence, but to get students to comprehend and produce language successfully and meaningfully. To limit teaching to the underlying system of a language is no guarantee that students will learn to do that. The precise relationship between the theoretical competence of an idealized speaker-hearer and the actual language performance of a specific human being is a highly tenuous matter, as any linguist will admit. For these reasons, it would be better for teachers to look towards theories of language use, at descriptions of language performance rather than those of language competence, for more immediately re..vant ideas about how best to present language in a classroom. It is more helpful to understand how language is actually used than how its underlying structure can be most efficiently described.

## Performance Grammars

Finding an appropriate performance grammar, however, presents its own difficulties. Most theoretical grammars, with their focus on competence, have little that is useful to tell teachers about language performance. In these theories, performance consists mainly of the residue that has not been amenable to linguistic investigations of competence, and it thus becomes a category invoked mainly to be dismissed. One must turn to psycholinguistics to find more positively wrought performance grammars. Even here, though, many grammars do not treat performance autonomously but explore it only as it correlates with competence. For example, these grammars concern very general, abstract rules of psychological processing that operate, as competence does, independently of any context. They also describe universals of psychological processing to match the search for universals of competence, and thus fail to investigate the possibility of cross-linguistic differences in performance. Both characteristics lessen the relevance of these grammars for teaching. What teachers need are performance grammars that describe how people actually comprehend and produce particular languages in particular situations.

Recent studies of language acquisition suggest an alternative. For some time, teachers have reviewed studies of language acquisition for ideas about what they might expect of their students in the classroom. The greater part of this research, following prevailing theory, has been designed to test notions of linguistic competence by establishing the extent to which a student's current performance is a correct or incorrect reflection of native speaker competence. More recently however, studies in language acquisition have pulled away from competence models and have begun to look at how language develops for use in social interaction. This research pays more attention to *how* something is learned rather than to *what* is learned, and thus examines the path to, rather than the goal of, language acquisition (Bickerton, 1983). Following that path can be illuminating for language teachers, for along the way we find common patterns among all types of language acquirers. It is this new direction in language acquisition research that currently offers the most help for language teachers, for it not only describes the ways people actually use language, but it also suggests ways that first, second *and* foreign language learning can be seen, and, in the last two cases, taught, as similar processes.


## Prefabricated Language

These current studies of language acquisition show that children pass through a stage in which they use a large number of unanalysed chunks of language in certain predictable social contexts; they use, in other words, a great deal of *prefabricated* language (Peters, 1983). Many early researchers thought these prefabricated chunks were distinct and somewhat peripheral to the main body of language, which they saw as the creative product of the systematic rules of competence (Brown, 1973; Clark, 1974). Others began to assign a more basic and creative role to these chunks, however. Hakuta, in a study of a Japanese child learning English, drew a distinction between prefabricated 'routines', which he described as 'unvarying chunks of language', and prefabricated 'patterns', which he described as 'segments of sentences which operate in conjunction with a moveable component, such as the insertion of a noun phrase or a verb phrase' (Hakuta, 1974: 284). He also suggested that these chunks were not isolated or peripheral to the creative rule-forming process, but in fact played a role in its development. Children seemed to use these chunks not only as memorized formulas but also as raw material for later segmentation and analysis in developing the rules of syntax. For example, children may initially use 'wannago' holophrastically as a memorized prefabricated routine in certain set situations, and then, after they become aware of similar phrases like 'wannaplay' and 'wannaget' in other contexts, they begin to analyse this phrase as a pattern with a moveable component, 'wanna + VP'. As children hear such moveable components in prefabricated patterns, they begin to analyse chunks into their separate pieces, and work their way to the actual rules of syntax. Wong-Fillmore (1976: 640), whose research is generally accepted as the most complete study of prefabricated speech in child second language acquisition, in fact claimed that 'the strategy of acquiring formulaic speech is central to the learning of language', that routines and patterns learned in the language acquisition process 'evolve directly into creative language'.

These descriptions of prefabricated language coincide neatly with other psycholinguistic research which shows that language learning, on all levels, takes place in two stages: a stage of 'item-learning' and a stage of 'system-learning':

The evidence shows learning taking place initially on an item by item basis at all levels of language. A child has to learn individual items by straightforward imitation to allow his mind to worry at, and play with (like a dog with a bone), such individual items in order to extract the system when he recognizes some part of the item being used in another utterance (phonology, intonation, morphology, and syntax) or the whole item being used in different situations or with different referents (semantics) . . . there is at least a strong possibility that some form of item-learning is an essential prerequisite to any type of system-learning (Cruttenden, 1981: 87).

The studies above concern only the language acquisition of children in fairly natural learning situations, so one might well doubt their relevance to adult language learning in more formal contexts. The few studies there are of prefabricated language in adult acquisition (such as VanPatten, 1986a, 1989) indicate otherwise, however. This is not unexpected, for there is no reason to think that adults would go about the learning task differently. Many characteristics of the language learning situation are the same for adults as for children and would make it likely that an adult learner would also find prefabricated language an efficient way to begin to acquire a new language system. On the one hand (and contrary to current emphases in linguistic theory), a great deal of language that people are exposed to every day is very routine and predictable, just as are the situations they encounter. This ritualization is simply characteristic of all aspects of human behaviour. On the other hand, there is always pressure for learners to produce more than they can, and they become discouraged when they can express only a few functions. Prefabricated chunks would allow for expression of functions that learners were yet unable to construct creatively from rules, simply because these chunks could be stored and retrieved whole when the situation called for them. Adults would even have an advantage over first language learners in making use of prefabricated language, for they would be immediately aware that these units could be analysed into smaller pieces by the process of segmentation at which they were already adept.

Intuitive judgements seem to be in accord with research evidence. Many people who have learned a foreign language in naturalistic circumstances remember a period of item-learning followed by one of system-learning, just as described above. My first phrases of survival Spanish, for example, were memorized routines like '*megusta*', '*muybien*', and '*mepareceque*', which later I learned to break into patterns with moveable pieces. Some learners have commented on the almost audible 'crack' when this break occurs:

Hearing again and again the question *Kore wa nan desu ka?* (What is this?) but never seeing it printed I conceived of *korewa* as a single word; it is spoken without pause. Some lessons later I learned that *wa* is a particle, an unchanging uninflected form, that marks the noun it follows as the topic of the sentence. Interestingly enough I did not, at once, reanalyze my word *korewa* and such others as *sorewa* and *arewa* into noun and particle forms. I did not do that until I started to hear such object forms as *kore o* and *sore o* and *are o* in which *o* marks the direct object. Then the truth dawned on me, and the words almost audibly cracked into *kore*, *sore*, and *are*, three demonstratives which took *wa* in the nominative form and *o* in the objective (Brown, 1973: 5).

## Teaching with Prefabricated Language

If a common characteristic of acquiring language performance is the progression from routine to pattern to creative language use, then we need to consider how this might be exploited in the classroom. One method of teaching prefabricated language would be to get students to make use of it in the same way as first language learners do, that is, by starting with a few basic fixed routines, which they then analyse as smaller, increasingly variable patterns, finally breaking them apart into individual words and thus finding their own way to the regular rules of syntax. More specifically, such a method might be put to work as follows. Pattern practice drills could first provide a way of gaining fluency with certain basic fixed routines (Peters, 1983). The challenge for the teacher would be to use such drills to allow confidence and fluency, yet not overdo them to the point that they became mindless exercise, as has often been the unfortunate result in strict audiolingualism. The next step would be to introduce the students to controlled variation in these basic phrases with the help of simple substitution drills, which would demonstrate that the chunks learned previously were not invariable routines but were instead patterns with open slots. The range of variation would then be increased, allowing students to analyse the patterns further. The goal is not to have students analyse just those chunks introduced in the lessons, of course, but to have them learn to segment and construct new patterns of their own by analogy with the kind of analysis they do in the classroom. It is when students learn this that creative control of the new language begins.

But there must be more. We not only have to ask *how* learners go about learning language, we need also ask *why* they learn it; and research clearly shows that the answer has to do with social motivation: children learn language as a part of a social interaction in which they have something they want to say. Language is best learned, that is, when it connects 'with our plans, with our most important memories and with our needs' (Stevick, 1976: 36). This socio-affective dimension provides the cognitive depth that is crucial to successful acquisition of language.

To include this affective dimension, we would design a beginning lesson to treat a single, predictable situation focused on some needed communicative function, and offer a few simple chunked phrases for dealing with that situation. Later materials would introduce the students to sets of more complex phrases that could also be used to express the same function, a kind of 'theme and variation' (Peters, 1983: 113), whose range of variation would broaden as learners became more skilled. These phrases would thus be presented in a cyclical rather than linear fashion, much as Wilkins (1976: 59) suggests for his notional-functional syllabus, so that students would return to the same functions throughout the course and learn to express them in an increasingly sophisticated manner. Many communicative language teaching activities would provide a framework for introducing these phrases, especially those exercises that have students consciously plan strategies for interacting with others (DiPietro, 1982).

What follows is an attempt to group prefabricated language in a way that will be pedagogically useful. These groups, revised from earlier work (Nattinger, 1980; 1986), are not traditional grammar or semantic categories, but are to some extent based on Wilkins's (1976) notional-functional categories, where emphasis is on the lexicon needed to perform specific speech functions. I have called these groups 'Social Interactions', 'Necessary Topics', and 'Discourse Devices', and list some examples of each below:

### Social Interactions

| | |
|---|---|
| Summoning: | 'excuse/pardon me' (with sustained intonation), 'hey/hi/hello, (name), how are you (doing)', 'lookit'. |
| Nominating a topic: | 'What's X?', 'Do you know/remember X?' |
| Checking comprehension: | 'O.K.?', 'all right?', '(Do you) understand (me)?' |
| Shifting a topic: | 'by the way', 'this is (a bit) off the subject/track, but X'. |
| Expressing politeness: | 'thanks (very much)', 'please', 'if you don't mind'. |

Requesting:             Modal verb + 'you' + action (i.e. 'Would
                        you (mind) X?'), 'May I X?'
Asserting:              'It is (a fact/the case that) X', 'I think/
                        believe that X'.
etc.

### Necessary Topics

Language:               'Do you speak X?', 'How do you say/spell X (in
                        Y)?', 'I (don't) speak X very well/a little'.
Autobiography:          'My name is X', 'I'm from X', 'I'm X (years old)'.
Time:                   'When is X?', 'at/it's X o'clock', 'for a long time/
                        X years', 'the X before/after Y'.
Quantity:               'How much/big is X?', '(not) a great deal', 'lots
                        of X'.
Location:               'Where/how far is X?', 'across from/next to X',
                        'to the right/left (of X)'.
Likes:                  'I like/enjoy X (a lot)', 'I don't like/enjoy X (at
                        all)', '(what)do you like to X?'
etc.

### Discourse Devices

Logical Connectors:     'thus', 'as a result (of X)', 'because (of) X',
                        'in spite of X'.
Exemplifiers:           'in other words', 'it's like X', 'for example',
                        'to give you an example'.
Evaluators:             'as far as I know/can tell', 'frankly', 'I guess',
                        'there's no doubt that X'.
Relators:               'X has (a lot)/doesn't have (much) to do with
                        Y', 'the (other) thing X is Y'.
Fluency Devices:        'you know', 'It seems (to me) that X', 'at any
                        rate', 'as a matter of fact'.
Summarizers:            'What I mean is (that) X', 'to make a long
                        story short', 'my point (here) is (that) X'.
etc.

Social Interactions and Discourse Devices provide patterns for the framework of the discourse, whereas Necessary Topics provide them for the subject at hand. Most linguistic encounters are composed of a patchwork of patterns from all three of these categories. For example, one of the most basic interactions at the beginning of a conversation is to get the attention of the person one is talking to. When that person responds to the summons, the second task is to get the partner to attend to the topic of discourse; the third is to offer information about the selected topic. In this way the participants co-operate to build a conversation. After the purpose of the conversation has been satisfied, the participants close the dialogue, and part. A brief but typical conversation might be:

**A:** Excuse me? (summons: SI)
**B:** Yes? (response to summons: SI)
**A:** the Saturday Market? (topic nomination: SI). Where is the Saturday Market, please? (location: NT) (politeness: SI)
**B:** I'm not sure but I think (assertion: SI) (evaluator: DD) (fluency device: DD) it's three blocks to the right, next to the Burnside Bridge (location: NT).
**A:** O.K. (acceptance: SI) Well (closing: SI), thanks very much (politeness: SI).
**B:** O.K. (acknowledgement: SI) So long (parting: SI).

Person A initiates the conversation by summoning the attention of B with the chunk 'excuse me', spoken with sustained intonation. B responds to the summons, and A then nominates a topic, 'the Saturday Market'. A then gets to the main point, which is to ask for the location of the market. B asserts an answer which also functions as an evaluator and fluency device (a fluency device because its length gives the speaker more time to plan for the next routine), and which precedes three short lexical phrases that describe location, 'three blocks', 'to the right', and 'next to the Burnside Bridge'. A indicates the answer is understood and moves to close. B acknowledges, and responds with a phrase for parting.

Students already 'know' these three categories of patterns and routines, of course. What they have to learn is how to produce them fluently in the new language, by using the right formulas on the right occasions.

## Further Research

As promising as a prefabricated language approach appears to be, there are many questions about it that have to be answered. Just what sorts of routinized language are used in particular encounters need to be explored and then assigned to appropriate categories. The role of prefabricated speech in classrooms is an urgent topic, yet investigation so far has dealt mainly with the prefabricated speech in academic lectures (Chaudron & Richards, 1986). The categories themselves must be evaluated, not only pedagogically but also empirically and theoretically.

It is quite possible that the distinction among Social Interactions, Necessary Topics and Discourse Devices obscures rather than clarifies, and that more realistic ways of grouping are necessary. Current interest in discourse analysis and social interaction will no doubt help provide answers to questions like these. There also remain uncertainties about the method for introducing these prefabricated patterns to students. It is clear that the best time to introduce controlled variation should come after students have automatic control of basic patterns but before these patterns have become fossilized and resistant to change. Just when such an optimum segmentation period occurs, though, needs to be investigated.

# 14  A role for communicative competence and the acquisition–learning distinction in translator training

DON KIRALY

*FAS, Universität Mainz, Germersheim, West Germany*

## Introduction

As the perceived need for multilingual professionals in the United States grows, courses in translation skills are being offered at more and more American colleges and universities. In fact, in the light of our students' increasing demand for more relevant, more practical and more marketable foreign language (FL) education, translation courses are rapidly becoming among the more popular offerings in university-level FL curricula. But while the field of FL education in general has greatly benefited from extensive research into psychological and social foundations of first and second language learning and use, very little has been published in the United States on what translation is, how it is performed, or how the ability to translate can be developed.

A basic premise of this paper is that translation can be seen and performed either as an act of communication or as a process of replacing linguistic material in a source language text with 'equivalent' material from a target language. An attempt will be made to demonstrate the importance of this distinction both for the practising translator and for the translator trainee. Reference will be made to translator training in West Germany, where translators have been trained in university-level courses for over 40 years and where a wealth of research has been done in the fledgling field of Translation Studies.

While some attempts have been made to apply knowledge gained in the area of second language acquisition (SLA) research to translation teaching (e.g. Hölz-Mäntärri, 1984; House, 1980; Sager, 1984; Königs, 1979; and Röhl, 1984) virtually no reference is made in works on translation teaching to the concepts of communicative competence and the acquisition–learning distinction which are at the heart of recent research into second language (L2) and FL learning in the United States. In this paper, the relevance of these two concepts to translation and to translator training will be shown. The linguistic theory of J. R. Firth, one of the earliest theoretical foundations of the communicative competence movement in SLA studies, will be used to help demonstrate the interdependence of language use, foreign language learning, translation and translation instruction.

## Towards a New Model of Translator Training

### Traditional translator training

In Western Europe, where translators have been trained on university courses since just after the Second World War, training tends to be based on a view of translation activity centred around the translation product. This training primarily involves the *ad hoc* production by students of translations with subsequent correction by instructors in so-called translation practice classes. Students are expected to learn the interlingual translation equivalents for words and grammatical constructions and to develop their ability to produce translation equivalents spontaneously in the foreign language or the mother tongue, as the case may be. This is, of course, a simplified scenario. Students generally must also take courses on the culture and history of the countries where their language is spoken and university programmes require, or at least recommend, that students plan an extended stay abroad sometime during their course of studies.

There is a vague general recognition that students cannot develop all the abilities they will need to become professional translators within the academic setting alone. Yet little research has been done into what students should or actually do acquire in the academic study of the language as opposed to a stay abroad. There are, however, remedial courses, designed to fill out students' 'knowledge' of the FL, that tend to correspond to traditional distinctions made in FL teaching: grammatical instruction, vocabulary memorization, pronunciation practice, and conversation practice.

The following quotation from a master's thesis written by a student on one of the West German translator training courses in 1984 will perhaps give a clearer picture of the atmosphere in which translator training takes place:

> I first became interested in this topic the day I realized, after having spent the entire day attending translation classes, that instead of being 'filled' with language, I had remained totally silent. In addition, my own personality (which was apparently superfluous in this situation), had once again remained outside the classroom. Sitting silently in a translation practice class, listening silently to translation suggestions and sometimes marking corrections on my paper; then listening silently to a lecture read aloud by an instructor; then in a seminar, listening silently to a paper read aloud by a student . . . then in a silent attempt in the cafeteria over a cup of coffee to pour fresh energy into myself in preparation for my afternoon classes; then my afternoon classes, equally silent, except for one class for students in their final semester, where there were only three students; then home to supper listening silently to the news in Spanish and reading a foreign language newspaper, and finally the evening and night time hours in my room, hunched silently over my translation texts—this summary of my day's activities may be a bit exaggerated, but my guess is that it is not atypical of the daily routine of student translators (Röhl, 1984: 6–7).

In short, a great deal of time is spent 'learning' and virtually none is spent using the language for self-expression or communication. This is the result of the dominant paradigm in translator training, which can be called the 'equivalence' or 'linguistic transfer' paradigm.

The equivalence paradigm underlying traditional translator training in Europe is exemplified in Catford (1965). According to Catford (1965: 1), the translator's main task consists of: 'the replacement of textual material in one language by equivalent material in another language'. He sees translation as the result of a search-and-replace operation in which the translator identifies formal equivalents and inserts them into a source language text. These formal equivalents can be found on the level of lexis by referring to previous translations (for example, bilingual dictionaries), or by consulting a 'competent bilingual', and on the level of syntax by identifying grammatical categories functioning in

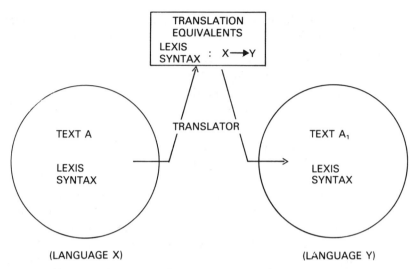

FIGURE 14.1 *Catford's view of the translation process*

approximately the same way in the economies of the source language and the target language. The translator's role is a rather mechanical one—the correct translation equivalents are in some sense waiting to be found by the translator. Figure 14.1 represents my interpretation of Catford's basic view of the translation process.

Catford does mention in passing that one cannot neglect the role of context in the translation process, just as some attention is paid to 'communicative activities' in many of the textbooks used in elementary FL classrooms today. In both cases the primary focus remains, however, on the implicit pre-eminence of grammatical and lexical elements.

The continued predominance of models similar to Catford's in translation teaching explains why translation courses and translator programmes are organized as they are. Student translators are simply expected to 'learn' the appropriate translation equivalents in different languages and to practise the skills of producing them spontaneously and incorporating them artfully into a translation text. From this viewpoint, the instructor, who is usually a former or practising translator or at least a functional bilingual in the respective languages, already knows the corresponding translation. equivalents and simply tries to pass that knowledge on to his students in what has been so aptly described by Ladmiral (1977) as a *'performance magistrale'*. This teaching technique involves some variation on the following theme:

A.  Instructor provides student with a text (generally an article or editorial from a newspaper in general translation courses).

B.  Students prepare a translation individually at home.

C.  In class, the instructor has various students read their translations of successive sentences aloud.

D.  The instructor informs students of the errors in the sentence translations.

E.  The instructor presents acceptable solutions or, in some cases, the definitive solution.

F.  Students mark changes to correspond to the instructor's corrections.

I contend that it is the nature of the underlying assumption that translation is a search for equivalents that perpetuates this teaching approach which in turn leads to the type of atmosphere so aptly described by Röhl above. The focus is on the lexical and syntactical elements in the final text and the formal equivalence relationship in which they stand to corresponding elements in the original text. There is little room for creative problem-solving or the systematic consideration of aspects of the translation situation beyond the most elementary linguistic levels.

### A communicative competence framework for translator training

The theoretical underpinnings of teaching for communicative competence underlying FL education—at least in theory, if not in practice—for over a decade, can be traced back at least as far as the linguistic theory of J. R. Firth, the esteemed representative of the British school of linguistics. Firth's work remained virtually unknown in the United States until interest began to develop around the communicative competence concept in the early 1970s. Firth is now widely recognized as one of the earliest modern linguists to incorporate what later became the essential principles of the communicative competence paradigm—the intricate interrelationship of form and function and of content and context in language use—into a theory of language. In Firth's (1968: 80) own words: 'the whole of our linguistic behavior is best understood if it is seen as a network of relations between people, things, and events'.

For Firth, the linguistic parts of language are intricately intertwined with the context of situation in which specific communicative utterances occur. Rather than throw out context as being irrelevant to the study of language, as other linguistic traditions have done, Firth proposed investigating the intimate relation between linguistic elements and context

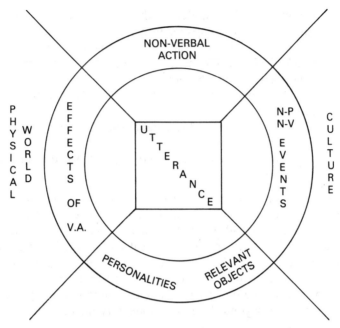

FIGURE 14.2 *Constituents of a typical context of situation: Personalities, Persons, Verbal Action, Non-verbal Action, Relevant Objects, Non-verbal, Non-personal Events, Effects of Verbal Action*

of situation. He describes the following as being constituents of a typical context of situation (Firth, 1968: 177):

1. Features of participants:
   A. Personalities (the interlocutors in a communicative act)
   B. Persons (individuals present but not actively communicating).
2. Verbal action, non-verbal action.
3. Relevant objects and non-verbal, non-personal events.
4. Effects of verbal action.

Firth's view of language interaction could perhaps be represented graphically as in Figure 14.2.

Taking Firth's theory of language use a step further, it is possible to view the distinction first made by Krashen between language acquisition and learning in the way shown in Figure 14.3. In this view, the learner traditionally studies elements and relationships within linguistic subsystems—generally syntax, semantics, morphology, phonology or lexis.

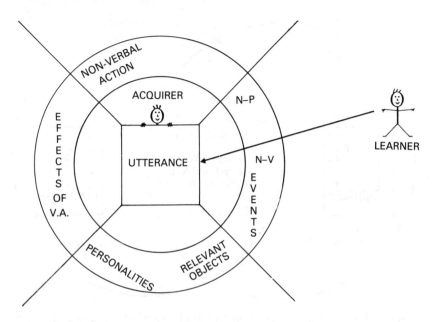

FIGURE 14.3 *Firth's context of situation* vis-à-vis *Krashen's acquisition-learning distinction*

This is primarily an intellectual process of consciously identifying regularities and elements that compose the sub-systems or identifying equivalence relationships between elements in different languages. The acquirer, on the other hand, finds himself in the middle of successive, real contexts of situation, using language for self-expression and communication.

On the basis of Firth's linguistic theory, including his constituents of a typical context of situation, and influenced by various other contributions to a communicative view of translation, I would like to propose a tentative model that I feel allows us to look at the translation process in a way that would ensure the incorporation of opportunities for acquisition as well as learning in translator training (Figure 14.4). In this view, the translator is an active participant in a multi-level communicative act. He is the receiver of the source language text as well as the co-creator of the target language text. He must indeed rely on his knowledge of syntax, vocabulary and style in the respective languages, but he must also have acquired or internalized enough of each language system to be able to relate both discourse and meaning on different levels within each

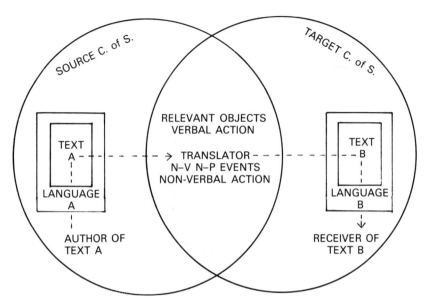

FIGURE 14.4 *An 'acquisitionist' model of the translation process. Constituents of a typical context of situation: Personalities, Persons, Verbal Action, Non-verbal Action, Relevant Objects, Non-verbal, Non-personal Events, Effects of Verbal Action*

language as well as across them. The translator needs to acquire communicative competence in addition to linguistic knowledge and linguistic manipulation skills in order to be able to relate to two complex contexts of situation and participate in them simultaneously. With the help of this model, we should be able to conceive of translation competence as a special type of communicative competence. If communicative competence is a major component of translation competence, then the implication is that translator trainees, like other FL students, have a need to acquire as well as to learn.

The model presented in Figure 14.4 could serve as a theoretical foundation for the development of translator training courses. The impact of such a change in viewpoint could be dramatic because if students as well as administrators and instructors view the act of translation as a communicative activity and the students' role as that of developing communicative translation competence through communicative translation tasks, then the focus of courses could move away from an obsession with the translation product itself and the relationship of bits of linguistic material between languages and towards developing the individual student's ability to interact appropriately and adequately as an active participant in communicative translation acts.

## Conclusions

Whether translation is or is not a communicative activity is to some extent a moot point—the translator may choose to deal with a translation task as if it were either a communicative act or a search for linguistic equivalents. A more relevant question is whether professional translators should translate texts or words, messages or linguistic signs. Similarly, FL students can attempt to learn linguistic rules and memorize translation equivalents, or they can try to acquire the FL— to develop sociolinguistic, discourse and strategic as well as grammatical competence. But in either case, the resulting competence will depend upon the approach taken by students in developing their translation competence, and consequently on the pedagogical model underlying the training course. We cannot expect our students to deal with the FL as a communicative tool if we present it as pure linguistic subject matter. Similarly, we cannot expect student translators to make much progress along the road to professional, communicative translation production if we present their task as a process of simply choosing linguistic equivalents and inserting them into an appropriate grammatical framework. Translator trainees, like all FL learners, need to acquire, as well as to learn.

# 15 Can foreign language learning be like second language acquisition? The curious case of immersion

LINDA SCHINKE-LLANO

*Millikin University, Decatur, IL, USA*

As is generally prudent, I will begin by stating what I do not intend to do in this paper before I specify my objectives. First, although the subject is of major interest and concern to me, I will not address the additional language learning of language *minority* children.[1] I overlook this large and important group to eliminate the variable of additive versus subtractive bilingualism (Lambert & Tucker, 1972) from the discussion. Instead, I focus on the additional language learning of language *majority* children, especially those of elementary school age. Second, I will not use the phrases 'second language acquisition' (SLA) and 'foreign language learning' (FLL) in the often-used senses of language learning which occurs in the target language speech community and in the native language speech community, respectively. Rather, I distinguish between the two according to their perceived products. That is, as an operating definition, I utilize the notions that SLA results in native-like use of the target language, and that FLL does not.

Disclaimers and clarifications aside, it is the intention of this paper to examine whether the process of additional language teaching can be modified so that the product more closely resembles SLA than FLL. Using immersion language education for the purpose of illustration, I will argue that environments facilitative of SLA can be approximated in the classroom. Further, I will argue that current classroom interaction research will help provide us with some of the tools necessary to make additional language learning as SLA-like as possible. As a result of this discussion, it is hoped that the relationship between SLA and FLL, as well as that between classroom and non-classroom learning, will be better delineated.

## Programmatic Approaches

Presently there are three primary programmatic approaches available to educators planning to implement additional language instruction for language majority children of elementary school age: FLEX, FLES and immersion. Each approach differs from the others with respect to several factors: its goals, its degree of integration with the total school curriculum, and the roles played by English and the target language (Schinke-Llano, 1985).

### FLEX

Introduced in the 1970s, foreign language experience (FLEX) courses have as their goal the exposure of children to additional languages, not the development of fluency (Rhodes & Schreibstein, 1983). As they are viewed as enrichment in nature, FLEX courses are supplementary to, rather than an integral part of, the total school curriculum. Because of the limited goals and enrichment characteristics of FLEX courses, the target language is used relatively infrequently in the classroom. Thus, English is used as the medium of instruction, with the target language functioning as the topic of discussion.

### FLES

Begun in the 1950s and currently enjoying a period of revitalization, foreign language in the elementary school (FLES) courses have broader goals than do FLEX courses with respect to both the level of proficiency and the number of skills to be developed. FLES courses encourage a degree of proficiency in listening and speaking; a lesser degree of proficiency in reading and writing; and the development of cultural awareness (Gray et al., 1984). Depending upon the school district involved, FLES courses can range from supplementary to an integral part of the school curriculum. Similarly, there is variation from course to course with respect to the use of native and target languages. Since attainment of certain levels of proficiency is a goal, more class time is devoted to using the target language than is the case in FLEX courses; in some instances, entire classes are conducted in the target language.

## Immersion

Created in Canada in the mid-1960s and later replicated in the United States, language immersion courses have four stated goals: continued development of English; academic achievement; proficiency in the target language in the four skill areas of listening, speaking, reading and writing; and appreciation of the target culture and its members (Lambert & Tucker, 1972; Campbell, 1984). Given the ambitiousness of the goals, immersion courses function as an integral part of the school curriculum. However, the nature of the integration varies along three dimensions: the 'degree of immersion'; the grade level of implementation; and the number of target languages involved (Schinke-Llano, 1984). For example, courses can be described as total or partial immersion depending upon whether the target language is used 100% at the outset or less (Genesee, 1984). Further, courses can be classified as early (kindergarten or first grade implementation); delayed (fourth or fifth grade implementation); or late (late elementary or early secondary school implementation) (Lapkin & Cummins, 1984). Finally, single or double immersion courses can exist, depending upon whether one or two target languages are incorporated. Regardless of the variation described, all immersion courses have one essential characteristic which distinguishes them from the other approaches discussed: namely, the target language serves as the medium of instruction in subject matter classes.

## Research Results

### FLEX

Given the distinctive characteristics of these three programmatic approaches to additional language teaching, what evidence do we have, if any, of their efficacy? With respect to FLEX courses, virtually no research has been conducted, presumably due to the recency of their development. I believe it safe to assume, however, that well-run FLEX courses can and do achieve their stated goal, that of exposing children to other languages and establishing in them a positive attitude towards the experience. Concerning what is of interest to us here, i.e. the development of native-like skills in another language, I believe it also prudent to assume that such an achievement would, by definition, not result from FLEX courses.

## FLES

While a great deal has been written about FLES courses, most of the articles are descriptive rather than evaluative. The empirical studies that do exist (e.g. Brega & Newell, 1965; Oneto, 1968; and Karabinus, 1976) suggest that in FLES courses students perform better in the long run on a number of measures than do students in more traditional foreign language (FL) courses. What we do not know, however, is how FLES students compare to native speakers of the target language. One suspects, however, that such comparisons would not be impressive.[2]

## Immersion

Unlike the two types of course just discussed, there is a considerable amount of research available on immersion language courses. Coming to us predominantly from Canada, the evidence in support of language immersion courses for language majority children is overwhelmingly positive. Regarding the objective of continued development in English, under no circumstances have there been differences between immersion and non-immersion students in oral skills (Swain, 1984). In the area of literacy-related skills, however, immersion students have performed better than (Genesee, 1974), as well as (Lapkin, 1982), or more poorly than (Barik *et al.*, 1977) their non-immersion counterparts depending upon the facet of literacy being measured.

With respect to the goal of academic achievement, early total immersion students perform equal to or better than their non-immersion peers in areas such as mathematics and science (Swain & Lapkin, 1982). The results for early partial and late immersion students are less consistent, however (Barik & Swain, 1976; 1977; 1978). Interestingly, cognitive benefits have been seen to accrue for immersion students in areas such as divergent thinking (Scott, 1973, reported in Lambert, 1984) and in IQ (Barik & Swain, 1976).

As for the objective of appreciation of the target culture and its members, immersion courses are clearly successful. Immersion students have more positive attitudes toward French Canadians than do their non-immersion English Canadian peers (Lambert & Tucker, 1972). Further, the perceived social distance between English and French Canadians is less for immersion students than for non-immersion students (Cziko *et al.*, 1979).

The final objective of language immersion courses, that of the development of proficiency in listening, speaking, reading and writing in the target language, appears to be the most problematic. On the one hand, immersion students consistently perform better in the target language than their non-immersion peers (Swain, 1984). On the other hand, when compared with native speakers of the target language, immersion students do not show native-like proficiency in speaking and writing (Genesee, 1978; Harley, 1979; 1982; Spilka, 1976). Further, they need six to seven years to reach native-like performance in listening and reading (Swain & Lapkin, 1982). In fact, in the United States, Plann (1976) identified a classroom register peculiar to immersion courses.

## Facilitative Second Language Acquisition Environments

Given the information we have at our disposal regarding these three types of language course, what is it about immersion courses that makes them the most effective in developing target language skills? Are the differences merely quantitative? That is, does immersion work best because students are on the course more hours per day than on the other courses? Or, are there qualitative differences as well? To answer these questions, we need to look at what current research and theory tell us about environments facilitative of SLA. By doing so, we will, in turn, shed light on the issue of whether facilitative SLA environments can be approximated in the classroom.

For decades, laymen and educators alike functioned under the assumption that sufficient exposure to a second language constituted the most important factor in its being learned. Further, throughout the history of second language teaching, there have been strong proponents of a pedagogical approach which entails analysing and memorizing the patterns and paradigms of the target language. Such an approach is best exemplified by the Audio Lingual Method, which represents the influence of both behavioural psychology and structural linguistics. Both of these beliefs, however, have been resoundingly criticized by SLA researchers and theoreticians.

Krashen (1981; 1982), for example, distinguishes between the *acquisition* and *learning* of a second language. Acquisition is natural and subconscious, akin to the process of first language acquisition. Learning, on the other hand, is a conscious studying of the rules, or grammar, of a language. Most importantly, according to Krashen, the acquisition process is superior to the learning process if native-like competence is desired by the student. This position is supported by Terrell (1977), as well. In his Natural Approach, Terrell advocates the acquisition of a second language in a context similar to that in which the first language is acquired, i.e. one in which students use the language for communicative purposes, rather than as an object of formal analysis. Further, Wells (1981) confirms that language learning is the result of interaction in meaningful contexts.

Just as the formal learning of a second language has been criticized, so has the notion of the importance of exposure to the target language. While exposure is necessary, it is by no means sufficient for SLA to occur. The key, hypothesizes Krashen (1981, 1982), is input. Not all of the target language available in the environment constitutes input, only that which the learner,[3] because of his or her limited proficiency, is able to 'take in' for processing. Optimal input meets several criteria. First and foremost, it is comprehensible. Moreover, for acquisition to occur, the input must contain structures slightly beyond current levels of competence $(i+1)$. Further, optimal input occurs in sufficient quantity for and is interesting and relevant to the learner. Similar to input in a first language situation, optimal input for a second language learner is not grammatically sequenced. Finally, 'tools' for conversational management are provided. That is, optimal input equips the learner with the linguistic means to function in the second language community despite limited proficiency.

Similarly to Krashen's criticisms of the importance of exposure, Long (1980a; 1981) contends that input, as characterized by Krashen, is a necessary but not sufficient prerequisite for SLA. The prerequisite which is both necessary and sufficient is interaction. By interacting verbally with members of the second language speech community, learners are able to negotiate meaning and elicit input which meets the criteria specified by Krashen. Without such interaction and the resultant negotiated input, competence in the second language is not achieved.

Related to the concepts of 'optimal input' and 'negotiated interaction' is that of *comprehensible output*. Swain (1983) emphasizes the need for providing students with frequent opportunities to produce and practise the target language in meaningful contexts. Comprehensible output on the part of the learner encourages interaction with native speakers which, in turn, assists in the negotiation of optimal input—all factors critical to the SLA process. Further, focusing on comprehensible output forces the learner to analyse the target language.

Also important to the acquisition of a second language, as mounting research evidence attests, is the presence of a silent period. It has been observed that children learning both first and second languages in natural settings undergo a period characterized by an absence of production in the target language. The explanation, of course, is that the child is establishing receptive skills before attempting productive ones. Methodologies, such as Total Physical Response (TPR), which incorporate a silent period, have been shown to be superior on a number of measures of English skills to more traditional ones that do not (Asher, 1972; 1977a; 1977b; Asher *et al.*, 1974). In addition to cognitive reasons for providing a silent period, there are affective ones as well. The silent period allows a student to begin production in a second language when he or she is psychologically 'ready'.

This last observation leads to the final aspect of a desirable second language environment to be discussed here. According to numerous theoreticians, researchers and methodologists (Krashen, 1982; Curran, 1976; Lozanov, 1979; Asher, 1977a; Brown, 1987), affective factors are a key variable in SLA. Learners who, for whatever reasons, feel uncomfortable, inhibited, or embarrassed simply do not perform as well in the target language as those who do not. Thus, an environment which helps the learner maintain a low affective filter (Krashen, 1981; 1982) is desirable.

Now that aspects of a second language environment which facilitate SLA have been discussed, it is necessary to determine whether immersion courses provide such a facilitative environment. Certainly, since the second language is used as the medium of instruction, rather than as the target, an environment is created which allows the student to *acquire*, not to *learn*, the language. Also, because of this defining characteristic of immersion education, input is provided in sufficient quantity, is not grammatically sequenced, and, it is assumed, provides the learner with the necessary conversational management tools appropriate for classroom interaction.

Next, since content area subjects are the targets of instruction, it is assumed that the input obtained is both interesting and relevant. Also, because of the nature of subject matter teaching, opportunities exist for the learner to produce comprehensible output and to interact with the teacher using the second language. Further, because immersion students comprise a homogeneous group with respect to second language skills, all content teaching is provided at their level of competence, thereby assuring comprehensible input.

Finally, two other aspects of a facilitative SLA environment are provided for in immersion courses. First, a silent period is allowed. Although the teacher speaks only the second language, students are allowed to express themselves in their first language. Communicative attempts in the second language are, of course, encouraged, but—in the case of early immersion courses—students are not expected to produce consistently in the target language until anywhere from the second half of the first year (Swain, 1984) to the second half of the second year (Lapkin & Cummins, 1984). Finally, it is precisely this initial lack of pressure to produce in the second language, coupled with the acceptance of the home language, which helps maintain a low affective filter for the learners.

It is evident from the preceding discussion that the design of immersion courses is such that all aspects of a facilitative SLA environment can be provided. Certain of the environmental aspects (e.g. low affective filter) are not unique to immersion courses. Further, the extent to which certain other aspects (e.g. interesting and relevant input) are developed is teacher-dependent. Yet, immersion education is uniquely suited to provide at least two key facilitative aspects—namely, an environment which fosters acquisition and which provides input in sufficient quantity. Thus, with respect to current theoretical constructs and recent research findings, immersion education is potentially, if not inherently, suited to provide a facilitative second language environment.

## Second Language Acquisition and Classroom Interaction

As a result of the previous discussion, one can see that immersion courses are both quantitatively and qualitatively different from the other types of additional language course currently available. Further, as immersion courses by their structure provide key characteristics essential to the SLA process, and as they have been empirically demonstrated to be effective, I argue that environments that are more facilitative of SLA than FLL can, indeed, be approximated in the classroom.

Despite this claim, we are left with the nagging problem that immersion students, no matter how superior they may be to their non-immersion counterparts, generally do not achieve native-like proficiencies in the target language. The question then becomes whether native-like abilities in an additional language can ever be achieved in a classroom setting. Genesee (1986: 237) thinks not, for he states: 'In fact it is unlikely that any student will attain totally native-like competence in a language if language learning and use are restricted to the school environment.'

In essence I agree with Genesee, for the school setting by nature provides students with the opportunity to use the target language in only a limited number of functions, as compared to the functional range both offered and required by the target language speech community. Yet, given the reality that the classroom constitutes the only opportunity for many, if not most, students to develop an additional language, I believe it counter-productive to conclude that a particular goal is unattainable. We have already seen that facilitative SLA environments can be approximated in the classroom. What remains to be determined—a large task, admittedly—is what can be done within these facilitative environments to ensure that the product more closely resembles SLA than FLL.

A fruitful area of research in this respect is that of the current investigations of classroom interaction. While interactional analysis in the classroom is not new to education in general or to the SLA field in particular, the recent studies attempt to identify not only what kinds of interaction occur in language classrooms, but also which of the interactions appear to facilitate SLA and which do not. Cummins (1980; 1981a), for example, argues that interactional tasks along two axes (context-embedded to context-reduced, and cognitively demanding to cognitively undemanding) are necessary to develop both basic interpersonal communicative skills (BICS) and cognitive academic language proficiency (CALP). Long & Porter (1985) focus on the pedagogical and psycholinguistic rationales for small-group work; they claim that it is an effective and desirable alternative to teacher-led interactions and to one-to-one conversations with native speakers. Doughty & Pica (1986) demonstrate that tasks requiring an exchange of information facilitate the conversational modification thought necessary for SLA. Further, they show that small-group and dyadic interactions result in greater interactional modifications than do teacher-led ones. Finally, Porter (1983) and Varonis & Gass (1983) conclude that non-native speaker–non-native speaker (NNS–NNS) dyads generate more conversational negotiation than do native speaker–non-native speaker (NS–NNS) dyads. Clearly, studies such as these can assist us in structuring the most effective language classes possible.

## Conclusion

Returning to the issues raised at the outset of this paper, I believe that environments facilitative of SLA can be approximated in the classroom. The curious case of immersion courses—wherein the products are clearly superior to FLL, yet not quite equivalent to SLA—demonstrates that such facilitative environments can, indeed, be provided. Further, while accepting the facts that classroom and non-classroom learning and that FLL and SLA can never be identical, I nevertheless claim that the process of additional language teaching—even within facilitative environments—can be modified so that the instructional product more closely resembles SLA than FLL. The exact nature of the needed modifications will become more evident as research in SLA, in general, and in classroom interaction, in particular, progresses.

## Notes to Chapter 15

1. I employ the neutral phrase 'additional language' where appropriate to avoid the connotations of 'foreign language' and 'second language', since it is precisely these concepts and their relationship that we are attempting to clarify.
2. It is not my intention to criticize either FLEX or FLES courses. Both have goals which are desirable and educationally sound, and both can achieve those goals if carefully implemented. However, in examining the question of whether environments facilitative of SLA can be approximated in the classroom, it is clear that neither type of course, by nature, can provide the optimal setting.
3. The generic term 'learner' is being used rather than the technically more appropriate 'acquirer'.

# 16   Conservation of language resources

RUSSELL N. CAMPBELL and KATHRYN J. LINDHOLM

*Center for Language Education and Research, University of California, Los Angeles, USA*

## Introduction

In an ecology-minded society such as ours the term *conservation* is readily understood. It suggests strategies to protect against the loss or diminution of endangered, highly valued resources. As its title suggests, this chapter is about the conservation of extremely valuable language resources that are now being foolishly squandered; namely,the high levels of language proficiency, in a wide variety of languages, brought to our schools each year by representatives of linguistic minority populations.

For example, a five-year-old Korean American student entering a public school kindergarten class in Los Angeles' Korea Town will have acquired, as have hundreds of other youngsters in this neighbourhood, a very high level of oral-aural proficiency in the native language of his parents and grandparents—Korean. If one were to collect and analyse samples of these children's performance in Korean, one would find that these children may well have mastered completely the phonological system of adult Korean speakers. They may have acquired nearly all of the morphological and syntactic rules necessary for sentence formation as well as those for the production and comprehension of conversational discourse. It would also be noted that they nearly always adhere to sociolinguistic rules determined by the relationship they have with their interlocutors; that is, there will be differences in their choice of lexicon, honorifics and even voice qualifiers and body-language depending upon their conversational partners. Like all normal five-year-old children, our hypothetical children will have acquired the bulk of the linguistic and sociolinguistic rules that would allow them to be counted among native speakers of their ancestral language.

Clearly, the linguistic abilities of children at this age are still interestingly different from those of mature adult speakers of Korean. There are still certain syntactic and discoursal rules missing in their repertoire that are not normally acquired until late childhood (Chomsky, 1969). More obvious, however, will be the absence of semantic networks that reflect experience and knowledge in the multitude of sociocultural, scholastic and occupational domains in which five-year-olds have never participated. And, of course, the typical child is not literate in Korean whereas the adult might well be. In spite of these differences, it cannot be denied that the level of linguistic accomplishment of the five-year-old is substantial. To help us better understand the magnitude of these accomplishments, we can speculate on how many years of typical university language courses would be required before the average English speaker might attain equal competence. One would guess, setting literacy skills aside, that it has rarely, if ever, been accomplished. For example, experience at the Defense Language Institute in Monterey, California, has shown that students who receive some 1400 hours of instruction over a period of 47 weeks, in addition to hundreds of hours of structured homework, will acquire a level of proficiency that would be rated a 2 or 2+ on the US Government Interagency Language Round Table Oral Proficiency Interview scale (Adams & Frith, 1979, cited in Lowe, 1982). This level of proficiency means that the student, *inter alia*, is

> [able] to satisfy routine social demands and limited work requirements. . . can get the gist of most conversations on nontechnical subjects and has a speaking vocabulary sufficient to respond simply with some circumlocutions; accent, though often quite faulty, is intelligible; can usually handle elementary constructions quite accurately but does not have a thorough or confident control of grammar (Lowe, 1982).

If a university student were to take Korean language courses five hours a week for 30 weeks each year for four years of her undergraduate career, she would have received only 600 hours of instruction and would be fortunate if her proficiency were rated in the 2/2+ range of proficiency. On the other hand, there is simply no doubt that our hypothetical five-year-olds would be rated, with the limitations suggested above, at the 3+/4 level on the same scale.

The obvious point of these extensive introductory remarks is to establish the dimensions of the resources represented in the competence of linguistic minority children in our schools. Clearly what has been described for hypothetical Korean American children is also true for countless numbers of children in other ethnolinguistic communities found in almost all urban centres in the United States. These children have already acquired, without the expenditure of community resources, what would take foreign language students in our schools and colleges thousands of hours to acquire, if in fact we had the instructional technology that would allow them to do so, at huge financial costs to taxpayers.

The question now is what does our society do first to conserve and then to enhance these enormous national resources? We already know the answer. We do very little. In fact, it is almost as if there were an unspoken national policy to do whatever is necessary to deny opportunities for the conservation of the competence held by these linguistic minority students. Our policy is basically 'subtractive' in nature: we seem to insist that linguistic minority children give up their ancestral languages as dues if they wish to become members of the generally monolingual English-speaking majority club. It is our contention that this is a seriously misguided policy, one that is contrary to the best interests of linguistic minority children with regard to their general education and progress towards acquiring proficiency in English, and with regard to our national interest given the renewed attention to the enhancement of our foreign language (FL) resources.

Fortunately, there is some evidence of efforts under way to counteract these contradictory tendencies. In this paper we will present brief descriptions of three different school programmes that represent instructional models that attempt to reverse the national trend; namely, programmes that provide linguistic minority children with opportunities to conserve the language skills acquired in their homes and communities and to continue normal language development toward the skills that are characteristic of mature, adult, literate, native speakers of their ancestral languages.

## Elementary Level Bilingual Immersion Education

One extremely promising experimental model of education that, among a host of other benefits, would permit substantial numbers of linguistic minority children to make normal progress towards the acquisition of a mature, educated level of proficiency in their home language, is bilingual immersion. Although this model is referred to by many names (e.g. 'language immersion', 'two-way immersion', 'two-way bilingual education'), the most common names are 'two-way bilingual immersion' or 'bilingual immersion'. Despite the variety of names, the programmes share a common definition:

> a program. . . which employs two languages, one of which is English, for the purposes of instruction and involves students who are native speakers of each of those languages. Both groups of students— limited English proficient (LEP) and English proficient (EP)—are expected to become bilingual. They learn curricula through their own language and through the second language, become proficient in the second language, and continue to develop skills and proficiency in their native language (New York State Education Department, 1986).

There are a number of goals for such a programme over and beyond the conservation and development of the linguistic minority students' first language (L1). These goals include high levels of scholastic achievement in both languages, earlier and more efficient acquisition of English language skills, high self-esteem, and positive attitudes toward both languages and the communities they represent (Lindholm, 1987). These outcomes, individually and collectively, are probably of greater importance to the education and welfare of minority students than the language conservation issue being addressed in this chapter. But, the added benefit of L1 conservation is an extremely precious by-product, one that is worthy of careful monitoring over the next few years to provide qualitative and quantitative information on the conditions that provide optimal language development opportunities for children on these programmes.

The basic instructional design of the bilingual immersion programme is, assuming English and Spanish as the two languages involved, as follows. First, in terms of student participants, there are roughly one-third English and two-thirds Spanish native speakers in each class. Second, in terms of language of instruction, Spanish is the primary language of instruction from kindergarten to second grade, but with some time—for example, 30 minutes a day in kindergarten and 60 minutes a day in first grade—dedicated to the development of English language proficiency and language arts. In grades two to three, approximately 20% of the curriculum is taught in English and in grades four through six, 50% of the instruction is in English. The two languages are never mixed within an instructional period. Each language is used as the medium of instruction for the subject matter employing all of the verbal skills, both oral and written, normally associated with each content area. It is therefore necessary for the students to develop linguistic and metalinguistic skills in both languages that will enable them to read academic texts, write acceptable essays and test responses, and be able to discuss subject-matter areas—mathematics, science and social studies—in both languages.

We are currently working with four California schools, each of which began implementation of a Spanish/English bilingual immersion programme in September, 1986. Our objective has been to help implement and to evaluate the bilingual immersion programmes. Initially, we worked with the California State Department of Education's Bilingual Education Office to develop the instructional characteristics that would further define the bilingual immersion model. We looked to the literatures on bilingual education, FL immersion education, L2 learning and teacher effectiveness for the instructional characteristics that underlie successful educational models. One important characteristic that emerged concerns the curriculum. Apparently, there must be integration of content and language instruction in the teaching of the core curriculum of the school; Spanish and English language arts components need to be included and integrated with the content. A second significant characteristic concerns language input; it must be comprehensible to the L2 learners but also challenging for the L1 speakers. Third, co-operative learning techniques are utilized to integrate students from both groups, to provide opportunities for using language (especially L2) and to create tasks wherein each student has an equal status. Fourth, there is a positive and reciprocal teacher–student interactional climate that utilizes a two-way interactional mode of instruction, and positive expectations for and interactions with all students. Finally, a home/school component is necessary to involve parents in the education of their children.

Our evaluation model is an interaction model (Cortés, 1986) which assumes that programme outcomes (academic achievement, language proficiency, psychosocial functioning) are the result of a complex interaction between societal factors (community background factors such as status of L1 and L2; and home background factors such as exposure to L2, parent educational background) and school factors (educational input characteristics such as purchase of Spanish materials, expectations for student success; instructional characteristics such as use of Spanish and English and integration of language and content; student characteristics such as language aptitude and motivation). The objective is not simply to determine programme outcomes, but to understand what interactions of societal and school factors influence particular programme outcomes. Furthermore, L2 learning paradigms involving transfer and metalinguistic strategies in different language proficiency contexts (e.g. contextualized versus decontextualized) are also under investigation in order better to understand the processes underlying how the variables interact to produce particular programme outcomes.

A total of 112 kindergarten ($n=58$) and first-grade ($n=54$) students participated in the first-year evaluation study. Data were gathered on English and Spanish proficiency with pre- and post-test measures; English and Spanish achievement, with pre- and post-test measures in Spanish; and perceived competence. In addition, the data collection included a parent questionnaire and a bilingual immersion staff questionnaire. Also, 20 kindergarten and 19 first-grade students, who were not enrolled in the bilingual immersion programme, were tested using the English achievement test.

In terms of the students' language development, all of the students made gains in both languages. Native language proficiency was high, with about two-thirds of the students rated at the Fluent Proficiency level, and one third at the Limited Proficiency level. L2 proficiency varied considerably, with some students rated at the Non-Proficiency level, others at the Limited Proficiency level, and still others at the Fluent Proficiency level. More Spanish-dominant students were fluent in the L2 than were English-dominant students.

Both the Spanish-dominant and English-dominant students scored at an average to above average level in achievement performance. The Spanish-dominant speakers scored in the average to above average range on Spanish achievement tests and made significant gains from the autumn to the spring. Even the English-dominant students scored well on the Spanish achievement tests; the kindergartners scored average in reading and slightly above average in maths, but the first graders scored above average in reading and well above average in maths. In addition, the first-graders made significant progress from the autumn to the spring. On English achievement tests, the Spanish-dominant kindergartners scored below average but the first-graders performed only slightly below average, and they did not differ significantly from the non-bilingual immersion students. The English-dominant kindergartners scored slightly below average, but the first-graders performed average in reading and language and slightly above average to well above average in maths. Furthermore, on every sub-test, the English-dominant kindergartners scored higher than the non-bilingual immersion students, with significantly higher scores in maths.

The students' perceived competence ratings were high in each of four domains (academic, peer, physical, and maternal); and attitudes toward the bilingual immersion programme were generally positive from the parents and teachers.

Several important points should be made about the results that have implications for the bilingual immersion model. First, the Spanish speakers at both grade levels made highly significant gains in English and the English speakers demonstrated some gain in English proficiency. Thus, despite the small amount of English instruction, most students were able to make gains in English language proficiency. Second, all students made gains in Spanish proficiency and the gains were highly significant for the Spanish-speaking kindergartners. These are important results because they demonstrate that the bilingual immersion model's assumptions related to language development were accurate; that is, Spanish speakers increased their level of Spanish proficiency and began to develop some proficiency in English, and English speakers did not lose their English proficiency while acquiring Spanish proficiency skills.

A second set of important points concerns the achievement performance of the students. First, the English-speaking students acquired enough content after only one year of instruction through Spanish to be able to score average to above average in a test normed for *native* Spanish speakers. Second, the Spanish speakers performed from average to above average on the Spanish achievement test, demonstrating a good level of performance for these students when tested in their native language. Third, the English-speaking kindergartners and the Spanish-speaking first-graders scored average to only slightly below average in reading and maths; and the English-speaking first-graders scored average to above average in reading, language and maths. The fact that these students were able to score this high in English, despite having received their instruction in Spanish, demonstrates that the students were acquiring the maths concepts in Spanish, and they were able to apply these concepts when tested in English. Thus, the achievement results also validate the achievement assumptions underlying the bilingual immersion model in that the model assumes that content that is learned in Spanish will be available in English as well. The fact that the students were able to score as well as they did demonstrates that the concepts were available to them in both languages. These findings were comparable to the results reported by the San Diego City Schools (Lindholm, 1987) and three other bilingual immersion programmes in California (Lindholm, 1987). The consistency of the findings across other school sites also adds validity to the achievement and language assumptions underlying the bilingual immersion model.

The characteristics of the bilingual immersion model are, of course, markedly different from most bilingual education programmes designed for linguistic minority children which seldom provide for the development and maturation of adult-level linguistic competence in the children's L1. Bilingual immersion education also differs from the highly successful foreign language immersion programmes which have provided extraordinary opportunities for linguistic majority children to acquire foreign languages. Bilingual immersion education would appear to offer both linguistic minority and majority children excellent academic and language acquisition opportunities and, of relevance here, we see no brighter prospects for the conservation of the valuable language resources discussed earlier than those to be gained through participation in a bilingual immersion programme.

## Secondary Level Bilingual Partial Immersion Programme

Another promising experimental model of education that would permit linguistic minority students the opportunity to develop a mature, educated level of proficiency in their home language is exemplified by the bilingual partial immersion programme at Mount Miguel High School, Grossmont Union High School District, in San Diego, California. The bilingual partial immersion programme was initiated in 1981 and is open to any interested incoming ninth-grader. Programme participants are divided into two streams: Intensive Spanish as a Second Language (ISSL) and Spanish for Native Speakers (SNS). The ISSL stream, which involves more exposure to Spanish language use and instruction than is practised in traditional Spanish foreign language courses since Spanish is used as the medium of instruction, demands a four-year commitment to Spanish (one hour per day, five days per week), enabling students to obtain more exposure to Spanish, particularly communicative input. For students in the SNS stream, Spanish is also the medium of instruction. Since SNS students enter the programme with varying degrees of oral-aural fluency but few have had any formal education in Spanish, SNS classes are intended to provide an opportunity for the development of Spanish academic language and literacy skills. Thus, the two streams of formal instruction in Spanish were designed to fulfil the differing needs for achieving Spanish academic proficiency in the two populations in this programme. After the first year, ISSL and SNS students participate together in one content course taught in Spanish each semester. All of the content courses satisfy graduation requirements. The curriculum design can be illustrated as follows:

| Year 1 | Year 2 | Year 3 | Year 4 |
|--------|--------|--------|--------|
| ISSL 1 | ISSL 2 | ISSL 3 | ISSL 4 |
| SNS 1  | SNS 2  | SNS 3  | SNS 4  |
|        | P.E.   | History | Government/Anthropology |

The third-year history course and the fourth-year government and anthropology courses are taught in alternating units of Spanish and English. P.E. is taught entirely in Spanish.

There are also traditional Spanish (hereafter SPANISH) foreign language courses taught at Mount Miguel, which focus on Spanish grammar and literacy largely using English as the medium of instruction.

We have been working with this bilingual partial immersion programme to help them examine the Spanish proficiency levels of SNS, ISSL and SPANISH students and to determine what factors are associated with high versus low Spanish proficient speakers in the programme.

A total of 236 ninth- to twelfth-grade students participated in the first year of data collection. Of these, 59 were in the SNS stream (17 in year 1, 24 in year 2, 11 in year 3, and 7 in year 4), 76 were in the ISSL stream (34 in year 1, 25 in year 2, 12 in year 3, and 5 in year 4), and 101 were in the SPANISH stream (53 in year 1, 30 in year 2, 15 in year 3, and 3 in year 4). Each student was administered the listening, reading and writing sub-tests of the Modern Language Association (MLA) Cooperative Foreign Language Test and a background questionnaire. The MLA speaking test was not included because it is very expensive to administer and score. The background questionnaire consists of four sections that record students' Spanish language background and exposure to Spanish, attitudes toward Spanish, motivation for learning or maintaining Spanish, and self-ratings of Spanish proficiency.

There are several characteristics which relate to the Spanish language experiences of the students in the different streams that are important in reporting and interpreting the results. In looking at their primary language, 82% of the SNS, 4% of the ISSL and 5% of the SPANISH students spoke Spanish as their first language. When the current home language is looked at, 29% of the SNS spoke only Spanish, 61% spoke both Spanish and English, and 10% used only English. Of the ISSL students, 3% used Spanish, 9% conversed in both Spanish and English, and the remainder spoke only English in the home. In the SPANISH group, none spoke only Spanish, 10% used both Spanish and English, and 90% conversed only in English in the home. What these data show is that most (90%) of the SNS students, 12% of the ISSL and 10% of the SPANISH students came from homes in which Spanish was used. Outside of the home, 93% of the SNS, 81% of the ISSL and only 45% of the SPANISH students reported that they used Spanish. These self-reported frequencies of Spanish use did not consider the amount of Spanish that was spoken at any particular time. Thus, SNS students may have held extended conversations whereas the ISSL or SPANISH students may have referred to the use of salutations or short phrases or sentences. The important point, though, is that twice as many ISSL students reported at least attempts to speak Spanish as did the SPANISH students outside of the home.

The results from two consecutive years of research are very consistent. They show that at every level and with almost every sub-test, the Mount Miguel students performed at or above what would be expected of them in listening, reading and writing in comparison with the MLA norming sample. In many cases, the ISSL and particularly the SNS groups scored much higher than the norming sample. In comparing the SNS, ISSL and SPANISH groups, where such comparisons were possible, the SNS group consistently scored higher than the ISSL group which scored higher than the SPANISH group. However, the difference between the ISSL and SPANISH groups was not always statistically significant.

In constructing a profile of the highly proficient Spanish speaker in the Mount Miguel bilingual partial immersion programme, several factors were evident. A proficient speaker was proficient in all three skills— listening, reading and writing—and could accurately assess his or her proficiency. In addition, the highly proficient speakers were exposed to and used more Spanish through interactions with others, watching Spanish TV programmes, and reading Spanish literature.

Perhaps more importantly, though, this study is one of the few that has addressed the native language proficiency of students who had previously received most, if not all, of their instruction in English and who wanted to develop their Spanish literacy skills. Thus, the results clearly show that the bilingual partial immersion programme is meeting its goals in providing native speakers with academic language and literacy skills in Spanish.

These findings are important for the L2 learning literature because of what they reveal about the Spanish proficiency levels of students who are educated in English. Most of the SPANISH, ISSL and SNS students who came from Spanish-speaking homes would be considered as native speakers of Spanish and second language learners of English. However, for most of these students, instruction has been through English to the exclusion of Spanish. Thus, in essence, they have more English than Spanish academic proficiency skills, especially decontextualized language skills. We would argue that these students need more investigative attention by second language learning researchers to determine how or whether they differ from other highly proficient Spanish speakers in their acquisition of high-level Spanish competencies. More information is needed about their process of Spanish language development and how best to design programmes of instruction that build on their existing language skills. This issue is complicated by the lack of tests that can adequately measure the Spanish language skills that these students possess.

Partial bilingual immersion programmes at the secondary level offer an extremely promising approach to conserve and build on the L1 proficiency skills of linguistic minority students while at the same time promoting high L2 proficiency skills for linguistic majority students. A partial bilingual immersion programme is also an excellent model to conserve the specialized language skills of highly proficient speakers who graduate from elementary-level bilingual immersion and foreign language immersion programmes.

## University Level Language Conservation Programme

Many American university campuses have high concentrations of students from diverse ethnolinguistic groups. The University of California at Los Angeles may be especially blessed in this regard in that there are large populations of students from several of these groups. While, for reasons discussed earlier in this paper, not all students in these ethnolinguistic groups have had the opportunity to acquire, maintain or develop linguistic competencies in their ancestral languages, it is evident that a substantial number have at least measurable proficiency in the languages of their forefathers. For many such students, these predominantly passive abilities constitute a resource that is valuable; one that might well serve as the basis on which to build toward high levels of productive skills at an advantageous rate and to a degree that might exceed those attained by more traditional approaches to foreign language education.

Recently, an experimental programme was designed and implemented at UCLA to provide Korean American students who have demonstrable levels of competence in spoken Korean an opportunity to acquire adult levels of linguistic and literacy skills in Korean. This programme permits registered Korean American students to enrol in an intensive Korean language programme jointly sponsored by UCLA and the Seoul National University (SNU). The first cohort of such students completed the intensive course designed for them during the Spring quarter of 1987. A second group went to Seoul in the spring of 1988.

The curriculum for the intensive course designed to meet the linguistic and literacy skill objectives was developed in collaboration with SNU Korean language teachers and faculty at UCLA in the departments of East Asian Languages and Cultures and Applied Linguistics. The programme of instruction includes many of the content-based features described earlier in this paper. It includes 30 hours of classroom instruction per week for ten weeks at SNU in Seoul. At least half of these hours are courses in Korean history, art, geography, literature and culture taught in a 'sheltered' version of Korean (i.e. language that is made comprehensible by limiting the initial input and accompanying communicative attempts with actions, objects, gestures, expressions, pictures and circumlocutions). In addition to classroom instruction, there are a number of problem-solving activities off-campus which require use of Korean, as well as residence in Korean homes while in Korea.

To evaluate the efficacy of this programme, data on each participant were collected. Pre-test data included Korean language proficiency, self-esteem, ethnolinguistic loyalties, as well as a host of other biographical data. The experiences of the students in and out of class were carefully monitored by an applied linguistics researcher, student diaries were also kept and analysed and post-tests were administered to ascertain gains in Korean language proficiency. These data, when completely analysed, will help to elucidate the contributions such a programme can make toward developing the students' competence and confidence in using Korean for subsequent academic, social or professional purposes. Also, the data will be analysed to examine the impact such an experience has on participants' views of themselves as representatives of this ethnolinguistic group and the impact that these attitudes may have on their success as Korean language acquirers.

We are, of course, optimistic that as a result of the experience with these populations, we will be able to demonstrate enormous strides toward the development of high-level language skills that are rarely attained in traditional university language courses. If we are proven correct, then one can confidently consider providing similar opportunities to Thai Americans, Polish Americans, and other ethnolinguistic groups.

## Discussion and Conclusion

These three model programmes differ in how they promote L1 conservation, but they do not differ in the importance that is attached to maintaining and developing the home language of linguistic minority students. The significance of developing the first language in the early elementary grades is critical for many linguistic minority students to expedite their learning of English and to facilitate their academic achievement (Cárdenas, 1984; Cummins, 1979; 1981b; Skutnabb-Kangas, 1981; Troike, 1986; Willig, 1985). If we subscribe to these L2 learning and bilingual education views, then L1 maintenance and development must be awarded a priority in the education of young linguistic minority children.

Our programme of research with the elementary-level and secondary-level bilingual immersion programmes follows a structural interaction model that attempts to look at the factors that lead to high versus low academic achievement and language proficiency. But, more importantly, we want to understand how student factors interact with instructional factors to facilitate students' development of their home languages. Furthermore, at the secondary level, we know very little about how best to integrate the results of first and second language learning research to inform us about how best to encourage the development of L1 academic proficiency of linguistic minority students in our schools.

One important factor to consider at the secondary and tertiary levels is that many of the students in the programmes cannot necessarily be classified as proficient speakers of their home language. While they are native speakers at varying levels, they have not advanced in their native language as they have in English. Many are much more fluent at an academic level in English than they are in their ancestral language. Second language learning researchers need to be aware of this population as one worthy of study. How does this population differ from the English monolingual population? How do their stages of development differ from those of English monolinguals beginning the study of a foreign language, or from English speakers who have had a few years of formal instruction or have acquired some language proficiency informally as a result of experiences in an L2 environment? These are issues that have not been adequately dealt with in the second language learning literature.

In conclusion, we have described three programmes at three different academic levels that are designed, in part, to support the conservation and development of linguistic minority students' home languages. These programmes are in their infancy. As we learn more about the critical factors in developing high-level literacy skills in linguistic minority students' ancestral languages, these programmes will be modified and replicated. We strongly believe that priority should be given to research that will teach us how we can most efficiently conserve the highly valuable language resources possessed by thousands of young people who could make major contributions toward resolution of our national foreign language resource deficits.

# 17 Contexts, processes, and products in second language acquisition and foreign language learning

BILL VANPATTEN and JAMES F. LEE

*University of Illinois at Urbana-Champaign, USA*

In this collection we have seen a rich array of research projects and thoughts on second language acquisition (SLA) and foreign language (FL) teaching. We have also seen at various points observations on how both research and teaching can or should be realized. It is time to return to our point of departure at the beginning of this volume and ask, 'Has this collection put any mega-order into the mega-inquiry?'

## Research and Theory

The first aspect of this collection that we would like to consider here is how some use or interpret the terms 'second language acquisition' and 'foreign language learning', particularly in terms of research issues. Is there a consensus on what these terms mean? The answer is, quite simply, 'no'. While Berns begins the volume with a discussion of the social context of language use, it is evident that not all authors make so careful a distinction. Some contributors maintain (either explicitly or implicitly, to be sure) that foreign language learning (FLL) is some type of SLA (Kramsch; Gass; Andersen; Eubank; Odlin). Others argue for a more restricted view of SLA that does not completely 'encompass' FLL (VanPatten). Still others find it useful to maintain a distinction (Wildner-Bassett) while others do not find that it is even necessary to consider the issue for their research purposes (Brooks; Bacon). While we mentioned before (see Introduction to Part I) that researchers' backgrounds colour their perspectives, we see in retrospect that whether or not one feels the need to distinguish between SLA and FLL is largely based upon one's particular research pursuits. If we envision language learning as a complex puzzle of interlocking pieces involving *contexts*, *processes* and *products*, then the following seem to fall out of the present volume's contributions.

First, a distinction between SLA and FLL is important when one's research domain is context. Specifically, social context, those situations in which language is *used*, has an impact on quality and quantity of language interaction(s), be it in the realm of input that the learner is exposed to or the output of the learner himself or herself.

Second, a distinction between SLA and FLL is of varying importance when it comes to processes, these being defined in two ways: psycholinguistic processes and psychosocial processes. The first is concerned with how learners build a grammatical system from the input that surrounds them; the latter is concerned with how learners (and their interlocutors) act during speech events and why they behave the way they do. In terms of psycholinguistics it would appear that the distinction is irrelevant. It is argued that the learner's language acquisition faculties do not change from environment to environment. However, in terms of psychosocial processes, the distinction might be important since pragmatic and communicative devices for language use seemingly do change from discourse context to discourse context.

Third, a distinction between SLA and FLL is useful in the discussion of product, both eventual proficiency gained and the relative impact of certain influences, e.g. first language influence. (We do not see in the present discussion that the process of first language influence actually changes from context to context; it is simply more present or less present in the product.)

As delineated here, these three areas can be viewed as an extension of Gass's division between variables internal and external to the learner, but we could take this discussion one step further. In Chapter 8, VanPatten made a detailed comparison of the output of two learners, one a classroom foreign language learner in the United States, another an adolescent residing in Puerto Rico. What emerged from the comparison were a distinction between superficial (output) differences and deep (processing) differences and the conclusion that context of learning results in superficial differences only. This is supported by Eubank's interpretation of the output differences between classroom and non-classroom acquisition of German negation.

In terms of building a theory of non-primary language acquisition, we might ask ourselves whether we are looking at or even *for* superficial or deep differences when examining learner data. To be sure, as VanPatten points out, superficial and deep should not be confused with unimportant and important, respectively. What is important in one situation or context, may not be so in another. Eubank, for example, finds the differences between the second and foreign language learners' outputs to be relatively unimportant since he is able to link them theoretically, i.e. they are traceable to the same source. However, Wildner-Bassett's output differences are indeed important as she seeks to examine what can be called 'pragmatic impact'. In short, for purposes of constructing a theory of *acquisition* the SLA–FLL distinction may be unimportant, but for purposes of understanding language *use*, it may be very important.

Recalling VanPatten's visual scheme in Chapter 2, we are inclined to agree that overlapping circles best captures this discussion. That is, FLL is neither contained by nor itself contains SLA. Rather, there is only part of FLL research that is relevant to SLA theory-building and that part must also overlap with research in English as a second language (ESL) and untutored language acquisition. FLL, on the other hand, as Kramsch points out, must be concerned with certain aspects of research that are not common to other domains of language learning, e.g. untutored language learning, pidgin formation. That is, FLL research must contain a substantial amount of classroom-orientated research.

## Language Teaching

In terms of language teaching and language curricula, we find that two general themes emerge. One is that theory-building can (and possibly should) be independent of pedagogy. Andersen, for example, explicitly claims that his discussion is not be construed as a programme for pedagogy, but rather as an outline for research. Eubank and Odlin likewise ignore the question of classroom procedure. On the other hand, some view research and teaching as closely related, either by suggesting that research 'expand its scope' to include more classroom-orientated issues (Kramsch), or by showing how research and theory might impact on what happens in the classroom (Savignon; Nattinger; Kiraly; and Schinke-Llano). In the latter case, the impact on the classroom is not necessarily viewed in the same way. Savignon views theory and research as having a broad impact on how teachers think about language learners and the outcomes of language learning. Her argument is that research is important for supporting or debunking beliefs, and from this research theory will emerge. Nattinger and Kiraly, on the other hand, find a tighter relationship, one in which specific aspects of research and theory have specific implications for curriculum development. Schinke-Llano follows Nattinger and Kiraly in looking for implications, but these implications are less specific. Her conclusion is that classrooms can and should be input- and acquisition-rich environments, with immersion-type classes being an example.

It is important to underscore an assumption underlying these various positions on teaching, an assumption that takes us back to theoretical and research issues. It would seem that, in deriving implications for the classroom from second language (L2) research/theory, one must assume that FLL and SLA are fundamentally the same, at least psycholinguistically, and that an L2 situation is in many respects superior to an FL situation. Indeed, Schinke-Llano makes this latter claim explicitly. What one does in deriving classroom implications from the research and theory is to make adjustments in the context so as to *facilitate* the processes involved in learning another language, i.e. one wants FL learners to *undergo* SLA in the classroom. This is an important point to emphasize since for years much of FL pedagogy has been built around an attempt to *overcome* the 'natural' psycholinguistic and psychosocial tendencies in language learning. The extreme form of contrastive analysis and audiolingualism's fear of errors are two such examples. In the implications for language teaching sampled in this collection, it is clear that 'natural' phenomena are not viewed negatively.

Not all in FL teaching would agree, to be sure. Higgs & Clifford (1982), Omaggio (1984; 1986), and Hammerly (1982; 1985) are but several examples of strong criticisms of pushing learners along 'natural' paths. The argument is that, unlike Schinke-Llano's claim, non-classroom L2 learning does not produce superior linguistic products and that 'unchecked' classroom learning produces equally 'bad' products.

As we reflect on these various positions, one aspect of the relationship between theory/research and teaching, and therefore, SLA and FLL, does emerge: that there are *constraints* on the effects of teaching. While an examination of major research findings is beyond the scope of these concluding remarks (but see VanPatten, forthcoming) we feel confident in suggesting that teaching a language cannot be haphazard or freely speculative. Language teaching must consider the results of research, it cannot ignore them. And at least some of the results of research are clearly not contextually bound. Thus, rather than dictate or even merely imply what should happen in the classroom, we prefer to think of theory and research as providing a set of principles that act as constraints on the range of classroom behaviours that are optimal for language learning. Teachers and curriculum designers are free to develop methodologies unique to their own and their language learners' needs, having only to check these methodologies against the set of principles derived from research.

It is perhaps important to illustrate with an example and then relate the discussion to the contributions presented in Part III. In VanPatten (forthcoming) a set of five principles are derived from research on non-primary language acquisition. Each principle is expanded and refined by a set of corollaries. Without getting into a discussion of the relevant L2 literature here, we present Principle 1 and its corollaries. Each should be self-explanatory.

> Principle 1. For successful language acquisition, learners need access to input that is communicatively and/or meaningfully orientated and comprehensible in nature.

>> Corollary 1. Learners cannot just receive input, they must interact with it to maximize the acquisition process(es). The type of appropriate and/or adequate interaction will change as the learner's ability with the L2 develops.

>> Corollary 2. Interaction with written input is crucial if learners are to avoid an extended plateauing phenomenon and if they are to broaden their discoursal skills (both written and oral).

>> Corollary 3. For early and early intermediate learners, input must not only be comprehensible, it must be comprehended with ease.

>> Corollary 4. By extension, degree and quality of language acquisition is partially determined by degree and quality of input received.

As we see it, Principle 1 and its corollaries do not tell a teacher what to do, nor do they suggest one particular methodology for the classroom. Instead, they act as a set of checks against which the curriculum designer and the classroom teacher can evaluate the method of their choice. Thus, the director of a language programme might ask 'Are we supplying both written and oral input that is comprehensible to the learner?' 'Is this

input varied and rich?' 'How are the learners asked to respond to the input?' and so on.

As we reflect on the contributions in Part III, and keeping in mind Kramsch's comments, we become aware that those seeking implications from L2 research really are not looking for mandates but for principles. They are not looking for the 'one way' to teach nor 'what to do on Monday morning'; rather, they seek knowledge about how learners go about the business of acquisition so that they can build curricula that do not 'fight the learner'. Schinke-Llano and Campbell & Lindholm are most clearly in line with this approach to the classroom and the former even serves as an example of how a curriculum might be evaluated against a set of principles. Kiraly and Nattinger do the same, but their particular curricula do not consider an entire set of principles. Instead, both authors focus on one particular aspect of language acquisition and then check curricula and teacher behaviours against it. In short, we believe we are in agreement with Savignon when she says that 'Teachers today look to research, both inside and outside the classroom, for insights regarding their role in the language learning process'; we, however, interpret 'insights' as principles.

## Conclusion

We readily acknowledge that our attempt to put mega-order into mega-inquiry has not provided a definitive response to the question of what the relationship is between SLA and FLL. Language acquisition is too complex for us to do so now and we further realize that both SLA and FLL must someday be 'reconciled' with child first language acquisition. We also readily admit that we have not touched upon all the possible research domains of language acquisition. We acknowledge, for example, that issues in language comprehension and strategies in communication are absent in the present discussion. Reading in another language is a fast-growing field of research, but we have not touched upon it in this volume. None the less, we hope to have underscored the notion that relating SLA and FLL is dependent upon background, goals, and the professional interests of language professionals. Whether the same or different, overlapping or exclusive, one embedded within the other, the relationship between SLA and FLL is a function of one's own purpose.

# References

ABNEY, S. 1986, Functional elements and licensing. Paper presented at GLOW-Colloquium, Gerona, Spain.

ACTON, W. 1983, Second language interpersonal communication: Paradigm and praxis. *Language Learning* 33, 193–215.

ADJÉMIAN, C. 1976, On the nature of interlanguage systems. *Language Learning* 26, 297–320.

ALGEO, J. 1960, Korean Bamboo English. *American Speech* 35, 117–23.

ALLWRIGHT, R. L. 1980, Turns, topics, and tasks: Patterns of participation in language learning and teaching. In D. Larsen-Freeman (ed.), *Discourse Analysis in Second Language Research* (pp. 165–87). Rowley, MA: Newbury House.

AMERICAN COUNCIL ON THE TEACHING OF FOREIGN LANGUAGES 1986, *ACTFL Proficiency Guidelines*. Hastings-on-Hudson, NY: ACTFL.

ANDERSEN, R. 1978, An implicational model for second language research. *Language Learning* 26, 221–82.

—— 1979a, The relationship between first language transfer and second language overgeneralization: Data from the English of Spanish speakers. In R. ANDERSEN (ed.), *The Acquisition and Use of Spanish and English as First and Second Languages* (pp. 43–58). Washington, DC: TESOL.

—— 1979b, Expanding Schumann's Pidginization Hypothesis. *Language Learning* 29, 105–19.

—— 1980, Creolization as the acquisition of a second language as a first language. In A. VALDMAN and A. HIGHFIELD (eds), *Theoretical Orientations in Creole Studies* (pp. 273–95). New York: Academic Press.

—— 1982, Determining the linguistic attributes of language attrition. In R. D. LAMBERT and B. FREED (eds), *The Loss of Language Skills* (pp. 83–188). Rowley, MA: Newbury House.

—— (ed.) 1983a, *Pidginization and Creolization as Language Acquisition*. Rowley, MA: Newbury House.

—— 1983b, Transfer to somewhere. In S. GASS and L. SELINKER (eds), *Language Transfer in Language Learning* (pp. 177–201). Rowley, MA: Newbury House.

—— 1984a, The One-to-One Principle of interlanguage construction. *Language Learning* 34, 77–95.

—— 1984b, What's gender good for, anyway? In R. ANDERSEN (ed.), *Second*

246

*Languages: A Cross-Linguistic Perspective* (pp. 77–99). Rowley, MA: Newbury House.

—— (ed) 1984c, *Second Languages: A Cross-Linguistic Perspective*. Rowley, MA: Newbury House.

—— 1986a, El desarrollo de la morfología verbal en el español como segundo idioma. In J. MEISEL (ed.), *Adquisición de lenguaje/Aquisicão da linguagem* (pp. 115–38). Frankfurt: Vervuert.

—— 1986b, Interpreting data: Second language acquisition of verbal aspect. Unpublished manuscript.

—— 1986c, The need for native language comparison data in interpreting second language data. Unpublished manuscript. Invited Forum Lecture, 1986 TESOL Summer Institute, Honolulu, HI.

ANDERSON, H. and RHODES, N. C. 1984, Immersion and other innovations in U.S. elementary schools. In S. J. SAVIGNON and M. S. BERNS (eds), *Initiatives in Communicative Language Teaching* (pp. 167–81). Reading, MA: Addison-Wesley.

ANTINUCCI, F. and MILLER, R. 1976, How children talk about what happened. *Journal of Child Language* 3, 169–89.

ASHER, J. 1972, Children's first languages as a model for second language learning. *Modern Language Journal* 56, 133–39.

—— 1977a, *Learning Another Language Through Actions: The Complete Teacher's Guidebook*. Los Gatos, CA: Sky Oaks Productions.

—— 1977b, Children learning another language: A developmental hypothesis. *Child Development* 48, 1040–48.

ASHER, J., KUSUDO, J. and DE LA TORRE, R. 1971, Learning a second language through commands: The second field test. *Modern Language Journal* 58, 24–32.

AUSUBEL, D., NOVAK, J. and HANESIAN, H. 1978, *Educational Psychology: A Cognitive View* (2nd edn). New York: Holt, Rinehart and Winston.

BACH, A. 1970, *Geschichte der deutschen Sprache*. Heidelberg, West Germany: Quelle and Meyer.

BACHMAN, L. and SAVIGNON, S. J. 1986, The evaluation of communicative language proficiency: A critique of the ACTFL oral interview. *Modern Language Journal* 70, 380–90.

BACON, S. C. 1985, The interaction of cognitive style and an oral interview for students of Spanish at the university level. Unpublished Ph.D. dissertation, Ohio State University.

BAIRD, B. and HEYNEMAN, J. 1982, A look at a company in-house English program. *JALT Newsletter* 16, 12–13.

BAKER, C. L. 1978, *Introduction to Generative-Transformational Syntax*. Englewood Cliffs, NJ: Prentice Hall.

BARIK, H. C. and SWAIN, M. 1976, A Canadian experiment in bilingual education: The Peel study. *Foreign Language Annals* 9, 465–79.

—— 1977, Report to the Elgin County Board of Education re: Evaluation of the 1976–1977 partial French immersion program in grades 5–7. Unpublished manuscript, Ontario Institute for Studies in Education, Toronto.

—— 1978, Evaluation of a bilingual education program in Canada: The Elgin study through grade six. *Cila Bulletin* 27, 32–58. (ERIC Document Reproduction Service No. ED 174 043.)

BARIK, H. C., SWAIN, M. and NWANUNOBI, E. 1977, English–French bilingual education: The Elgin study through grade five. *Canadian Modern Language Review* 33, 459–75.

BAUSCH, K. R. 1986, Fremdsprachendidaktik. In U. AMMON, N. DITTMAR and K. J. MATTHEIER (eds), *Sociolinguistics. An International Handbook of the Science of Language and Society* (pp. 1–37). New York: Walter de Gruyter.

BAUSCH, K. R. and KÖNIGS, F. G. 1983, Lernt oder erwirbt man Fremdsprachen im Unterricht? Zum Verhältnis von Sprachlehrforschung und Zweitsprachenerwerbsforschung. *Die Neueren Sprachen* 82, 308–36.

—— 1985, (Er)werben und (er)lernen. Eine Antwort und zwei Antworten. *Die Neueren Sprachen* 84, 218–33.

BAUSCH, K. R., KÖNIGS, F. and KOGELHEIDE, R. (eds) 1986, *Probleme und Perspektiven der Sprachlehrforschung*. Frankfurt: Scriptor.

BELLACK, A.A., KLIEBARD, H. M., HYMAN, R. T. and SMITH, F. L. 1966, *The Language of the Classroom*. New York: Teachers College Press.

BERETTA, A. 1987, The Bangalore project: Description and evaluation. In S. J. SAVIGNON and M. S. BERNS (eds), *Initiatives in Communicative Language Teaching II* (pp. 83–106). Reading, MA: Addison-Wesley.

BERNHARDT, E. 1986, Proficient texts or proficient readers? *ADFL Bulletin* 18, 25–28.

BERNS, M. 1987, Why language teaching needs the sociolinguist. Paper presented at the Illinois TESOL/BE Conference, Champaign, IL.

—— 1988, The cultural and linguistic context of English in West Germany. *World Englishes* 7.

BERWICK, R. C. 1985, *The Acquisition of Syntactic Knowledge*. Cambridge, MA: MIT Press.

BIALYSTOK, E. 1979, Explicit and implicit judgements of grammaticality. *Language Learning* 29, 81–103.

BICKERTON, D. 1977, Pidginization and creolization: Language acquisition and language universals. In A. VALDMAN (ed.), *Pidgin and Creole Linguistics* (pp. 49–69). Bloomington, Indiana: University Press.

—— 1983, Introduction. In T. HEUBNER, *A Longitudinal Analysis of the Acquisition of English* (pp. xxi–xxix). Ann Arbor, MI: Karoma.

BICKERTON, D. and GIVÓN, T. 1976, Pidginization and syntactic change: From SXV and VSX to SVX. In S. SEEVER, C. WALKER and S. MUFWENE (eds), *Papers from the Parasession on Diachronic Syntax* (pp. 9–39). Chicago: Chicago Linguistics Society.

BIRDSONG, D. 1987, On the question of negative evidence in second language acquisition. Paper presented at the annual meeting of the American Association of Applied Linguistics, San Francisco, CA.

—— 1988, Second language acquisition theory and the logical problem of the data. Paper presented at the Second Language Research Forum, Honolulu, HI.

BLEY-VROMAN, R. 1989, What is the logical problem of foreign language learning? In S. GASS and J. SCHACHTER (eds), *Linguistic Perspectives in Second Language Acquisition*. Cambridge: Cambridge University Press.

—— in press, The logical problem of foreign language learning. *Linguistic Analysis*.

BLOOM, L., LIFTER, K. and HAFITZ, J. 1980, Semantics of verbs and the development of verb inflection in child language. *Language* 56, 386–412.

BLUM-KULKA, S. and OLSHTAIN, E. 1986, Too many words: Length of utterance and pragmatic failure. *Journal of Pragmatics* 8, 47–61.

BOCK, J. K. and WARREN, R. 1985, Conceptual accessibility and syntactic structure in sentence formation. *Cognition* 21, 47–67.

BOHANNON, J. and STANOWICZ, L. in press, The issue of negative evidence: Adult responses to children's language errors. *Developmental Psychology*.

BOURDIEU, P. 1982, *Ce que parler veut dire*. Paris: Fayard.

BOWERMAN, M. 1985, What shapes children's grammar? In D. I. SLOBIN (ed.), *The Cross-Linguistic Study of Language Acquisition*, Vol. 2 (pp. 1257–1319). Hillsdale, NJ: Lawrence Erlbaum.

—— 1987, Commentary: Mechanisms of language acquisition. In B. MACWHINNEY (ed.), *Mechanisms of Language Acquisition* (pp. 443–66). Hillsdale, NJ: Lawrence Erlbaum.

BREEN, M. 1985, The social context for language learning—a neglected situation? *Studies in Second Language Acquisition* 7, 135–58.

BREEN, M. and CANDLIN, C. 1980, The essentials of a communicative curriculum in language teaching. *Applied Linguistics* 1, 89–112.

BREGA, E. and NEWELL, J. M. 1965, Comparison of performance by 'FLES' program students and regular French III students on Modern Language Association tests. *The French Review* 39, 433–38.

BROCK, C., CROOKES, G. and DAY, R. 1986, The differential effects of corrective feedback in native speaker–nonnative speaker conversation. In R. DAY (ed.), *Talking to Learn: Conversations in Second Language Acquisition* (pp. 229–36). Rowley, MA: Newbury House.

BROOKS, N. 1966, Language teaching: The new approach. *Phi Delta Kappa* 47, 357–59.

BROWN, H. D. 1987, *Principles of Language Learning and Teaching* (2nd edn). Englewood Cliffs, NJ: Prentice Hall Regents.

BROWN, R. 1973, *A First Language: The Early Stages*. Cambridge, MA: Harvard University Press.

BRUNER, J. 1985, Vygotsky: A historical and conceptual perspective. In J. V. WERTSCH (ed.), *Culture, Communication and Cognition* (pp. 21–34). Cambridge: Cambridge University Press.

BYBEE, J. L. 1985, *Morphology*. Amsterdam/Philadelphia: John Benjamins.

CAMPBELL, R. N. 1984, The immersion approach to foreign language teaching. In J. LUNDIN and D. P. DOLSON (eds), *Studies on Immersion Education: A Collection for United States Educators* (pp. 114–43). Sacramento, CA: California Department of Education, Office of Bilingual Bicultural Education. (ERIC Document Reproduction Service No. ED 239 509.)

CANADIAN PARENTS FOR FRENCH 1986, *The CPF Immersion Directory, 1986*.

CANCINO, H. 1976, Grammatical morphemes in second language acquisition— Marta. Unpublished qualifying paper, Harvard University.

CÁRDENAS, J. A. 1984, The role of native language instruction in bilingual education. *NABE Journal* 8, 1–10.

CATFORD, J. C. 1965, *A Linguistic Theory of Translation*. London: Oxford University Press.

CAZDEN, C., JOHN, V. P. and HYMES, D. (eds) 1972, *Functions of Language in the Classroom*. New York: Teachers College Press.

CHAUDRON, C. 1983, Foreigner talk—An aid to learning? In H. W. SELIGER and

M. H. LONG (eds), *Classroom Oriented Research in Second Language Acquisition* (pp. 127–45). Rowley, MA: Newbury House.

—— 1985, A method for examining the input/intake distinction. In S. GASS and C. MADDEN (eds), *Input in Second Language Acquisition* (pp. 285–300). Rowley, MA: Newbury House.

—— 1986, The interaction of quantitative and qualitative approaches to research: A view of the second language classroom. *TESOL Quarterly* 26, 709–17.

—— 1988, *Second Language Classrooms: Research on Teaching and Learning.* New York: Cambridge University Press.

CHAUDRON, C. and RICHARDS, J. 1986, The effect of discourse markers on the comprehension of lectures. *Applied Linguistics* 7, 113–27.

CHOMSKY, C. 1969, *The Acquisition of Syntax in Children from 5 to 10.* Cambridge, MA: MIT Press.

CHOMSKY, N. 1965, *Aspects of the Theory of Syntax.* Cambridge, MA: MIT Press.

—— 1981a, *Lectures on Government and Binding.* Dordrecht: Foris.

—— 1981b, Markedness and core grammar. In A. BELLETTI, L. BRANDI and L. RIZZI (eds), *Theory of Markedness in Generative Grammar: Proceedings of the 1979 GLOW Conference* (pp. 123–46). Pisa: Scuola Normale Superiore di Pisa.

—— 1986, *Knowledge of Language.* New York: Praeger.

CHUN, A., DAY, R., CHENOWETH, A. and LUPPESCU, S. 1982, Types of errors corrected in native–non-native conversations. *TESOL Quarterly* 16, 537–47.

CLAHSEN, H. 1982, *Spracherwerb in der Kindheit.* Tübingen: Gunter Narr Verlag.

—— 1984a, The acquisition of German word order: A test case for cognitive approaches to L2 development. In R. ANDERSEN (ed.), *Second Languages: A Cross-Linguistic Perspective* (pp. 219–242). Rowley, MA: Newbury House.

—— 1984b, Der Erwerb von Kasusmarkierungen in der Kindersprache. *Linguistische Berichte* 89, 1–31.

—— 1987, Connecting theories of language processing and (second) language acquisition. In C. PFAFF (ed.), *First and Second Language Acquisition Processes* (pp. 103–16). Cambridge, MA: Newbury House.

CLAHSEN, M., MEISEL, J. and PIENEMANN, M. 1983a, *Deutsch als Fremdsprache.* Tübingen: Gunter Narr Verlag.

—— 1983b, *Deutsch als Zweitsprache. Der Spracherwerb ausländischer Arbeiter.* Tübingen: Gunter Narr Verlag.

CLAHSEN, H. and MUYSKEN, P. 1986, The accessibility of universal grammar to adult and child learners—A study of the acquisition of German word order. *Second Language Research* 2, 93–119.

CLARK, H. H. and CLARK, E. V. 1977, *Psychology and Language: An Introduction to Psycholinguistics.* New York: Harcourt Brace Jovanovich.

CLARK, R. 1984, Performing without competence. *Journal of Child Language* 1, 1–10.

COMRIE, B. 1981, *Language Universals and Linguistic Typology.* Chicago: University of Chicago Press.

CONRAD, A. and FISHMAN, J. 1977, English as a world language: The evidence. In J. FISHMAN, R. COOPER and A. CONRAD (eds), *The Spread of English* (pp. 3–76). Rowley, MA: Newbury House.

COOK, V. 1985, Chomsky's universal grammar and second language learning. *Applied Linguistics* 6, 19–44.

COPPIETERS, R. 1987, Competence differences between native and native-like nonnative speakers. *Language* 63, 544–73.

CORDER, S. P. 1973, *Introducing Applied Linguistics*. Harmondsworth: Penguin.

CORTÉS, C. E. 1986, The education of language minority students: A contextual interaction model. In *Beyond Language: Social and Cultural Factors in Schooling Language Minority Students* (pp. 3–33). Los Angeles: Evaluation, Dissemination and Assessment Center, California State University.

COULMAS, F. 1981, *Routine im Gespräch*. Linguistische Forschungen, Bd. 29. Wiesbaden: Athenaion.

CRUTTENDEN, A. 1981, Item-learning and system learning. *Journal of Psycholinguistic Research* 10, 79–88.

CUMMINS, J. 1979, Linguistic interdependence and the educational development of bilingual children. *Review of Educational Research* 49, 222–51.

—— 1980, The entry and exit fallacy in bilingual education. *NABE Journal* 4, 25–59.

—— 1981a, Four misconceptions about language proficiency in bilingual education. *NABE Journal* 5, 31–45.

—— 1981b, The role of primary language development in promoting educational success for language minority students. In *Schooling and Language Minority Students: A Theoretical Framework* (pp. 3–49). Los Angeles: Evaluation, Dissemination and Assessment Center, California State University.

CURRAN, C. 1976, *Counseling Learning in Second Languages*. East Dubuque, IL: Counseling Learning Publications.

CZIKO, G. A., LAMBERT, W. and GUTTER, R. 1979, French immersion programs and students' social attitudes: A multidimensional investigation. *Working Papers on Bilingualism* 19, 13–28.

DAHL, Ö. 1979, Typology of sentence negation. *Linguistics* 17, 79–106.

DALGADO, S. R. 1906, Dialecto Indo-Portugués do norte. *Revista Lusitana* 9, 142–66, 193–228.

DAWKINS, R. M. 1916, *Modern Greek in Asia Minor*. Cambridge: Cambridge University Press.

DAY, R. R. (ed.) 1986, *Talking to Learn: Conversation in Second Language Acquisition*. Rowley, MA: Newbury House.

DIPIETRO, R. 1982, The open-ended scenario: A new approach to conversation. *TESOL Quarterly* 16, 15–20.

DITTMAR, N. 1981, 'Regen bisschen pause geht'—More on the puzzle of interference. Unpublished manuscript, Free University of Berlin.

DIXON, R. M. W. 1972, *The Dyirbal Language of Northern Queensland*. Cambridge: Cambridge University Press.

DOMINGUE, N. 1971, Bhojpuri and Creole in Mauritius: A study of linguistic interference and its consequences in regard to synchronic variation and language change. Unpublished Ph.D. dissertation, University of Texas at Austin.

DOUGHTY, C. and PICA, T. 1986, 'Information Gap' tasks: Do they facilitate second language acquisition? *TESOL Quarterly* 20, 305–25.

DULAY, H. and BURT, M. K. 1974, A new perspective on the creative construction processes in child second language acquisition. *Language Learning* 24, 253–78.

DULAY, H., BURT, M. and KRASHEN, S. D. 1982, *Language Two*. New York: Oxford University Press.

DUPLESSIS, J., SOLIN, D., TRAVIS, L. and WHITE, L. 1987, UG or not UG, that is the question: A reply to Clahsen and Muysken. *Second Language Research* 3, 56–75.
ECKMAN, F. 1988, Markedness and the contrastive analysis hypothesis. *Language Learning* 27, 315–30.
EDELHOFF, C. 1981, Theme-oriented English teaching. Text varieties, media, skills, and project-work. In C. CANDLIN (ed. and trans.), *The Communicative Teaching of English* (pp. 49–62). London: Longman.
EDMONDSON, J. A. 1982, *Einführung in die Transformationssyntax des Deutschen.* Tübingen, West Germany: Gunter Narr Verlag.
EDMONDSON, W. 1981, *Spoken Discourse: A Model for Analysis.* London: Longman.
—— 1985, Discourse worlds in the classroom and in foreign language learning. *Studies in Second Language Acquisition* 7, 159–68.
EDMONDSON, W., HOUSE, J., KASPER, G. and STEMMER, B. 1984, Learning the pragmatics of discourse: A project report. *Applied Linguistics* 5, 113–27.
ELLIS, R. 1985, *Understanding Second Language Acquisition.* Oxford: Oxford University Press.
ERICKSON, F. and SHULTZ, J. 1981, When is a context? Some issues and methods in the analysis of social competence. In J. GREEN and C. WALLAT (eds), *Ethnography and Language in Educational Settings* (pp. 147–60). Norwood, NJ: Ablex.
—— 1982, *The Counselor as Gatekeeper: Social Interaction in Interviews.* New York: Academic Press.
EUBANK, L. 1987, The acquisition of German negation by formal language learners. In B. VANPATTEN, T. DVORAK and J. LEE (eds), *Foreign Language Learning: A Research Perspective* (pp. 33–51). Cambridge, MA: Newbury House.
FAERCH, C., HAASTRUP, K. and PHILLIPSON, R. 1984, *Learner Language and Language Learning.* Clevedon, Avon: Multilingual Matters.
FATHMAN, A. 1978, ESL and EFL learning: Similar or dissimilar? In C. BLATCHFORD and J. SCHACHTER (eds), *On TESOL '78: EFL Policies, Programs, Practices.* Washington, DC: TESOL.
FELIX, S. 1978, *Linguistische Untersuchungen zum natürlichen Zweitsprachenerwerb.* Munich: Wilhelm Fink.
—— 1981, The effect of formal instruction on second language acquisition. *Language Learning* 31, 81–112.
—— 1984, Two problems of language learning: On the interaction of universal grammar and language growth. Unpublished manuscript, University of Passau.
FELIX, S. and HAHN, A. 1985, Fremdsprachenunterricht und Sprachewerbsforschung. *Die Neueren Sprachen* 84, 191–206.
FERGUSON, C. 1966, National sociolinguistic profile formulas. In *Sociolinguistics: Proceedings of the UCLA Sociolinguistic Conference 1964.* The Hague: Mouton.
FINER, D. and BROSELOW, E. I. 1987, Second language acquisition of reflexive binding. *NELS* 16.
FIRTH, J. 1968, *Selected Papers of J. R. Firth.* London: Indiana University Press.
FLANDERS, N. A. 1970, *Analyzing Teaching Behavior.* Reading, MA: Addison-Wesley.

FLYNN, S. 1987, *A Parameter-Setting Model of L2 Acquisition: Experimental Studies in Anaphora*. Dordrecht: D. Reidel.

FODOR, J. 1983, *The Modularity of Mind*. Cambridge, MA: MIT Press.

FRAWLEY, W. and LANTOLF, J. P. 1985, Second language discourse: A Vygotskyan perspective. *Applied Linguistics* 6, 174–89.

FRECHETTE, E. 1976, Directions of research in the 1970s. In G. A. JARVIS (ed.), *An Integrative Approach to Foreign Language Teaching: Choosing Among the Options* (pp. 351–95). Skokie, IL: National Textbook Company.

FREED, B. 1980, Talking to foreigners versus talking to children: Similarities and differences. In R. SCARCELLA and S. KRASHEN (eds), *Research in Second Language Acquisition* (pp. 19–27). Rowley, MA: Newbury House.

—— 1984, Proficiency in context: The Pennsylvania experience. In S. J. SAVIGNON and M. S. BERNS (eds), *Initiatives in Communicative Language Teaching* (pp. 211–40). Reading, MA: Addison-Wesley.

GAIES, S. 1977, The nature of linguistic input in formal second language learning: Linguistic and communicative strategies in ESL teachers' classroom language. In H. D. BROWN, R. CRYMES and C. YORIO (eds), *Teaching and Learning English as Second Language: Trends in Research and Practice. On TESOL '77* (pp. 204–12). Washington, DC: TESOL.

—— 1979, Linguistic input in first and second language learning. In F. ECKMAN and A. HASTINGS (eds), *Studies in First and Second Language Learning* (pp. 185–93). Rowley, MA: Newbury House.

GALAMBOS, S. and GOLDIN-MEADOW, S. 1983, Learning a second language and metalinguistic awareness. In A. CHUKERMAN, M. MARKS and J. RICHARDSON (eds), *Papers from the Nineteenth Regional Meeting* (pp. 117–133). Chicago: Chicago Linguistic Society.

GARDNER, R. and LAMBERT, W. 1972, *Attitudes and Motivation in Second Language Learning*. Rowley, MA: Newbury House.

GASS, S. 1979, Second language acquisition and language universals. In R. DIPIETRO, W. FRAWLEY and A. WEDEL (eds), *The First Delaware Symposium on Language Studies*. Newark: University of Delaware Press.

—— 1987, The resolution of conflicts among competing systems: A bidirectional perspective. *Applied Psycholinguistics* 8, 329–50.

—— 1988a, Integrating research areas: A framework for second language studies. *Applied Linguistics* 9, 198–217.

—— 1988b, Approaches to language universals: Will the relevant one please stand up? Plenary address, Second Language Research Forum, Honolulu, HI.

—— in press, A possible role for explicit grammar instruction. In R. PHILLIPSON, E. KELLERMAN, L. SELINKER and M. SWAIN (eds), *Papers in Memoriam for Claus Faerch*. Clevedon, Avon: Multilingual Matters.

GASS, S. and MADDEN, C. (eds) 1985, *Input in Second Language Acquisition*. Rowley, MA: Newbury House.

GASS, S. and SELINKER, L. (eds) 1983, *Language Transfer in Language Learning*. Rowley, MA: Newbury House.

GASS, S. and VARONIS, E. M. 1984, The effect of familiarity on the comprehensibility of nonnative speech. *Language Learning* 34, 65–89.

—— 1985a, Variation in native speaker modification to nonnative speakers. *Studies in Second Language Acquisition* 7, 37–58.

—— 1985b, Task variation in nonnative/nonnative negotiation of meaning. In S.

Gass and C. Madden (eds), *Input in Second Language Acquisition* (pp. 149–61). Rowley, MA: Newbury House.

—— 1985c, Miscommunication in native/nonnative conversation. *Language in Society* 14, 327–43.

—— 1986, Sex differences in NNS/NNS interactions. In R. R. Day (ed.), *Talking to Learn: Conversation in Second Language Acquisition* (pp. 327–51). Rowley, MA: Newbury House.

—— 1988, Conversational interactions and the development of an L2. Paper presented at the annual meeting of TESOL, Chicago, IL.

—— 1989, Incorporated repairs in non-native discourse. In M. Eisenstein (ed.), *Variation and Second Language Acquisition*. New York: Plenum Press.

Genesee, F. 1974, An evaluation of the English writing skills of students in French immersion programs. Unpublished manuscript, Protestant Schools of Greater Montreal.

—— 1978, A longitudinal evaluation of an early immersion school program. *Canadian Journal of Education* 3, 31–50.

—— 1984, Historical and theoretical foundations of immersion education. In J. Lundin and D. P. Dolson (eds), *Studies on Immersion Education: A Collection for United States Educators* (pp. 32–57). Sacramento: California Department of Education, Office of Bilingual Bicultural Education. (ERIC Document Reproduction Service No. ED 239 509.)

—— 1986, The baby and the bathwater, or What immersion has to say about bilingual education. *NABE Journal* 10, 227–54.

Gilbert, G. 1983, Transfer in second language acquisition. In R. Andersen (ed.), *Pidginization and Creolization as Language Acquisition* (pp. 168–80). Rowley, MA: Newbury House.

Givón, T. (ed.) 1983, *Topic Continuity in Discourse*. Amsterdam: John Benjamins.

—— 1984, Universals of discourse structure and second language acquisition. In W. Rutherford (ed.), *Language Universals and Second Language Interaction* (pp. 110–39). Amsterdam: John Benjamins.

Gleitman, L. 1981, Maturational determinants of language growth. *Cognition* 10, 103–14.

Goodlad, J. 1984, *A Place Called School: Prospects for the Future*. St Louis, MO: McGraw-Hill.

Goodman, M. 1971, The strange case of Mbugu. In D. Hymes (ed.), *Pidginization and Creolization of Languages* (pp. 243–54). Cambridge: Cambridge University Press.

Gray, T., Rhodes, N., Campbell, R. and Snow, M. 1981, *Comparative Evaluation of Elementary School Foreign Language Programs: Final Report*. Washington, DC: Center for Applied Linguistics. (ERIC Document Reproduction Service No. ED 238 255.)

Green, J. 1983a, Exploring classroom discourse: Linguistic perspectives on teaching learning processes. *Educational Psychologist* 18, 180–99.

—— 1983b, Research on teaching as a linguistic process: A state of the art. In E. Gordon (ed.), *Review of Research in Education 10* (pp. 152–252). Washington, DC: American Educational Research Association.

Green, J. and Bloome, D. 1983, Ethnography and reading: Issues, approaches, criteria and findings. *National Reading Conference Yearbook* 32, 6–30. Rochester, NY: National Reading Conference.

Green, J. and Harker, J. 1982, Gaining access to learning: Conversational, social and cognitive demands on group participation. In C. WILKINSON (ed.), *Communicating in the Classroom* (pp. 183–221). New York: Academic Press.

GREEN, J. and SMITH, D. 1983, Teaching and learning: A linguistic perspective. *Elementary School Journal* 83, 353–91.

GREEN, J. and WALLAT, C. 1981, Mapping instructional conversations. In J. GREEN and C. WALLAT (eds), *Ethnography and Language in Educational Settings* (pp. 161–205). Norwood, NJ: Ablex.

GREEN, J. and WEADE, R. 1985, Reading between the words: Social cues to lesson participation. *Theory into Practice* 24, 14–21.

—— 1987, In search of meaning: A sociolinguistic perspective on lesson construction and reading. In D. BLOOME (ed.), *Literacy and Schooling*. Norwood, NJ: Ablex.

GREENBERG, J. 1966, Some universals of grammar with particular reference to the order of meaningful elements. In J. GREENBERG (ed.), *Universals of Language* (pp. 73–113). Cambridge, MA: MIT Press.

GREGG, K. 1989, Second language acquisition theory: The case for a generative perspective. In S. GASS and J. SCHACHTER (eds), *Linguistic Perspectives in Second Language Acquisition*. Cambridge: Cambridge University Press.

—— 1988, Epistemology without knowledge: Schwartz on Chomsky, Fodor and Krashen. *Second Language Research* 4, 66–80.

GREMMO, M., HOLES, H. and RILEY, P. 1978, *Taking the Initiative: Some Pedagogical Applications of Discourse Analysis*. University of Nancy: CRAPEL.

GUTHRIE, E. 1984, Intake, communication, and second language teaching. In S. J. SAVIGNON and M. S. BERNS (eds), *Initiatives in Communicative Language Teaching* (pp. 34–54). Reading, MA: Addison-Wesley.

HAIDER, H. and PRINZHORN, M. (eds) 1986, *Verb Second Phenomena in Germanic Languages*. Dordrecht: Foris.

HAKES, D. 1980, *The Development of Metalinguistic Abilities in Children*. Berlin: Springer Verlag.

HAKUTA, K. 1974, Prefabricated patterns and the emergence of structure in second language acquisition. *Language Learning* 24, 287–97.

—— 1976, A case study of a Japanese child learning English as a second language. *Language Learning* 26, 321–51.

HAMILTON, S. 1982, The social side of schooling: Ecological studies of classrooms and schools. *Elementary School Journal* 83, 313–34.

HAMMERLY, H. 1982, *Synthesis in Second Language Teaching*. Blaine, WA: Second Language Publications.

—— 1985, *An Integrated Theory of Language Teaching*. Blaine, WA: Second Language Publications.

HARDER, P. 1980, Discourse and self-expression—on the reduced personality of the second language learner. *Applied Linguistics* 1, 262–70.

HARLEY, B. 1979, French gender rules in the speech of English-dominant, French-dominant, and monolingual French-speaking children. *Working Papers on Bilingualism* 19, 129–56.

—— 1982, Age-related differences in the acquisition of the French verb system by anglophone students in French immersion programs. Unpublished Ph.D. dissertation, University of Toronto.

HARLEY, B. and SWAIN, M. 1984, The interlanguage of immersion students

and its implications for second language teaching. In C. A. DAVIES and
A. P. R. HOWATT (eds), *Interlanguage* (pp. 291–311). Edinburgh: Edinburgh
University Press.

HATCH, E. (ed.) 1978a, *Second Language Acquisition: A Book of Readings*.
Rowley, MA: Newbury House.

HATCH, E. 1978b, Discourse analysis and second language acquisition. In E.
HATCH (ed.), *Second Language Acquisition: A Book of Readings* (pp.
401–35). Rowley, MA: Newbury House.

—— 1983a, *Psycholinguistics*. Rowley, MA: Newbury House.

—— 1983b, Simplified input and second language acquisition. In R. ANDERSEN
(ed.), *Pidginization and Creolization as Language Acquisition* (pp. 64–86).
Rowley, MA: Newbury House.

HATCH, E., FLASHNER, V. and HUNT, L. 1986, The experience model and language
teaching. In R. R. DAY (ed.), *Talking to Learn: Conversation in Second
Language Acquisition* (pp. 5–22). Rowley, MA: Newbury House.

HAWKINS, B. 1981, Papiamentu: A study in nonnative use. Unpublished paper,
UCLA.

—— 1985, Is an 'appropriate response' always so appropriate? In S. GASS and
C. MADDEN (eds), *Input in Second Language Acquisition* (pp. 162–78).
Rowley, MA: Newbury House.

HAWKINS, J. 1983, *Word Order Universals*. New York: Academic Press.

HEESCHEN, V. 1978, The metalinguistic vocabulary of a speech community in the
highlands of Irian Jaya (West New Guinea). In A. SINCLAIR, R. JARVELLA
and W. LEVELT (eds), *The Child's Conception of Language* (pp. 155–87).
Berlin: Springer Verlag.

HEIDELBERGER FORSCHUNGSPROJEKT 'Pidgin Deutsch' 1975, *Sprache und Kommuni-
kation ausländischer Arbeiter*. Kronberg/Taunus: Scriptor.

HELGESEN, M. 1987, Playing in English: Games in the L2 classroom in Japan. In
S. SAVIGNON and M. BERNS (eds), *Initiatives in Communicative Language
Teaching II* (pp. 205–25). Reading, MA: Addison-Wesley.

HENNE, H. and REHBOCK, H. 1979, *Einführung in die Gesprächsanalyse*. Berlin:
de Gruyter.

HENZL, V. 1973, Linguistic register of foreign language instruction. *Language
Learning* 23, 207–22.

—— 1979, Foreigner talk in the classroom, *IRAL* 17, 159–65.

HERNÁNDEZ PEÑA, F. 1984, *Teorías psico-sociolingüísticas y su aplicación a la
adquisición del español como lengua materna*. Madrid: Siglo XXI.

HIGGS, T. V. (ed.) 1984, *Teaching for Proficiency: The Organizing Principle*.
Lincolnwood, IL: National Textbook Company.

—— 1985, The Input Hypothesis: An inside look. *Foreign Language Annals* 18,
197–203.

HIGGS, T. V. and CLIFFORD, R. 1982, The push toward communication. In T. V.
HIGGS (ed.), *Curriculum, Competence and the Foreign Language Teacher*
(pp. 57–79). Lincolnwood, IL: National Textbook Company.

HÖLZ-MÄNTÄRRI, J. 1984, Sichtbarmachung und Beurteilung translatorischer
Leistungen bei der Ausbildung von Berufstranslatoren. In W. WILSS and
G. THOME (eds), *Die Theorie des Übersetzens und ihr Aufschlusswert für
die Übersetzungs- und Dolmetschdidaktik* (pp. 176–85). Tübingen, West
Germany: Gunter Narr Verlag.

HOUSE, J. 1980, Übersetzen im Fremdsprachenunterricht. In S. POULSEN and

W. WILSS (eds), *Angewandte Übersetzungswissenschaft* (pp. 7–17). Aarhus, Denmark: Aarhus.

—— 1984, Some methodological problems and perspectives in contrastive discourse analysis. *Applied Linguistics* 5, 245–54.

—— 1986, Cross-cultural pragmatics and foreign language teaching. In K. R. BAUSCH, F. KÖNIGS and R. KOGELHEIDE (eds), *Probleme und Perspektiven der Sprachlehrforschung* (pp. 281–95). Frankfurt: Scriptor.

HUANG, J. and HATCH, E. 1978, A Chinese child's acquisition of English. In E. HATCH (ed.), *Second Language Acquisition: A Book of Readings* (pp. 118–31). Rowley, MA: Newbury House.

HUEBNER, T. 1979, Order-of-acquisition versus dynamic paradigm: A comparison of method in interlanguage research. *TESOL Quarterly* 13, 21–28.

—— 1983, *A Longitudinal Analysis of the Acquisition of English*. Ann Arbor, MI: Karoma.

—— 1985, System and variability in interlanguage syntax. *Language Learning* 35, 141–63.

HYLTENSTAM, K. 1977, Implicational patterns in interlanguage syntax variation. *Language Learning* 27, 383–411.

HYMES, D. 1972, On communicative competence. In J. B. PRIDE and J. HOLMES (eds), *Sociolinguistics: Selected Readings* (pp. 269–93). Harmondsworth: Penguin Books.

IVIR, V. 1981, Formal correspondence versus translation equivalence revisited. *Poetics Today* 2, 51–59.

JACKSON, J. 1974, Language identity of the Colombian Vaupés Indians. In R. BAUMAN and J. SHERZER (eds), *Explorations in the Ethnography of Speaking* (pp. 50–64). Cambridge: Cambridge University Press.

JACOBSEN, T. 1986, ¿Aspecto antes que tiempo? Una mirada a la adquisición temprana del español. In J. MEISEL (ed.), *Adquisición del lenguaje/Aquisição da linguagem* (pp. 97–114). Frankfurt: Vervuert.

JANSEN, B., LALLEMAN, J. and MUYSKEN, P. 1981, The Alternation Hypothesis: Acquisition of Dutch word order by Turkish and Moroccan foreign workers. *Language Learning* 31, 315–36.

JORDENS, P. 1980, Interlanguage research: Interpretation or explanation. *Language Learning* 30, 195–207.

—— 1987, The acquisition of word order in Dutch and German as L1 and L2. Paper presented at the Second Language Research Forum, Los Angeles.

KACHRU, B. 1983, *The Indianization of English: The English Language in India*. Delhi: Oxford University Press.

KACHRU, Y. 1986, Applied linguistics and foreign language teaching: A non-Western perspective. *Studies in the Linguistic Sciences* 16, 35–52.

KARABINUS, R. 1976, Report of foreign language instruction differences in grades 5, 6 and 7. Unpublished manuscript, Hinsdale Public Schools, Hinsdale, IL.

KASPER, G. 1982, Teaching induced aspects of interlanguage discourse. *Studies in Second Language Acquisition* 4, 99–113.

—— 1986, Zur Prozeßdimension in der Lernersprache. In K. R. BAUSCH, F. KÖNIGS and R. KOGELHEIDE (eds), *Probleme und Perspektiven der Sprachlehrforschung* (pp. 197–224). Frankfurt: Scriptor.

KELLERMAN, E. 1977, Towards a characterization of the strategy of transfer in second language learning. *Interlanguage Studies Bulletin* 2, 58–145.

—— 1983, Now you see it, now you don't. In S. GASS and L. SELINKER (eds), *Language Transfer in Language Learning* (pp. 112–34). Rowley, MA: Newbury House.

—— 1984, The empirical evidence for the influence of L1 on interlanguage. In A. DAVIES, C. CRIPER and A. P. R. HOWATT (eds), *Interlanguage*. Edinburgh: Edinburgh University Press.

KLEIN, W. and DITTMAR, N. 1979, *Developing Grammars*. Berlin: Springer Verlag.

KÖNIGS, F. 1979, *Übersetzung in Theorie und Praxis: Ansatzpunkte für die Konzeption einer Didaktik der Übersetzung*. Bochum, West Germany: Seminar für Sprachlehrforschung der Ruhruniversität Bochum.

KOOPMAN, H. 1984, *The Syntax of Verbs*. Dordrecht: Foris.

KOORDINIERUNGSGREMIUM IM DFG, SCHWERPUNKT SPRACHLEHRFORSCHUNG (ed.) 1983, *Sprachlehr und Sprachlernforschung: Begründung einer Disziplin*. Tübingen: Gunter Narr Verlag. Reviewed by C. Kramsch in *Modern Language Journal* 70, 169–71.

KOSTER, J. 1975, Dutch as a SOV language. In A. KRAAK (ed.), *Linguistics in the Netherlands 1972–1973* (pp. 165–77). Assen/Amsterdam: Van Gorcum.

KRAMSCH, C. 1981, *Discourse Analysis and Second Language Teaching*. Washington, DC: Center for Applied Linguistics.

—— 1985, Classroom interaction and discourse options. *Studies in Second Language Acquisition* 7, 169–83.

—— 1986, From language proficiency to interactional competence. *Modern Language Journal* 70, 366–72.

KRASHEN, S. D. 1981, *Second Language Acquisition and Second Language Learning*. Oxford: Pergamon Press.

—— 1982, *Principles and Practice in Second Language Acquisition*. New York: Pergamon Press.

—— 1984, Immersion: Why it works and what it has taught us. *Language and Society* (pp. 61–64). Ottawa: Ministry of Supply and Services.

KRASHEN, S. D. and TERRELL, T. D. 1983, *The Natural Approach. Language Acquisition in the Classroom*. Hayward, CA: The Alemany Press (and New York: Pergamon Press).

KUMPF, L. 1984, Temporal systems and universality in interlanguage: A case study. In F. ECKMAN, L. BELL and D. NELSON (eds), *Universals of Second Language Acquisition* (pp. 132–43). Rowley, MA: Newbury House.

KUWAHATA, M. 1984, The negation system in the interlanguage of a Japanese speaker. Unpublished master's thesis, UCLA.

LADMIRAL, J. R. 1977, La traduction dans le cadre de l'institution pédagogique. *Die Neueren Sprachen* 5, 489–516.

LAMBERT, R. D. 1987, The case for a national foreign language center: An editorial. *Modern Language Journal* 71, 1–11.

LAMBERT, W. 1984, An overview of issues in immersion education. In J. LUNDIN and D. P. DOLSON (eds), *Studies on Immersion Education: A Collection for United States Educators* (pp. 8–30). Sacramento, CA: California State Department of Education, Office of Bilingual Bicultural Education. (ERIC Document Reproduction Service No. ED 239 509.)

LAMBERT, W. and TUCKER, G. R. 1972, *Bilingual Education of Children: The St Lambert Experiment*. Rowley, MA: Newbury House.

LANGE, D. 1987, Developing and implementing proficiency oriented tests for a new language requirement at the University of Minnesota: Issues and problems for implementing the ACTFL/ETS/ILR Proficiency Guidelines. In A. VALDMAN (ed.), *Proceedings of the Symposium on the Evaluation of Foreign Language Proficiency* (pp. 275–90). Bloomington, IN: Committee for Research and Development in Language Instruction, Indiana University.

LANTOLF, J. and FRAWLEY, W. 1986, Oral proficiency testing: A critical analysis. *Modern Language Journal* 70, 337–45.

LAPKIN, S. 1982, The English writing skills of French immersion pupils at grade five. *Canadian Modern Language Review* 39, 24–33.

LAPKIN, S. and CUMMINS, J. 1984, Canadian French immersion education: Current administrative and instructional practices. In J. LUNDIN and D. P. DOLSON (eds), *Studies on Immersion Education: A Collection for United States Educators* (pp. 58–86). Sacramento, CA: California State Department of Education, Office of Bilingual Bicultural Education. (ERIC Document Reproduction Service No. ED 239 509.)

LAPKIN, S. and SWAIN, M. 1984, Research update. *Language and Society* (pp. 48–54). Ottawa: Ministry of Supply and Services.

LARSEN-FREEMAN, D. 1975, The acquisition of grammatical morphemes by adult ESL students. *TESOL Quarterly* 9, 409–19.

—— 1976, An explanation for the morpheme acquisition order of second language learners. *Language Learning* 26, 125–34.

—— (ed.) 1980, *Discourse Analysis in Second Language Research*. Rowley, MA: Newbury House.

—— 1985, State of the art on input in second language acquisition. In S. GASS and C. MADDEN (eds), *Input in Second Language Acquisition* (pp. 433–44). Rowley, MA: Newbury House.

LEE, J. F. 1987a, Morphological factors influencing pronominal reference assignment by learners of Spanish. In T. MORGAN, J. LEE and B. VANPATTEN (eds), *Language and Language Use: Studies in Spanish* (pp. 221–32). Lanham, MD: University Press of America.

—— 1987b, The Spanish subjunctive: An information processing perspective. *Modern Language Journal* 71, 50–57.

LEE, J. F. and MUSUMECI, D. 1988, On hierarchies of reading skills and text types. *Modern Language Journal* 72: 173–87.

LENNEBERG, E. H. 1967, *Biological Foundations of Language*. New York: John Wiley & Sons.

LE PAGE, R. B. and TABOURET-KELLER, A. 1985, *Acts of Identity: Creole-based Approaches to Language and Ethnicity*. Cambridge: Cambridge University Press.

LESLAU, W. 1945, The influence of Cushitic on the Semitic languages of Ethiopia. *Word* 1, 59–82.

LI, C. 1984, From verb-medial analytic language to verb-final synthetic language: A case of typological change. In C. BRUGMAN *et al.* (eds), *Proceedings from the Tenth Annual Meeting of the Berkeley Linguistics Society* (pp. 307–23). Berkeley, CA: Berkeley Linguistics Society.

LIGHTBOWN, P. 1983, Exploring relationships between developmental and instructional sequences in L2 acquisition. In H. SELIGER and M. LONG (eds), *Classroom Oriented Research in Second Language Acquisition* (pp. 217–45). Rowley, MA: Newbury House.

—— 1985a, Can language acquisition be altered by instruction? In K. HYLTENSTAM and M. PIENEMANN (eds), *Modelling and Assessing Second Language Acquisition* (pp. 101–12). Clevedon: Multilingual Matters.

—— 1985b, Great expectations: Second language acquisition research and classroom teaching. *Applied Linguistics* 6, 174–89.

LIGHTFOOT, D. 1981, Explaining syntactic change. In N. HORNSTEIN and D. LIGHTFOOT (eds), *Explanation in Linguistics* (pp. 209–40). London: Longman.

LINDHOLM, K. 1987, *Directory of Bilingual Immersion Programs: Two-Way Bilingual Education for Language Minority and Majority Students. Educational Report No. 8.* Los Angeles: Center for Language Education and Research, UCLA.

LITTLEWOOD, W. 1983, Contrastive pragmatics and the foreign language learner's personality. *Applied Linguistics* 4, 200–06.

LONG, M. H. 1980a, Input, interaction and second language acquisition. Unpublished Ph.D. dissertation, UCLA.

—— 1980b, Inside the 'Black Box': Methodological issues in classroom research on language learning. *Language Learning* 30, 1–42.

—— 1981, Input, interaction, and second language acquisition. *Annals of the New York Academy of Sciences* 379, 259–78.

—— 1983a, Does second language instruction make a difference? *TESOL Quarterly* 17, 359–82.

—— 1983b, Inside the 'Black Box': Methodological issues in classroom research on language learning. In H. W. SELIGER and M. H. LONG (eds), *Classroom Oriented Research in Second Language Acquisition* (pp. 3–36). Rowley, MA: Newbury House.

LONG, M. H. and PORTER, P. 1985, Group work, interlanguage talk, and second language acquisition. *TESOL Quarterly* 19, 207–28.

LONG, M. H. and SATO, C. 1983, Classroom foreigner talk discourse: form and functions of teachers' questions. In H. W. SELIGER and M. H. LONG (eds), *Classroom Oriented Research in Second Language Acquisition* (pp. 268–85). Rowley, MA: Newbury House.

LOWE, PARDEE JR 1982, The U.S. government's foreign language attrition and maintenance experience. In R. D. LAMBERT and B. F. FREED (eds), *The Loss of Language Skills* (pp. 176–89). Rowley, MA: Newbury House.

LOWENBERG, P. H. 1984, English in the Malay archipelago: Nativization and its functions in a sociolinguistic area. Ph.D. dissertation, Unversity of Illinois at Urbana-Champaign.

LOZANOV, G. 1979, *Suggestology and Outlines of Suggestopedy.* New York: Gordon and Breach.

LUJÁN, M., MINAYA, L. and SANKOFF, D. 1984, The Universal Consistency Hypothesis and the prediction of word order acquisition stages in the speech of bilingual children. *Language* 60, 343–71.

MACK, M. 1986, A study of semantic and syntactic processing in monolinguals and fluent early bilinguals. *Journal of Psycholinguistic Research* 15, 463–88.

MAGURA, B. 1984, Style and meaning in African English: A sociolinguistic analysis of South African and Zimbabwean English. Ph.D. dissertation, University of Illinois at Urbana-Champaign.

MALEY, A. 1984, 'I got religion'—Evangelism in language teaching. In S. J. SAVIGNON and M. S. BERNS (eds), *Initiatives in Communicative Language Teaching* (pp. 79–86). Reading, MA: Addison-Wesley.

MANZINI, R. and WEXLER, K. 1985, Parameters, learnability and binding theory. Unpublished manuscript, University of California, Irvine.

MAY, R. 1985, *Logical Form*. Cambridge, MA: MIT Press.

McHOUL, A. 1978, The organization of formal talk in the classroom. *Language in Society* 7, 183–213.

McLAUGHLIN, B. 1987, *Theories of Second Language Learning*. London: Edward Arnold.

—— 1988, Restructuring. Plenary address, Second Language Research Forum, Honolulu, HI.

MEHAN, H. 1979, *Learning Lessons: Social Organization in the Classroom*. Cambridge, MA: Harvard University Press.

MEISEL, J. 1980, Linguistic simplification. In S. FELIX (ed.), *Second Language Development: Trends and Issues* (pp. 13–40). Tübingen: Gunter Narr Verlag.

—— 1983, Transfer as a second language strategy. *Language and Communication* 3, 11–46.

—— (ed.) 1986, *Adquisición del lenguaje/Aquisicão da linguagem*. Frankfurt: Vervuert.

MORROW, P. 1987, The users and uses of English in Japan. *World Englishes* 6, 49–62.

MÜHLHÄUSLER, P. 1986, *Pidgin and Creole Linguistics*. Oxford: Basil Blackwell.

MUYSKEN, P. 1984, The Spanish that Quechua speakers learn: L2 learning as norm-governed behavior. In R. ANDERSEN (ed.), *Second Languages: A Crosslinguistic Perspective* (pp. 101–19). Rowley, MA: Newbury House.

NAGARA, S. 1972, *Japanese Pidgin English in Hawaii: A Bilingual Description*. Honolulu: University of Hawaii Press.

NATTINGER, J. 1980, A lexical phrase grammar for ESL. *TESOL Quarterly* 14, 337–44.

—— 1986, Lexical phrases, functions, and vocabulary acquisition. *The Ortesol Journal* 7, 1–14.

NEUFELD, G. 1980, On the adult's ability to acquire phonology. *TESOL Quarterly* 14, 285–98.

NEW YORK STATE EDUCATION DEPARTMENT 1986, *Applications for New Grants for Two-Way Bilingual Education Programs*. Albany, NY: Office of State Printing.

NIEDZIELSKI, P. 1979, Le contexte, le raisonnement et l'institution dans l'apprentis- age individualise de la lecture. *The French Review* 52, 575–83.

ODLIN, T. 1986, On the nature and use of explicit knowledge. *IRAL* 24, 123–44.

—— 1988, Language transfer. Unpublished manuscript.

—— 1989, On the recognition of transfer errors. Paper presented to the Annual TESOL Conference, San Antonio, TX, March.

OHTANI, T. 1978, Adult education: A brief history of teaching and study of business English in Japan. In I. KOIKE *et al.* (eds), *The Teaching of English in Japan*. Tokyo: Eichosha.

OMAGGIO, A. 1984, The proficiency oriented classroom. In T. HIGGS (ed.), *Teaching for Proficiency: The Organizing Principle* (pp. 43–84). Lincolnwood, IL: National Textbook Company.

—— 1986, *Teaching Language in Context: Proficiency-Oriented Instruction*. Boston: Heinle & Heinle.

ONETO, A. J. 1968, *FLES Evaluation: Language Skills and Pupil Attitudes in the*

*Fairfield, Connecticut Public Schools*. Hartford, CT: Connecticut State Department of Education. (ERIC Document Reproduction Service No. 023 333).

PECK, S. 1978, Child–child discourse in second language acquisition. In E. HATCH (ed.), *Second Language Acquisition: A Book of Readings* (pp. 383–400). Rowley, MA: Newbury House.

PETERS, A. M. 1977, Language learning strategies: Does the whole equal the sum of the parts? *Language* 53, 560–73.

—— 1983, *The Units of Language Acquisition*. Cambridge: Cambridge University Press.

—— 1985, Language segmentation: Operating principles for the perception and analysis of language. In D. I. SLOBIN (ed.), *The Cross-Linguistic Study of Language Acquisition*, Vol. 2 (pp. 1029–67). Hillsdale, NJ: Lawrence Erlbaum.

PFAFF, C. 1985, On input and residual L1 transfer effects in Turkish and Greek children's grammar. In R. W. ANDERSEN (ed.), *Second Languages: A Crosslinguistic Perspective* (pp. 271–298). Rowley, MA: Newbury House.

—— 1987, Functional approaches to interlanguage. In C. PFAFF (ed.), *First and Second Language Acquisition Processes* (pp. 81–102). Cambridge, MA: Newbury House.

PICA, T. 1983, Adult acquisition of English as a second language under different conditions of exposure. *Language Learning* 33, 465–97.

—— 1985, Linguistic simplicity and learnability: implications for language syllabus design. In K. HYLTENSTAM and M. PIENEMANN (eds), *Modelling and Assessing Second Language Acquisition* (pp. 137–151). Clevedon, Avon: Multilingual Matters.

—— 1987, Second language acquisition, social interaction and the classroom. *Applied Linguistics* 8, 3–21.

PIENEMANN, M. 1981, *Der Zweitsprachenerwerb ausländischer Arbeiterkinder*. Bonn: Bouvier.

—— 1985, Learnability and syllabus construction. In K. HYLTENSTAM and M. PIENEMANN (eds), *Modelling and Assessing Second Language Acquisition* (pp. 23–75). Clevedon, Avon: Multilingual Matters.

—— 1987, Properties of formal and natural SLA. Paper presented at the SLA-FLL Conference, University of Illinois at Urbana-Champaign, 3–4 April.

PINKER, S. 1979, Formal models of language learning. *Cognition* 1, 217–18.

—— 1984, *Language Learnability and Language Development*. Cambridge, MA: Harvard University Press.

—— 1987, Resolving a learnability paradox in the acquisition of the verb lexicon. Lexicon Project Working Papers 17, Center for Cognitive Science, MIT.

PLANN, S. 1976, The Spanish immersion program: Toward native-like proficiency or a classroom dialect. Unpublished master's thesis, UCLA.

PLATT, J., WEBER, H. and HO, M. L. 1984, *The New Englishes*. London: Routledge and Kegan Paul.

PORTER, P. 1983, Variations in the conversations of adult learners of English as a function of the proficiency level of the participants. Unpublished Ph.D. dissertation, Stanford University.

RHODES, N. C. and SCHREIBSTEIN, A. R. 1983, *Foreign Language in the Elementary School: A Practical Guide*. Washington, DC: Center for Applied Linguistics. (ERIC Document Reproduction Service No. ED 225 403.)

RICHARDS, J. and SUKIWAT, M. 1983, Language transfer and conversational competence. *Applied Linguistics* 4, 113–25.

RILEY, P. 1977, Discourse networks in classroom interaction: Some problems in communicative language teaching. *Mélanges Pédagogiques*, University of Nancy: CRAPEL.

RIVERS, W. 1972, Talking off the tops of their heads. *TESOL Quarterly* 6, 71–81.

RÖHL, M. 1984, Ansätze zu einer Didaktik des Übersetzens. Unpublished master's thesis, Fachbereich Angewandte Sprachwissenschaft, Universität Mainz.

ROSANSKY, E. 1976, Methods and morphemes in second language research. *Language Learning* 26, 409–25.

ROUCHDY, A. 1980, Languages in contact: Arabic-Nubian. *Anthropological Linguistics* 22, 334–44.

RUTHERFORD, W. 1983, Language typology and language transfer. In S. GASS and L. SELINKER (eds), *Language Transfer in Language Learning* (pp. 358–70). Rowley, MA: Newbury House.

—— 1984, Description and explanation in interlanguage syntax: State of the art. *Language Learning* 34, 127–55.

—— 1986, Grammatical theory and L2 acquisition: A brief overview. *Second Language Studies* 2: 1–15.

SACKS, H., SCHEGLOFF, E. and JEFFERSON, G. 1974, A simplest systematics for the organization of turn taking for conversation. *Language* 50, 696–735.

SAGER, J. 1984, Reflections on the didactic implications of an extended theory of translation. In S. POULSEN and W. WILSS (eds), *Angewandte Übersetzungswissenschaft*. Aarhus, Denmark: Aarhus.

SATO, C. 1986, Conversation and interlanguage development: Rethinking the connection. In R. R. DAY (ed), *Talking to Learn: Conversation in Second Language Acquisition* (pp. 23–45). Rowley, MA: Newbury House.

SAVIGNON, S. J. 1971, A study of the effect of training in communicative skills as part of a beginning college French course on student attitude and achievement in linguistic and communicative competence. Ph.D. dissertation, University of Illinois at Urbana-Champaign.

—— 1983, *Communicative Competence: Theory and Classroom Practice*. Reading, MA: Addison-Wesley.

—— 1985, Evaluation of communicative competence: The ACTFL Provisional Proficiency Guidelines. *Modern Language Journal* 69, 129–34.

SAVIGNON, S. J. and BERNS, M. S. 1984, *Initiatives in Communicative Language Teaching*. Reading, MA: Addison-Wesley.

—— 1987, *Initiatives in Communicative Language Teaching II*. Reading, MA: Addison-Wesley.

SCARCELLA, R. and HIGA, C. 1981, Input, negotiation and age difference. *Language Learning* 31, 409–37.

SCHACHTER, J. 1988, Second language acquisition and its relationship to universal grammar. *Applied Linguistics* 9.

SCHEGLOFF, E. 1968, Sequencing in conversational openings. *American Anthropologist* 70, 1075–95.

SCHEGLOFF, E. and SACKS, H. 1973, Opening up closings. *Semiotica* 8, 289–327.

SCHERER, G. and WERTHEIMER, M. 1964, *A Psycholinguistic Experiment in Foreign Language Teaching*. New York: McGraw-Hill.

SCHINKE-LLANO, L. 1983, Foreigner talk in content classrooms. In H. W. SELIGER and M. H. LONG (eds), *Classroom Oriented Research in Second Language Acquisition* (pp. 146–65). Rowley, MA: Newbury House.

—— 1984, Programmatic and instructional aspects of language immersion programs. Unpublished manuscript, SRA Technologies, Mountain View, CA.

—— 1985, *Foreign Language in the Elementary School: The State of the Art.* Englewood Cliffs, NJ: Prentice Hall Regents.

SCHMIDT, A. 1985, *Young People's Dyirbal.* Cambridge: Cambridge University Press.

SCHMIDT, R. 1988, The role of consciousness in second language learning. Plenary address, Second Language Research Forum, Honolulu, HI.

SCHUCHARDT, H. 1883, Kreolische Studien III: Über das Indoportugiesische von Diu. *Sitzungberichte der Kaislerlichen Akademie der Wissenschaften zu Wien (philosophische-historische Klasse).*

—— 1889, Zum Indoportugiesischen von Mahé und Cannanore. *Zeitschrift für Romanische Philologie* 13, 516–24.

SCHWARTZ, B. 1986, The epistemological status of second language acquisition. *Second Language Research* 2, 120–59.

—— 1988, Testing between UG and problem-solving models of SLA: Developmental sequence data. Paper presented at Second Language Research Forum, Honolulu, HI.

SCOTT, S. 1973, The relation of divergent thinking to bilingualism: Cause or effect? Unpublished manuscript, McGill University, Montreal.

SCRIBNER, S. and COLE, M. 1981, *The Psychology of Literacy.* Cambridge, MA: Harvard University Press.

SELIGER, H. 1980, Utterance planning and correction behavior: Its function in the grammar construction process for second language learners. In H. DECHERT and M. RAUPACH (eds), *Toward a Cross-Linguistic Assessment of Speech Production* (pp. 87–99). Frankfurt: Verlag Peter D. Lang.

SELIGER, H. W. and LONG, M. H. (eds) 1983, *Classroom Oriented Research in Second Language Acquisition.* Rowley, MA: Newbury House.

SELINKER, L. 1969, Language transfer. *General Linguistics* 9, 67–92.

—— 1972, Interlanguage. *International Review of Applied Linguistics* 10, 209–31.

SELLS, P. 1985, *Lectures on Contemporary Syntactic Theories.* Stanford University: Center for the Study of Language and Information.

SHARWOOD SMITH, M. 1981, Consciousness-raising and the second language learner. *Applied Linguistics* 2, 59–68.

—— 1986, Comprehension vs. acquisition: Two ways of processing input. *Applied Linguistics* 7, 239–56.

SIEGEL, J. 1987, *Language Contact in a Plantation Environment: A Sociolinguistic History of Fiji.* Cambridge: Cambridge University Press.

SIMÕES, M. C. P. and STOEL-GAMMON, C. 1979, The acquisition of inflections in Portuguese: A study of the development of person markers on verbs. *Journal of Child Language* 6, 53–67.

SINCLAIR, J. and COULTHARD, R. 1975, *Towards an Analysis of Discourse.* Oxford: Oxford University Press.

SKUTNABB-KANGAS, T. 1981, *Bilingualism or Not: The Education of Minorities.* Clevedon, Avon: Multilingual Matters.

SLOBIN, D. I. 1973, Cognitive prerequisites for the development of grammar. In

C. I. FERGUSON and D. I. SLOBIN (eds), *Studies of Child Language Development* (pp. 175–276). New York: Holt, Rinehart and Winston.

—— 1977, Language change in childhood and history. In J. MACNAMARA (ed.), *Language Learning and Language Thought* (pp. 185–214). New York: Academic Press.

—— 1982, Universal and particular in the acquisition of language. In E. WANNER and L. R. GLEITMAN (eds), *Language Acquisition: The State of the Art* (pp. 128–70). Cambridge: Cambridge University Press.

—— 1985a, Cross-linguistic evidence for the language-making capacity. In D. I. SLOBIN (ed.), *The Cross-Linguistic Study of Language Acquisition*, Vol. 2 (pp. 1157–1256). Hillsdale, NJ: Lawrence Erlbaum.

—— 1985b, *The Cross-Linguistic Study of Language Acquisition*. Hillsdale, NJ: Lawrence Erlbaum.

SMITH, I. 1977, Sri Lanka Creole Portuguese phonology. Unpublished Ph.D. dissertation, Cornell University.

SMITH, P. D. 1970, *A Comparison of the Cognitive and Audiolingual Approaches to Foreign Language Instruction: The Pennsylvania Foreign Language Project*. Philadelphia: Center for Curriculum Development.

SMITH, S. 1987, Second language teaching in the business world: Communicative English course content in Germany. In S. SAVIGNON and M. BERNS (eds), *Initiatives in Communicative Language Teaching II* (pp. 107–123). Reading, MA: Addison-Wesley.

SNOW, C. 1987, Beyond conversation: Second language learners' acquisition of descriptions and explanation. In J. P. LANTOLF and A. LABARCA (eds), *Research in Second Language Learning: Focus on the Classroom* (pp. 3–16). Norwood, NJ: Ablex.

SORENSON, A. P. 1967, Multilingualism in the northwest Amazon. *American Anthropologist* 69, 670–84.

SPILKA, I. 1976, Assessment of second language performance in immersion programs. *Canadian Modern Language Review* 32, 543–61.

SRIDHAR, K. K. and SRIDHAR, S. N. 1986, Bridging the paradigm gap: Second language acquisition theory and indigenized varieties of English. *World Englishes* 5, 3–14.

STANLAW, J. 1982, English in Japanese communicative strategies. In B. KACHRU (ed.), *The Other Tongue: English Across Cultures* (pp. 168–97). Urbana: University of Illinois Press.

STENSON, N. 1975, Induced errors. In J. SCHUMANN and N. STENSON (eds), *New Frontiers in Second Language Learning* (pp. 54–70). Rowley, MA: Newbury House.

—— 1981, *Studies in Irish Syntax*. Tübingen: Gunter Narr Verlag.

STERN, H. H. 1983, *Fundamental Concepts of Language Teaching*. Oxford: Oxford University Press.

—— 1984, The immersion phenomenon. *Language and Society* (pp. 4–7). Ottawa: Ministry of Supply and Service.

STEVICK, E. 1976, *Memory, Meaning and Method*. Rowley, MA: Newbury House.

STICKEL, G. 1970, *Untersuchungen zur Negation im heutigen Deutschen*. Braunschweig: Vieweg.

SUN, C. F. and GIVÓN, T. 1985, On the so-called SOV word order in Mandarin Chinese. *Language* 61, 329–51.

SWAIN, M. 1983, Communicative competence: Some roles of comprehensible output in its development. Paper presented at the Tenth University of Michigan Conference in Applied Linguistics, Ann Arbor.

—— 1984, A review of immersion education in Canada: Research and evaluation studies. In J. LUNDIN and D. P. DOLSON (eds), *Studies on Immersion Education: A Collection for United States Educators* (pp. 87–112), Sacramento, CA: California Department of Education, Office of Bilingual Bicultural Education. (ERIC Document Reproduction Service No. ED 239 509.)

—— 1985, Communicative competence: Some roles of comprehensible input and comprehensible output in its development. In S. GASS and C. MADDEN (eds), *Input in Second Language Acquisition* (pp. 235–53). Rowley, MA: Newbury House.

SWAIN, M. and LAPKIN, S. 1982, *Evaluating Bilingual Education: A Canadian Case Study*. Clevedon, Avon: Multilingual Matters.

TARONE, D., SWAIN, M. and FATHMAN, A. 1976, Some limitations to the classroom application of current SLA research. *TESOL Quarterly* 10, 19–31.

TARONE, E. 1977, Conscious communication strategies in interlanguage: A progress report. In H. D. BROWN, R. CRYMES and C. YORIO (eds), *Teaching and Learning English as Second Language: Trends in Research and Practice. On TESOL '77* (pp. 194–203). Washington, DC: TESOL.

—— 1980, Communication strategies, foreigner talk, and second language acquisition. Paper presented at the annual meeting of TESOL, San Francisco.

TAYLOR, H. 1987, The word order of three Dutch FL students. Unpublished term paper, UCLA.

TERRELL, T. D. 1977, A natural approach to second language acquisition and learning. *Modern Language Journal* 6, 325–37.

TESCHNER, R. V. 1987, A profile of the specialization and expertise of lower division foreign language program directors in American universities. *Modern Language Journal* 71, 28–35.

THIERSCH, C. 1978, Topics in German syntax. Ph.D. dissertation, MIT.

THOMAS, J. 1983, Cross-cultural pragmatic failure. *Applied Linguistics* 4, 91–112.

—— 1984, Cross-cultural discourse as 'Unequal Encounter': Towards a pragmatic analysis. *Applied Linguistics* 5, 226–35.

THOMASON, S.G. 1981, Are there linguistic prerequisites for contact-induced language change? Paper presented at the 1981 Milwaukee Linguistics Symposium, Milwaukee, WI. ED 205054.

—— 1983, Genetic relationship and the case of Ma'a (Mbugu). *Studies in African Linguistics* 14, 195–231.

THOMASON, S. G. and KAUFMAN, T. 1988, *Language Contact, Creolization and Genetic Linguistics*. Berkeley: University of California Press.

THOMPSON, S. 1978, Modern English from a typological point of view: Some implications of the function of word order. *Linguistische Berichte* 54, 19–35.

TRÉVISE, A. 1986, Is is transferable, topicalization? In E. KELLERMAN and M. SHARWOOD SMITH (eds), *Crosslinguistic Influence in Second Language Acquisition* (pp. 186–206). New York: Pergamon Press.

TRÉVISE, A. and NOYAU, C. 1984, Adult Spanish speakers and the acquisition of French negation forms: Individual variation and linguistic awareness. In R. ANDERSEN (ed.), *Second Languages: A Crosslinguistic Perspective* (pp. 165–89). Rowley, MA: Newbury House.

TROIKE, R. C. 1986, Improving conditions for success in bilingual education programs. Prepared for the Committee on Education and Labor, US House of Representatives.

TURNER, D. 1979, The effect of instruction on second language learning and second language acquisition. In R. ANDERSEN (ed.), *The Acquisition and Use of Spanish and English as First and Second Languages* (pp. 107–116). Washington, DC: TESOL.

VAN LIER, L. 1988, *The Classroom and the Language Learner: Ethnography and Second Language Classroom Research*. London: Longman.

VAN RIEMSDIJK, H. and WILLIAMS, E. 1986, *Introduction to the Theory of Grammar*. Cambridge, MA: MIT Press.

VANPATTEN, B. 1984, Morphemes and processing strategies. In F. ECKMAN, L. BELL and D. NELSON (eds), *Universals of Second Language Acquisition* (pp. 88–98). Rowley, MA: Newbury House.

—— 1985a, The acquisition of *ser* and *estar* by adult classroom learners: A preliminary investigation of transitional stages of competence. *Hispania* 68, 399–406.

—— 1985b, Communicative value and information processing in second language acquisition. In P. LARSON, E. JUDD and D. MESSERSCHMIDT (eds), *On TESOL '84, A Brave New World for TESOL* (pp. 89–99). Washington, DC: TESOL.

—— 1986a, Second language acquisition research and the learning/teaching of Spanish: Some research findings and implications. *Hispania* 69, 202–16.

—— 1986b, The ACTFL Proficiency Guidelines: Implications for grammatical accuracy in the classroom? *Studies in Second Language Acquisition* 8, 56–67.

—— 1987a, Classroom learners' acquisition of *ser* and *estar*: Accounting for developmental patterns. In B. VANPATTEN, T. R. DVORAK and J. F. LEE (eds), *Foreign Language Learning: A Research Perspective* (pp. 61–75). Cambridge, MA: Newbury House.

—— 1987b, On babies and bathwater: Input in foreign language learning. *Modern Language Journal* 71, 156–64.

——1988, How juries get hung: Problems with the evidence for a focus on form in teaching. *Language Learning* 38, 243–60.

——1989, Can learners attend to content and form while listening to the L2? *Hispania* 72, 409–17.

—— in press, X + Y = Utterance. In M. PIENEMANN (ed.), *Explaining Interlanguage Development*. Clevedon: Multilingual Matters.

—— forthcoming, Second language acquisition and language teaching.

VANPATTEN, B., DVORAK, T. R. and LEE, J. F. (eds) 1987, *Foreign Language Learning: A Research Perspective*. Cambridge, MA: Newbury House.

VARONIS, E. and GASS, S. 1983, 'Target Language': Input from non-native speakers. Paper presented at the annual meeting of TESOL, Toronto.

—— 1985, Non-native/non-native conversations: A model for negotiation of meaning. *Applied Linguistics* 6, 71–90.

VYGOTSKY, L. S. 1962, *Thought and Language*. Cambridge, MA: MIT Press.

WAGNER-GOUGH, J. and HATCH, E. 1975, The importance of input data in second language acquisition studies. *Language Learning* 25, 297–308.

WARDHAUGH, R. and BROWN, H. D. 1976, *A Survey of Applied Linguistics*. Ann Arbor: University of Michigan Press.

WELLS, G. 1981, *Learning Through Interaction: The Study of Language Development*. New York: Cambridge University Press.

WESCHE, W. and READY, D. 1983, Foreigner talk discourse in the university classroom. Paper presented at the Tenth University of Michigan Conference on Applied Linguistics, Ann Arbor.

WEXLER, K. and CULICOVER, P. 1980, *Formal Principles of Language Acquisition*. Cambridge, MA: MIT Press.

WHITE, L. 1987, Against comprehensible input: The Input Hypothesis and the development of L2 competence. *Applied Linguistics* 8, 95–110.

WILDNER-BASSETT, M. 1984, *Improving Pragmatic Aspects of Learners' Interlanguage*. Tübingen: Gunter Narr Verlag.

—— 1986, Sicherheitsinseln im Kommunikationsfluss: Gesprächsroutinen und Strategien für Deutsch als Alltags- und Wirtschaftssprache. In K. R. BAUSCH, F. KÖNIGS and R. KOGELHEIDE (eds), *Probleme und Perspektiven der Sprachlehrforschung* (pp. 181–95). Frankfurt: Scriptor.

—— in press, The clanger phenomenon and the foreign language learner. *International Review of Applied Linguistics*.

—— in preparation, *Generating and Executing Communicative Plans: Routines and their Applications for Language Acquisition* (working title).

WILKINS, D. 1976, *Notional Syllabuses*. Oxford: Oxford University Press.

WILLIG, A. 1985, A meta-analysis of selected studies on the effectiveness of bilingual education. *Review of Educational Research* 55, 269–317.

WISS, C. 1987, Issues in the assessment of learning problems in children from French immersion programs: A case study illustration in support of Cummins. *Canadian Modern Language Review* 43, 302–13.

WODE, H. 1981, *Learning a Second Language*. Tübingen: Gunter Narr Verlag.

—— 1985, Die Revolution frisst ihre Eltern. *Die Neueren Sprachen* 84, 206–18.

WOLFSON, N. and JUDD, E. (eds) 1983, *Sociolinguistics and Language Acquisition*. Rowley, MA: Newbury House.

WONG-FILLMORE, L. 1976, The second time around: Cognitive and social strategies in second language acquisition. Unpublished Ph.D dissertation, Stanford University.

—— 1979, Individual differences in second language acquisition. In C. J. FILLMORE, D. KEMPLER and W. S.-Y. WANG (eds), *Individual Differences in Language Ability and Language Behaviour* (pp. 203–28). New York: Academic Press.

YOROZUYA, R. and OLLER, J. 1980, Oral proficiency scales: Construct validity and the halo effect. *Language Learning* 30, 135–53.

ZOBL, H. 1980a, Developmental and transfer errors: Their common bases and (possibly) differential effects on subsequent learning. *TESOL Quarterly* 14, 469–79.

—— 1980b, The formal and developmental selectivity of L1 influence on L2 acquisition. *Language Learning* 30, 43–57.

—— 1983, L1 acquisition, age of L2 acquisition and the learning of word order. In S. GASS and L. SELINKER (eds), *Language Transfer in Language Learning* (pp. 205–21). Rowley, MA: Newbury House.

—— 1986a, Word order typology, lexical government, and the prediction of multiple, graded effects in L2 word order. *Language Learning* 36, 159–83.

—— 1986b, A functional approach to the attainability of typological targets in L2 acquisition. *Second Language Studies* 2, 16–32.

# Index

*Note*: FL = foreign language; FLL = foreign language learning; L1 = first language; L2 = second language; SLA = second language acquisition. References in *italics* indicate tables or figures.

Acculturation Hypothesis ix
Accuracy, in FLL 71, 145, 151, 187–8, 190
Acquisition
  –compared with learning 35, 182, 186, 208, 212–13, *213*, 220–1
  –deep/superficial differences 133, 241–2
  –L1 19, 245
  –natural, *see* SLA
  –theory 15, 17–18, 25—6, 73–5, 91–2, 185–97, 242
  –unified theory 69–70
  –variables 15, 29, 46, 241
    external 38–43
    internal 34–8, 170
  *see also* adult; child; classroom; FLL; input; operating principles
*ACTFL Proficiency Guidelines* 170, 178, 187–8
Adjacency Requirement 93n.
Adult, language acquisition 39–40, 109–10, 181–2, 192, 201
Affect, and SLA 222–3
Agreement, subject-verb 60
Agreement markers 56, *57*
Algeo, J. 102
Allwright, R.L. 194
Amharic 106–7
Analysis
  –contrastive 23, 95, 185, 243
  –discourse 65, 103, 153, 194, 206
  –interactional 30, 153, 194, 199, 224
  –qualitative 119
  –quantitative 29–30, 119–20, *121*, 121–2

Andersen, R. ix, 15–16, 45–68, 119–20, 122, 125, 129, 132, 242
Articles, encoding 52
Aspect, acquisition 60
Associative principle 84–5, 87–92
Attention principles 49
Attrition, language 95, *99*, 104, 115
Audiolingualism 192, 194, 198, 202, 220, 243
Authentic Language Plus Model 45
Awareness, metalinguistic 70, 96, 108, 109–12, 113–14, 115–16

Bach, A. 93n.
Bacon, S.C. 71, 170–80
Baker, C.L. 81–2
Bangalore Communicational Teaching Project (CTP) 195
Bantu languages 107
Beck, Maria 93n.
Behaviour, language, *see* discourse
Behaviourism 187–8
Beretta, A. 192, 195–6
Berns, M. 1–2, 3–11, 69, 182–3, 196, 240
Bhojpuri, Mauritius 105, *113*
Bialystok, E. 111
Bias, distributional, *see* cognitive operating principles
Bickerton, D. 62, 63
Bickerton, D. & Givón, T. 100–1, 103, 108
Bilingualism
  –and competence 37
  –in English 8, 98
  –United States 182–3

Binding Conditions 84
Birdsong, D. 39
Bley-Vroman, R. 39
Blum-Kulka, S. & Olshtain, E. 43
Bock, J.K. & Warren, R. 111
Bourdieu, P. 31
Bowen, Donald 23
Bowerman, M. 68n.
Breen, M. 145, 154
Breen, M. & Candlin, C. 192
Brooks, F.B. 71, 153–69
Brooks, N. 192
Brown, R. 48, 73–4, 83, 202
Bruner, J. 31
Buber, Martin 30
Bull, William 23
Bybee, J.L. 59–60

Campbell, R.N. & Lindholm, K.J. 182–3, 226–39, 245
Cancino, H. 63–4
Cancino, H. & Hakuta, K. 64
Catford, J.C. 209–10, 210
Cazden, C., et al. 194
Chaudron, C. 34, 193–4
Child
  –L1 proficiency 226–31
  –language acquisition 39, 73–4, 110, 182, 200–1
Chomsky, N. 39, 93n.
Chunks, speech, see speech, prefabricated
Clahsen, H. 49–50, 51, 74–5, 77, 79–81, 83–5, 87, 91
Clahsen, H. & Muysken, P. 92n.
Clahsen, H. et al. 77
Clark, H.H. & Clark, E.V. 46
Classroom
  –and clitic use 118–19, 124–5, 127–8, 130–3, 131
  –and cognitive operating principles 50, 52–3, 60, 64, 66
  –communication oriented 170–1, 196–7
  –effect on acquisition ix, x, 4–5, 15, 30–3, 35–7, 185–6
  –language production 38
  see also discourse; input; interaction; SLA research

Clitics 52, 56, 56, 61, 70, 118–39, 121
  –form 125–9, 126
  –position 129–30
  –use strategies 122–5
Cognition, development 219
Cognitive operating principles 49, 51–64, 66–7
  –distributional bias 58–9
  –formal determinism 55–8, 61, 68n.
  –multifunctionality principle 32, 53–5, 56
  –one-to-one principle 51–4, 55, 58
  –relevance 59–60
  –relexification 62–4
  –transfer to somewhere principle 61, 63–4
Cognitive-interactionist model 47–8, 66–7
Colorado Project 194
Communication
  –in FLL 4–7, 154–5, 157–8, 161–7, 170–8, 187–9, 221
  –as means of instruction 50, 170–1, 191, 196, 221–2
  –in SLA 47
Competence 4, 10–11, 23, 36, 47
  –communicative 30, 32, 182, 187–92, 194, 196–7, 208
  in translator training 211–15
  –grammatical 35, 37, 119, 191, 192, 198–9
  –native-like 223–4
  –pragmatic 140–52
  –productive 37–8
  –underlying 80, 81–5
Completeness 36–8
Consistency condition 92n.
Contact, language 99, 104, 106–7, 109, 113, 113–16
Context 15–16, 28–9, 34–7, 42–3, 64, 70, 112, 118, 197
  –cline of 1, 9–11, 69
  –dichotomy of 1, 7–8, 10
  –and immersion courses 220–3, 225
  –and pragmatics 141
  –social 31, 140–52, 155–65, 166–7, 240, 241–2
  of transfer 113–15
  –and translation 210, 211–14, 212, 213, 214

see also input; interaction,
   situational frame
Conventions, learning 140–1
Coppieters, R. 37, 38
Copula, in learner language 22
Correction 41, 71, 112, 144–6, 157–62,
   164, 188–90
   –and translation training 208–9, 211
Correctness 114, 144, 198
Coulmas, F. 141–2, 152
Creoles, creation 67n.
Cruttenden, A. 201
Cues 41, 42
Cummins, J. 224
Curriculum, and FLL 4, 181, 182,
   243–5
Cushitic languages 106–7

Dahl, Ö 84, 93n.
Dalgado, S.R. 106, 112
Data
   –elicitation 71
   –FLL 15, 77, 120–3, 141–4, 153–5,
   171, 189–90, 192
   in SLA theory 69, 71, 150–1
   –scarcity 108–9
   –SLA 21–2, 30, 31, 69, 119–23,
   141, 144–5, 151
Day, D. et al. 40
Deficit, resource 182, 227–8, 239
Denativization 47–8
Determiners, in learner language 82
Determinism, formal, see cognitive
   operating principles
Discourse
   –acquisition of patterns 32, 198–206
   –classroom 71, 153–65, 166–7
   –worlds of 141–52, 149
Dittmar, N. 77
Domain, FL 5, 6, 9–10
Doughty, C. & Pica, T. 224
Dulay, H. & Burt, M.K. 68n.
DuPlessis, J. et al. 77, 88
Dyirbal, Young Peope's 98–9, 99,
   105, 108, 113

Eckman, 68n.
Edelhoff, C. 6
Edmondson, J.A. 81–2
Edmondson, W. 142, 152n.

Edmondson, W. et al. 43
Ellis, R. 17, 26
English
   –child acquisition 73–4
   –as FL 1, 52, 55, 60–1, 242
   –as international language 5, 6–7,
   9–10
   –Korean Bamboo 102, 113
   –and language learning contexts 4–8
   –as link language 6, 7–8
   –non-native varieties ix, 3–8
   see also India; Japan; SLA; West
   Germany; word order
Enrichment, FL as 217
Equivalence paradigm 209–11, 210,
   215
Erickson, F. & Shultz, J. 40–1
Error, learner 36, 38–9, 112, 157–62,
   185, 188–90
Eubank, L. 69–70, 73–94, 241–2
Evidence
   –negative 38–41, 73, 78–9, 80–1, 84,
   112
   –positive 39, 82, 85, 164
Exposure
   –in FLL 98, 128, 131, 197, 218
   –in SLA 48, 70, 220–1, 233–5
Extendibility condition 73–5, 78–9,
   80–1, 85, 91

Feedback, see evidence, negative
Felix, S. 77, 87, 192
Ferguson, C. 4
Fijian, Pidgin 104, 113
Firth, J.R. 208, 211–13, 213
FL teaching 18–19, 27–8, 30, 242–5
Flanders, N.A. 194
FLES (foreign language in the
   elementary school) courses 217–18,
   219
FLEX (foreign language experience)
   courses 217, 218–19
FLL
   –definitions 17–18, 27–33, 117n.,
   182, 216, 240–1
   –and L2 learning 34–44, 66, 114,
   116, 181, 187–91, 241–3
   –and social interaction 153–69
   –and terminal 2 188–90

FLL research ix, 13–14, 15–16
–concept of language 30
–concept of learning 30–3, 165,
  191–3, 196
–education in 23, 27–33, 242–3
–methods 29–30, 153
–neglect of acquisition 22–4
–object 29
–producer-consumer relationship *18*,
  18–19, 20, 23–4
–and SLA research viii–ix, 13–16,
  17–19, 24–6, *25*, 27, 69, 185,
  193–7
Fluency, L2 35
Form, and meaning 22, 52–5, 58, 64,
  167, 186
Fossilization 54–5, 188–90
Frame, situational, *see* interaction,
  situational frame
Frechette, E. viii
Freed, B. 93n.
French, acquisition 52, 55, 61, 192

Gaies, S. 194
Gardner, R. & Lambert, W. 194
Gass, S.M. 15–16, 34–44, 241
Gass, S.M. & Madden, C. 20, 21
Gass, S.M. & Varonis, E.M. 64
Genesee, F. 224
German, acquisition 49–50, 51–2, 55,
  69–70, 73–92, 242
Givón, T. 117n.
Goodlad, J. 196
Government-Binding (GB) Theory 74,
  81–3
Grammar
  –in FLL 4, 35, 37, 38–9, 118–19,
    131–2, 188–90, 198
  –performance 199–200
  –universal 81–5, 86–7, 115
Green, J. & Wallat, C. 156
Greenberg, J. 108
Gregg, K. 39
Guthrie, E. 194

Hakuta, K. 49, 200
Hammerly, H. 186, 194, 243
Harder, P. 147–8
Hatch, E. 64, 65

Hawaiian Pidgin English 62–3, 98,
  100–2, *102*, *113*, 115
Hawkins, Barbara 65–6
Hawkins, J. 108
Heeschen, V. 108
Helgesen, M. 4–5, 9
Hernández, Piña F. 134n.
Higgs, T.V. viii–ix
Higgs, T.V. & Clifford, R. 188–90,
  243
Huang, J. & Hatch, E. 49
Huebner, T. 101
Hui, 107
Hymes, D. 170

Illinois, University of 192–3
Immersion 143, 191, 194–5, 216–25,
  243
  –bilingual 182–3, 238
    early 228–33
    late 233–6
  –goals 218, 224
  –and language proficiency 219–20,
    223–4
  –partial 233–6
India, English in 1, 7–8, 9
Indo-Portuguese 106–7, 112
Inferencing 155, 162, 167
Input
  –classroom 41–3, 48–50, 54–9, 63–4,
    118, 125, 130, *131*, 133, 233
  –communicative 19–21, 24, 124,
    244–5
  –and context 74
  –extra-classroom 1, 24, 118, *131*
  –in FLL and SLA 41–3, 49, 53,
    194, 222–3
  –and L1 acquisition 73–4
  –and learning of negation 82–3, 85,
    86–8, 90–1
  –natural 45, 75, 125, 221
Input Hypothesis viii, 68n.
Interaction
  –classroom 5, 20–1, 30, 38, 42, 71,
    118, 124, 182, 186, 191, 197
    and cognitive operating principles
      48, 50, 64, 66
    and discourse worlds 145–8,
      150–1
    and SLA 36, 223–4, 225, 243, 244

–extra-classroom 1, 24, 43, 49, 64, 118, 120, 151, 221
–and negative evidence 40
–situational frame 141–52, 167
–social, and FLL 153–69, 199, 203–4, 206
Interference 19, 97, 189
Interlanguage
–development 14, 47–8, 50, 51–5, 58–64, 69, 78, 122
–pragmatic competence 140–52
–rules 35
Interlocutor effect 226

Jackson, J. 114
Japan, English in 1, 4–5, 9
Jordens, P. 77, 93n.

Kachru, Y. ix
Kasper, G. 35–6
Kellerman, E. 116, 117n.
Kiraly, D. 182, 207–15, 243, 245
Klein, W. & Dittmar, N. 77
Knowledge, and skill 43
Koopman, H. 83
Korean
–Bamboo English 102, *113*
–language conservation 236–7
Kramsch, C.J. 15, 16, 27–33, 71, 140, 141–2, 152, 187, 196, 242, 245
Krashen, S.D. viii, 35, 68n., 182, 192, 194, 212–13, *213*, 220–1

Ladmiral, J.R. 210
Lado, Robert 23
Lambert, R.D. 191
Language
–authentic 45, 67
–concept of 30
–conservation of resources 183, 226–39
–focused/unfocused 113–15
–minority 182–3
–prefabricated 200–5
–second 1, 3, 8–10
Language Acquisition Device 31
Language Acquisition Support System 31
Larsen-Freeman, D. 20, 22, 64, 68n.

Le Page, R.B. & Tabouret-Keller, A. 113–14
Learnability condition 73–5, 78, 80, 84–5, 91
Learning
–co-operative 230
–concept of 30–3
–interactional 38
–item/system 200–1
–resistance to 85
see also acquisition
Lee, J.F. 132, 134n.
Lenneberg, H.E. 49
Lexis, transfer of, 116
Li, C. 107
Lightbown, P. 31, 192
Lightfoot, 93n.
Linguistics
–in FLL 23, 27
–in SLA 22
Listening skills 4
Long, M.H. 29–30, 64, 192, 221
Long, M.H. & Porter, P. 224
Lowe, P. 227
Luján, M. *et al.* 103–4, 108

Ma'a 107
Mack, M. 37
Maley, A. 190
Markedness Differential Hypothesis 68n.
May, R. 92
Meaning
–and context 155, 166–7
–and learning 170, 221
Meisel, J. 50, 93n., 101, 103
Memory, in language acquisition 49, 50
Method, teaching ix, 152, 165, 167, 181–2, 194–7, 242–4
–in FLL 23, 27–8, 71, 111–12, 186–92
–in SLA 52–3
Minorities, linguistic, language competence 226–39
Mixing, language 114–15
Molano, Elisa 132
Monitor Theory viii–ix
Morpheme, acquisition 21–2, 61

Morphology
  –transfer 96
  –verb 21–2, 52, 58–9, 60, 110
Motivation, for language learning 5,
  6–7, 11, 35, 203
Move Alpha 82, 86
Mühlhäusler, P. 101
Multifunctionality, see cognitive
  operating principles
Muysken, P. 103–4

Nagara, S. 100
Nativization Model ix, 47–8, 51
Nattinger, J.R. 181, 198–206, 243, 245
Negation
  –acquisition 53–4, 55, 242
  –final state 75–9
  –FLL 89–91
  –German 69–70, 73–92
  –and processing constraints 79–81
  –SLA 86–9
  –stage-one 83
Negotiation 38, 145–6, 192, 221
Nubian, Cairo 105, 108, 113

Odlin, T. 70, 95–117, 242
Omaggio, A. 188, 243
One-to-one principle, see cognitive
  operating principles
Operating principles, see cognitive
  operating principles
Output, learner 37–8, 79, 221–2,
  241–2

Papiamentu, acquisition 65–6
Parameters
  –institutional 31
  –setting 14, 18, 82–4, 86
Participation, classroom 155, 167
Patterns, speech, see speech,
  prefabricated
Peck, S. 64
Pennsylvania Project 194
Performance 81, see also grammar,
  performance
Personality, reduced learner 147–8,
  150–2
Peters, A.M. 48–9
Phrase structure 81–3
Pica, T. 134n.

Pidgins 62–3, 100–2, 104
Pienemann, M. 50, 68n.
Pinker, S. 73, 91
Plann, S. 220
Policy, language 182–3
Politzer, Robert 23
Porter, P. 224
Pragmatics, contrastive 140–52, 242
Prescriptivism 198
Process, language x, 48–50, 51,
  199–200, 241
  –constraints on 74–5, 79–81
  –and context 35, 69, 243
Production, L2 learner 37–8, 49,
  221–2, 241–2
Proficiency
  –cognitive academic language
    (CALP) 224
  –learner 27, 37, 100, 108–9, 181,
    187–90, 218–19, 223–4
  –native language 226–38
  –testing 170–80
Profiles
  –performance 188–9
  –sociolinguistic 4–8, 10
Pronoun
  –form 125–9
  –personal 52
  –stressed 122, 124
  see also clitics
Pronunciation 10
Psycholinguistics
  –and FLL ix, 189, 199, 200, 241
  –in SLA viii, 28, 46, 48–50, 51, 241
Psychology, faculty 74, 81

Quechua, influence of 98, 103, 110

Relevance, see cognitive operating
  principles
Relexification, see cognitive operating
  principles
Repair 63, 66
Repertoire, learner 147–8
Risk-taking, in interaction 150–1, 192
Rivers, Wilga 171, 192
Röhl, M. 209, 211
Role, social, in interaction 71,
  143–51, 161, 171
Rouchdy, A. 105

Rules
 –in classroom learning 50
 –interlanguage 35, 52, 73
 –transformational 82, 86
Rutherford, W. 96–8, 105, 108, 109,
 115

Savignon, S.J. 23, 181, 185–97, 242–3,
 245
Schachter, J. 36
Schinke-Llano, L. 182, 216–25, 243,
 245
Schmidt, R. 105, 108
Schuchardt, H. 106
Schumann, ix
Schwartz, B. 39, 77, 88
Segmentation 181, 200–1, 206
Self-parody, by learner 150–1
Seliger, H. 144
Seliger, H. & Long, M.H. 64
Selinker, L. 97
Siegel, J. 104
Silent period 222–3
Skill
 –basic interpersonal communicative
 (BICS) 224
 –and knowledge 43
SLA x, 117n, 182
 –definitions 216, 240–1
 –and L2 learning 34–44, 66, 114,
 116, 186, 242–3
 –patterns in 181
 –theory 74, 197
 see also cognitive operating
 principles; cognitive-interactionist
 model; process, language
SLA research
 –classroom application 31–2, 45–6,
 54–5, 59, 63–4, 66–7, 185–6,
 193–4
 –concentration on English 15, 23
 –context of ix
 –as cross-linguistic 19, 21–2
 –and FLL research viii–ix, 13–16,
 17–19, 24–6, 25, 27, 69, 73, 181,
 185, 193
 –and learning context 34, 74, 197
 –methods 29–30
 –role of 13–14, 20, 28
Slobin, D.I. 49, 51, 53, 59–60

Smith, I., 106
Smith, S. 7
Sociolinguistics
 –and language acquisition 3, 10–11,
 196
 see also profiles
Spanish
 –Andean 102–4, 108, 110, 113
 –as FL 1, 54, 56, 61, 70, 118–37,
 157, 167–9, 171
 –as L2 233–6
 –verb morphology 21–2, 52, 58–9,
 60
Speech
 –prefabricated 122, 124, 127–8, 181,
 198–206
 –quality 172, 173, 173, 174
 –quantity 172, 173, 174, 174
 –skills 4, 32, 170–2
Speech community x, 1, 4, 8–10, 43
Sridhar, K.K. & Sridhar, S.N. ix
Stenson, N. 35–6
Stern, H.H. 1, 4, 194
Stevick, E. 203
Stockwell, Robert 23
Storage principles 49
Strategies
 –Canonical Order (COS) 79–81
 –in clitic use 122–5, 123, 129
 –communication 64–6
 –Initial Finalization (IFS) 79–81
 –learning 32, 79–81
 –S-NEG 80–1
 –Subordinate Clause 93n.
Style shifting 71
Styles, learning 32
Subset Principle 83–4, 85
Sun, C.F. & Givón, T. 107
Swain, M. 37–8, 221
Syntax
 –acquisition 200, 202
 –and transfer 95–104

Tarone, D. et al. 31
Tarone, E. 64
Task, learning 35–6
Teachers
 –and correction 112
 –talk 125, 153, 194
 –training 15, 31, 34, 152

Teaching
 –constraints on 243–4
 –and research ix, 10, 15, 18, 32–3
Tense, acquisition 60
Terrell, T.D. 221
Testing, oral 71, 170–80
Tests, of method 195
Textbook, and language acquisition 32
Thomas, J. 148
Thomason, S.G. 96, 107
Thomason, S.G. & Kaufman, T. 107
Topic
 –choice 71, 170
 –development 172–3, *173*, 174–8,
  *176*
 –shifting 150, 162–3, 164, 203
Topicalization 79, 101, 115
Total Physical Response 21, 222
Transfer 61, 70, 95, 125
 –borrowing 96, 98, 104–5, 106–7,
  115, 117n.
 –lexical 116
 –linguistic, in translation 209
 –negative 112, 113, 115
 –substratum 96, 99–104, 106–7, 115,
  117n.
 *see also* context, social; word order
Transfer to somewhere principle, *see*
 cognitive operating principles
Translation, definition 207
Translator, training 4, 182, 207–15
Trévise, A. 112

United States
 –FLL in 27, 191
 –language policy 182–3
 –language resources 226–39
 –SLA in 21, 27

Universals, language 69–70, 95–8,
 101, 108, 116
Use, language 70–1, 198–9

VanPatten, B. ix, 13–14, 15–16,
 17–26, 70–1, 118–39, 241–2, 244
VanPatten, B. & Lee, J.F. 240–5
Variables, *see* acquisition, variables
Varieties, language 10
Varonis, E. & Gass, S. 224

Welch, J. 179n.
Wells, G. 194, 221
West Germany
 –English in 1, 6–7, 9
 –FLL/SLA research in 27
 –translator training 207–8, 209
Wexler, K. & Culicover, P. 82
White, L. 39
Wildner-Bassett, M. 71, 140–52, 242
Wilkins, D. 203
Wolfson, N. & Judd, E. 64
Wong-Fillmore, L. 49, 200
Word order
 –English 42–3, 61, 63
 –French 61, 112
 –German 49–50, 51, 77–84, 86–90
 –Italian 42–3
 –multiple underlying orders 83–4,
  86
 –Spanish 56, 102–4, 122, 129–30,
  *131*
 –transfer 70, 96–116, *98*, *99*, *113*
  infrequency of 107–13, 115–16

X-bar theory 82, 83

Zobl, H. 61, 96–8, 108, 111, 115